Creative Regions in Europe

Creative and cultural industries, broadly defined, are now considered by many policymakers across Europe at the heart of their national innovation and economic development agenda. Similarly, many European cities and regions have adopted policies to support and develop these industries and their local support infrastructures. However, this policy-making agenda implicitly incorporates (and indeed often conflates) elements of cultural and creative industries, the creative class, and so on, which are typically employed without due consideration of the context. Thus, a better understanding is required. To this end, this book features eight research chapters that are split evenly with regard to geographical focus between the United Kingdom and the continental Europe (the latter covering Spain, Germany, France, Luxemburg and Belgium individually and in combination). There is also a similar division in terms of those focusing primarily on the policy level (the chapters by Clifton and Macaulay, Mould and Comunian, Pareja-Eastaway and Pradel i Miquel, and Perrin) and those of the individual creative actor (the chapters by Alfken et al., Bennett et al., Wedemeier, and Brown). This book was previously published as a special issue of *European Planning Studies*.

Nick Clifton is a Professor of Economic Geography and Regional Development at Cardiff School of Management, Cardiff Metropolitan University, UK. His main research interests lie in the fields of regional economics, small business and entrepreneurship, networks, business strategy, innovation and creativity. In particular, he is interested in how firms use networks to acquire knowledge and innovate, and the factors that influence the location choices of creative individuals.

Caroline Chapain is a Lecturer in Economic Development, Birmingham Business School, University of Birmingham, UK. Her main research interests include creativity, innovation, creative industries, local and regional economic developments, and public policies. Recently, she has been doing increasing research looking at the links between the economic, cultural and social objectives sustaining creative practices and the role of new media.

Roberta Comunian is a Lecturer in Cultural and Creative Industries Department of Culture, Media and Creative Industries, King's College London, UK. Her main research interests include the relationship between public and private investments in the arts, art and cultural regeneration projects, cultural and creative industries, and creativity and competitiveness. She has also undertaken research on the role of higher education in the creative economy and the career opportunities and patterns of creative graduates in United Kingdom.

Creative Regions in Europe

Edited by
Nick Clifton, Caroline Chapain and
Roberta Comunian

LONDON AND NEW YORK

First published 2016
by Routledge
2 Park Square, Milton Park, Abingdon, Oxon, OX14 4RN, UK

and by Routledge
711 Third Avenue, New York, NY 10017, USA

Routledge is an imprint of the Taylor & Francis Group, an informa business

© 2016 Taylor & Francis

All rights reserved. No part of this book may be reprinted or reproduced or utilised in any form or by any electronic, mechanical, or other means, now known or hereafter invented, including photocopying and recording, or in any information storage or retrieval system, without permission in writing from the publishers.

Trademark notice: Product or corporate names may be trademarks or registered trademarks, and are used only for identification and explanation without intent to infringe.

British Library Cataloguing in Publication Data
A catalogue record for this book is available from the British Library

ISBN 13: 978-1-138-68364-8

Typeset in Times
by diacriTech, Chennai

Publisher's Note
The publisher accepts responsibility for any inconsistencies that may have arisen during the conversion of this book from journal articles to book chapters, namely the possible inclusion of journal terminology.

Disclaimer
Every effort has been made to contact copyright holders for their permission to reprint material in this book. The publishers would be grateful to hear from any copyright holder who is not here acknowledged and will undertake to rectify any errors or omissions in future editions of this book.

Contents

Citation Information vii
Notes on Contributors ix

Introduction: Creative Regions in Europe—Challenges and Opportunities for Policy 1
Nick Clifton, Caroline Chapain and Roberta Comunian

1. Home from Home? Locational Choices of International "Creative Class" Workers 12
Julie Brown

2. Hung, Drawn and Cultural Quartered: Rethinking Cultural Quarter Development Policy in the UK 32
Oli Mould and Roberta Comunian

3. Creativity, Cohesion and the 'Post-conflict' Society: A Policy Agenda (Illustrated from the Case of Northern Ireland) 46
Nick Clifton and Tony Macaulay

4. Living Hand to Mouth: Why the Bohemian Lifestyle Does Not Lead to Wealth Creation in Peripheral Regions? 66
Sophie Bennett, Steven McGuire and Rachel Rahman

5. Towards the Creative and Knowledge Economies: Analysing Diverse Pathways in Spanish Cities 80
Montserrat Pareja-Eastaway and Marc Pradel i Miquel

6. Creative Regions on a European Cross-Border Scale: Policy Issues and Development Perspectives 99
Thomas Perrin

7. Factors Explaining the Spatial Agglomeration of the Creative Class: Empirical Evidence for German Artists 114
Christoph Alfken, Tom Broekel and Rolf Sternberg

CONTENTS

8. Creative Professionals, Local Amenities and Externalities: Do Regional Concentrations of Creative Professionals Reinforce Themselves Over Time?   140
   Jan Wedemeier

   Index   159

Citation Information

The chapters in this book were originally published in *European Planning Studies*, volume 23, issue 12 (December 2015). When citing this material, please use the original page numbering for each article, as follows:

Chapter 1
Home from Home? Locational Choices of International "Creative Class" Workers
Julie Brown
European Planning Studies, volume 23, issue 12 (December 2015) pp. 2336–2355

Chapter 2
Hung, Drawn and Cultural Quartered: Rethinking Cultural Quarter Development Policy in the UK
Oli Mould and Roberta Comunian
European Planning Studies, volume 23, issue 12 (December 2015) pp. 2356–2369

Chapter 3
Creativity, Cohesion and the 'Post-conflict' Society: A Policy Agenda (Illustrated from the Case of Northern Ireland)
Nick Clifton and Tony Macaulay
European Planning Studies, volume 23, issue 12 (December 2015) pp. 2370–2389

Chapter 4
Living Hand to Mouth: Why the Bohemian Lifestyle Does Not Lead to Wealth Creation in Peripheral Regions?
Sophie Bennett, Steven McGuire and Rachel Rahman
European Planning Studies, volume 23, issue 12 (December 2015) pp. 2390–2403

Chapter 5
Towards the Creative and Knowledge Economies: Analysing Diverse Pathways in Spanish Cities
Montserrat Pareja-Eastaway and Marc Pradel i Miquel
European Planning Studies, volume 23, issue 12 (December 2015) pp. 2404–2422

CITATION INFORMATION

Chapter 6
Creative Regions on a European Cross-Border Scale: Policy Issues and Development Perspectives
Thomas Perrin
European Planning Studies, volume 23, issue 12 (December 2015) pp. 2423–2437

Chapter 7
Factors Explaining the Spatial Agglomeration of the Creative Class: Empirical Evidence for German Artists
Christoph Alfken, Tom Broekel and Rolf Sternberg
European Planning Studies, volume 23, issue 12 (December 2015) pp. 2438–2463

Chapter 8
Creative Professionals, Local Amenities and Externalities: Do Regional Concentrations of Creative Professionals Reinforce Themselves Over Time?
Jan Wedemeier
European Planning Studies, volume 23, issue 12 (December 2015) pp. 2464–2482

For any permission-related enquiries please visit:
http://www.tandfonline.com/page/help/permissions

Notes on Contributors

Christoph Alfken is a Researcher at the Institute of Economic and Cultural Geography, Leibniz University of Hanover, Hannover, Germany.

Sophie Bennett is a Lecturer in the School of Management and Business, Aberystwyth University, Aberystwyth, UK.

Tom Broekel is a Junior Professor at the Institute of Economic and Cultural Geography, Leibniz University of Hanover, Hannover, Germany.

Julie Brown is a Lecturer in the School of Communications and Marketing, Southampton Solent University, Southampton, UK.

Caroline Chapain is a Lecturer in Economic Development, Birmingham Business School, University of Birmingham, UK. Her main research interests include creativity, innovation, creative industries, local and regional economic developments, and public policies. Recently, she has been doing increasing research looking at the links between the economic, cultural and social objectives sustaining creative practices and the role of new media.

Nick Clifton is a Professor of Economic Geography and Regional Development at Cardiff School of Management, Cardiff Metropolitan University, UK. His main research interests lie in the fields of regional economics, small business and entrepreneurship, networks, business strategy, innovation and creativity. In particular, he is interested in how firms use networks to acquire knowledge and innovate, and the factors that influence the location choices of creative individuals.

Roberta Comunian is a Lecturer in Cultural and Creative Industries Department of Culture, Media and Creative Industries, King's College London, UK. Her main research interests include the relationship between public and private investments in the arts, art and cultural regeneration projects, cultural and creative industries, creativity and competitiveness. She has also undertaken research on the role of higher education in the creative economy and the career opportunities and patterns of creative graduates in Unite Kingdom.

Tony Macaulay is a Management Consultant at Macaulay Associates Network, Belfast, Northern Ireland.

NOTES ON CONTRIBUTORS

Steven McGuire is a Professor of Business and Public Policy (Business and Management) and the Head of School (School of Business, Management and Economics), University of Sussex, Sussex, UK.

Oli Mould is a Lecturer in the Department of Geography, Royal Holloway, University of London, Egham, UK.

Montserrat Pareja-Eastaway is an Associate Professor in the Department of Economic Theory, University of Barcelona, Barcelona, Spain.

Thomas Perrin is a Lecturer in the Faculty of Geography and Planning, University Lille 1, Research Centre TVES, Villeneuve d'Ascq, France.

Marc Pradel i Miquel is an Assistant Professor in the Department of Sociology Theory, University of Barcelona, Barcelona, Spain.

Rachel Rahman is a Senior Lecturer in the Psychology Department, Aberystwyth University, Aberystwyth, UK.

Rolf Sternberg is a Professor in the Institute of Economic and Cultural Geography, Leibniz University of Hanover, Hannover, Germany.

Jan Wedemeier is a researcher in the Hamburg Institute of International Economics (HWWI), Bremen, Germany.

Introduction: Creative Regions in Europe—Challenges and Opportunities for Policy

NICK CLIFTON,* CAROLINE CHAPAIN** & ROBERTA COMUNIAN[†]

*Cardiff School of Management, Cardiff Metropolitan University, Cardiff, UK, **Business School, University of Birmingham, Birmingham, UK, [†]Department of Culture, Media and Creative Industries, King's College London, UK

Creative Industries and Creative Class in Europe: Different Understandings, Roles and Objectives to Support Development at Local and Regional Levels

It has been almost 20 years since the election of the New Labour government in the United Kingdom in 1997 triggered a new role for culture within the economy (Smith, 1998) via the establishment of a new definition and measuring framework for the creative industries sector (DCMS, 1998, 2000), emphasising their contribution to economic growth. The emergence of this economic creative industries rhetoric in the rest of Europe is slightly more recent, as illustrated by the evolution of the European Commission (EC) position on this topic. While the EC was also considering the role of the cultural industries in supporting employment at the end of the 1990s (EP, 1999), it was not until the second part of the 2000s that European institutions started associating the word 'creative' to the then cultural sectors—which became the cultural and creative sectors—giving more focus to their direct economic contribution (EC, 2007). This shift was associated with the production of increasing economic evidence (KEA, 2006; ERICARTS, 2010; Power, 2011; European Cluster Observatory, 2013; Ketels and Protsiv, 2014; TERA, 2014; Fleming, 2015) and the adoption of policy initiatives to support the cultural and creative sectors through mainstream European Union (EU) support programmes (EP, 2013) such as the structural fund (EU, 2012) or specific budgets, i.e. Creative Europe (Creative Europe, 2013) or the European Cultural and Creative Industries Alliance (see www.eccia.eu).

Nevertheless, despite this shift in terminology and an increased focus on the direct economic contribution of cultural and creative sectors, the EC approach to support these sectors still retained non-economic objectives, such as the promotion of cultural diversity and literacy (Creative Europe, 2013) and the use of culture and creativity to support cultural development, social well-being and innovation, education and lifelong learning, and environmental sustainability, with these seen as cultural and creative spillovers (EU, 2012). This is in line with the ongoing research demonstrating the non-economic impacts of the arts and the cultural and creative industries (Matarosso, 1997; CEBR, 2013; Fleming, 2015), and is also reiterated in the latest United Nations creative economy report (UN, 2013). This debate has been reinforced by the view that the creative industries are driving profound structural changes in the economy and society (Hartley et al., 2013). As a consequence, despite an overwhelming economic drive in the last 10 years, policy initiatives supporting the Cultural and Creative Industries tend to emanate from the cultural, economic and planning spheres (Andres and Chapain, 2013, 2015), thus taking into account their various impacts and spillovers. In addition, there has been a continuing debate on the best way to capture the creative industries and their impacts, both nationally, as illustrated by the revised approach adopted in the United Kingdom in the last 5 years (see Chapain and Hargreaves, 2016, for a review), and with regard to the creative economy globally (see UN, 2013, for a review). This debate has been fuelled by the success of the creative class discourse promoted by Richard Florida (2002), which instead of focusing on firms and industries, argued for the importance of the role played by creative individuals and creative occupations (not necessarily artistic) as a motor of economic development in cities and regions. This essentially argues that economic outcomes are ultimately linked to places' ability to attract and retain mobile creative individuals. The 'quality of place' factors valued by these people are suggested to be tolerance and openness to different ethnic, racial and lifestyle groups, an authentic and attractive built environment, high levels of social cohesion, and the opportunity to take part in (or at least consume) a variety of cultural activities and related amenities. The presence of this creative class is then assumed implicitly to provide distinct advantages to regions in generating innovations, growing and attracting high-technology industries, and spurring economic growth.

Significantly, the pioneering work of Florida was undertaken with reference to the North American context. There is, however, growing empirical evidence that the European context does have significant implications for the trans-national applicability of the creative class thesis (Clifton, 2008; Asheim, 2009; Boschma and Frisch, 2009; Hansen and Niedomysl, 2009; Andersen et al., 2010a, 2010b; Martin-Brelot et al., 2010; Huggins and Clifton, 2011; Clifton et al., 2013; Clifton and Macaulay, 2015). In particular, Musterd and Gritsai (2013) have highlighted the relative lack of worker mobility in the European context, and are sceptical regarding the role played by soft factors relative to that of personal networks. More generally, there has been a significant critique of the creative class model around the apparent fuzziness of concepts, the nature of causality and its manifest attractiveness to policymakers who in turn began to adopt it in a largely off-the-shelf manner from the early to mid-2000s as a quick fix for their various urban problems (see Peck, 2005, for an extensive critique).

Finally, various national governments across Europe have adopted the creative discourse in their policies (Braun and Lavanga, 2007); cities and regions have played (and continue to do so) a key role in the development of these policies (Hall, 2000; Florida, 2002; EC, 2010; Musterd and Kovacs, 2013) due to the fact that the CCIs tend to cluster in space (Chapain et al., 2010; Power, 2011; Ketels and Protsiv, 2014) in order to benefit from both economies of scale and agglomeration, that is the various actors present at the different stages of the creative value chain from university graduates to creative workers, brokers, public institutions, arts galleries, theatres, creative associations as well as access to other local and regional economic actors. Within this historical development and policy backdrop, some interesting dynamics have emerged across Europe, which has shaped the understanding and analysis of the creative industries and the creative class, which we suggest have been driven more by regional agendas than national or European interventions.

Thus, the following drivers behind the emergence of a 'creative regions' agenda across Europe are identified:

The use of the creative industries and/or the creative class as a catalyst (to new regional economic dynamics and identities), which made regions (and city regions) the ideal settings for an increasing neo-liberal agenda of growth and development via CCIs;
A strong policy drive heavily linked to economic growth and innovation agendas, also encompassing cultural, social and environmental agendas, building on the wider impacts that the CCIs and creativity generate; as such, creative activities and occupations are targeted by a wide range of policy interventions and public sector investments;
A new focus on employment and work—as a response to previous needs for economic re-structuring reinforced by the 2008–2009 economic crisis—which often favoured a positive representation of creative employment but has largely failed to connect to the issue of representation, skills and job security at the national level and migration at the national, European and international levels.

These various understandings, objectives and drivers and their relative success are discussed within the various chapters of the book. On the one hand, authors such as Afken et al. and Wedermeir discuss the contribution of the creative class to regional economic development, whereas Brown explores the migration strategies of creative individuals, and Clifton and Macaulay examine how the location of creative individuals may or may not reinforce processes of social cohesion. On the other hand, Bennet et al., Mould and Comunian, Pareja-Eastaway and Pradel i Miquel, and Perrin discuss how the creative industries contribute to wider cultural and/or economic development or wider planning and regeneration strategies across various geographical contexts.

The Creative Class and the Creative Industries as Catalyst: Emerging Creative Regions

The shift towards neo-liberal policy-making as orthodoxy has been well documented within the field of regional development and beyond (Brenner et al., 2012; Haughton et al., 2013; Boland, 2014), exemplified by a focus on growth and the benchmarking of competitiveness via policies emphasising competitive bidding, attracting potential 'customers' (companies, tourists, mobile knowledge workers), urban planning involving spaces for consumption, recreation, cultural events, nightlife and artistic districts, plus high quality residential areas (for a comprehensive review see Sager, 2011). Many regions have thus adopted the standard suite of neo-liberal development policies in a more or less off-the-shelf fashion. Moreover, this policy-making agenda implicitly incorporates (and indeed often conflates) elements of cultural and creative industries, the creative class and so on, which are typically employed without due consideration of context (Chapain and Comunian, 2010; Clifton et al., 2013; Andres and Chapain, 2015), or indeed the more subtle aspects of the underlying drivers (Clifton, 2008). While previous reviews have considered whether there is evidence for a European perspective in relation to creative industries and the associated policy frameworks (Comunian et al., 2014), and examined the discontinuities and commonalities between different spatial scales of analysis (Chapain et al., 2013), there is a need to unpack the role of creativity within the prevailing policy-making climate described above. More generally, what is the broader meaning therein of 'attractive places' with regard to their external projection to the wider world (Clifton, 2014)?

The Role of Policy and Local and Regional Interventions

Considering the case studies presented in this book, but also looking beyond these at various European programmes—such as the wide range of INTERREG programmes that have supported local and interregional cooperation in relation to CCIs (Suwala, 2010)—it is clear that from the very start that regional policy was seen as a major factor for the development and support of CCIs. This was very visible in the United Kingdom after 1997 as the (now disbanded) Regional Development Agencies (RDAs) became protagonists of numerous initiatives to facilitate creative start-ups and promote them to market, as well as shaping the regional cultural regeneration of cities via creative clusters and cultural quarters, as questioned also by Mould and Comunian in this book. The range of interventions is well illustrated in an early article by Jayne (2005) and was perfectly summarised by Oakley in this quote:

> no region of the country, whatever its industrial base, human capital stock, scale or history is safe from the need for a 'creative hub' or 'cultural quarter' (OAKLEY, 2004, p. 68)

Similar trends have been observed for both the creative industries and the creative class in Western, Central and Eastern Europe (Musterd and Kovacs, 2013). While the relative advantages and disadvantages that different regional settings might offer to CCIs can be evidenced for various cities and regions (as Chapain and Comunian, 2010, do for the West Midlands and North-East of England) and/or with regard to the creative class (Clifton et al., 2013; Musterd and Gritsai, 2013), the role played by policy in these contexts is undeniable. From the interest of some leading UK and European city regions in defining and positioning themselves as 'creative'—with Barcelona as one of the front runners in Europe on marking its creative potential (Richards and Wilson, 2007)—the emphasis on creative class and the CCIs has expanded to include emerging regions, rural and smaller regions (Bell and Jayne, 2010; McGranahan et al., 2011; Gibson, 2012; Stryjakiewicz et al., 2013; Rozentale and Lavanga, 2014; Slee et al., 2015).

Comunian et al. (2010) articulate the relationship between locations and the creative economy in relation to four main assets: hard infrastructure, governance, soft infrastructure and markets. While they specifically consider the question of governance and creative policies, the other assets play an important role in local and regional policy interventions to support the creative economy. In relation to infrastructure, many cities and regions have seen the development of new buildings or refurbishment of old ones to provide spaces for the attraction and/or retention of local creative industries and workers and to foster creative consumption through the consumption of heritage, visual arts and performing arts for residents and tourists (Evans, 2009; Andres and Chapain, 2013, 2015). Public policy has a particular role to play in this type of infrastructural investment as the nature of CCIs—comprising mainly small and medium size companies—makes these impossible to undertake as part of their business models. In addition, these interventions are linked to wider cultural, social and environmental objectives in terms of regeneration in some deprived areas (Andres and Chapain, 2013, 2015). Public intervention is also critical in relation to investment in higher education infrastructure and knowledge/educational platforms, supporting the development of creative professionals (Comunian et al., 2015), whereas policies supporting other local and regional infrastructure such as transport can also be seen as important in giving access to markets and labour (Chapain and Comunian, 2010). However, policies have also an important role to play in relation to supporting soft infrastructure. Here, we can think of not only the importance of local creative networks and interaction platforms (Comunian, 2011; Musterd and Gritsai, 2013), but also the importance of place branding (Clifton, 2014) or the new emphasis on financial tools to support start-ups or creative products development (Perez Monclus, 2015). Finally, policies are instrumental in supporting the development of creative markets, for example, through commissioning (Comunian and Mould, 2014) or through financial schemes that allow borrowing to support the purchase of art or other creative outputs. Ultimately, the attraction and retention of creative individuals and firms are at the heart of all these interventions.

The value of and linkages between economic, cultural, social and other types of interventions to support either the creative industries or the creative class are highlighted in many of the chapters in the book (including Brown, Clifton and Macaulay, Mould and Comunian, Perrin, and Pareja-Eastaway and Pradel i Miquel). These contributions bring to the fore the potential contradictions and dualities of many local, regional and national creative policy interventions in Europe: on the one hand, an interest in and commitment to protecting and promoting cultural identities, heritage and cultural values to preserve and develop the cultural landscape of cities and regions and, on the other hand, the related expected socio-economic outcomes attached to these investments.

Creative Employment: Panacea or Placebo

Another key feature of the development of the creative regions discourse and intervention agenda has to be linked to the emphasis on creative employment. The attention towards work and employment has to be connected both with the attention of policy towards measuring the role of creative occupations and creative industries as a new employment sector—in many regions and countries which had previously been affected by unemployment and economic restructuring—as well as with the popularity of the creative class (Florida, 2002) theory in the early to mid-2000s leading the wider creative economy discourse (Bakhshi et al., 2013; UN, 2013).

In the United Kingdom, there has been a strong trajectory of growth in employment in the sector, initially within the creative industries themselves, but, since 2010, incorporating the creative occupations embedded in the rest of the economy (DCMS, 2010, 2015a). The data have supported policy investment and advocacy towards the creative industries and economy and its potential to provide employment in areas which have suffered from decline and restructuring (Comunian and Jacobi, 2015). As such, employment within the creative industries increased from 0.93 to 1.71 million jobs from 1997 to 2013 (84%), whereas the creative economy (i.e. creative industries plus creative occupations within the rest of the economy) grew from 1.81 to 2.62 million jobs (45%) over the same period. This growth in the creative economy was four times higher than the growth in jobs within the entire economy, supporting the idea that the creative economy is a pathway to growth and an alternative to job decline in the manufacturing sector, for example. However, these overall figures hide some very different trajectories with some strong creative sectors, like design and information technology and software growing at a very fast rate (over 15% from 2011 to 2013, for example) and others creative sectors suffering from job losses, like publishing, crafts, and museums and galleries showing negative trends (−15.8%, −4.9% and −5.9% respectively, from 2011 to 2013). As such, as detailed analysis of the social groups and individuals who make up this workforce highlight, access, equality and diversity appear to remain an issue across the creative sectors (DCMS, 2015b). Similar distinctive patterns across countries and industries can be observed in recent European creative statistics as well (TERA, 2014). Furthermore, as argued in Bennett et al. in this book, the livelihood and working conditions—as well as social security—of cultural workers and independent producers are often overlooked both in academic research and in policy intervention.

The positive projection of cultural and creative work as a new panacea to support local and regional development, even for lagging regions, has generated a fierce battle between cities and regions to attract and retain these jobs. The start of this debate is linked to the analysis of the North American context presented by Florida (2002). However, much of his work has been adapted and translated to a range of European national and regional mapping documents and publications, as discussed previously. The debate has expanded to require a closer reflection on the specificity of attraction dynamics and location choices in different countries, as the contributions of Julie Brown, Christoph Alfken, Tom Broekel and Rolf Sternberg in this volume highlight.

The Chapters

This edited book aims to present and critically discuss approaches that address the role of cities and regions in relation to the development of the creative class and the creative industries, but also considers the current challenges and opportunities that might emerge from different contexts in doing so, depending upon the activities targeted, that is industries or workers, and the objectives of policymakers and their expected outcomes.

The book features eight chapters, split evenly with regard to geographical focus between the United Kingdom and continental Europe (the latter covering Spain, Germany, France, Luxemburg and Belgium individually and in combination). There is also a similar division in terms of those focusing primarily on the policy level (the chapters of Clifton and Macaulay, Mould and Comunian, Pareja-Eastaway and Pradel i Miquel, and Perrin) and those of the individual creative actors (the chapters of Alfken et al., Bennett et al., Wedemeier, and Brown). There is also diversity within the United Kingdom–focused chapters.

The first of these, by Julie Brown, provides a micro-level, qualitative analysis of the motivations, experiences and migration trajectories of a subset of the creative class working in the music and visual and performing arts sector in the city of Birmingham, UK. Birmingham represents an example of a European 'second-tier' city emulating 'creative city' policies, and one that is potentially well placed to attract international talent due to its culturally diverse population and reputation for tolerance. Overall, she finds clear evidence that in reality, the migration decisions of such people depend on a much broader range of factors than simply the quality of place or diversity and tolerance. These are typically related to higher education and personal and career development opportunities; thus she suggests that policies focusing on subjective concepts of place's attractiveness are unlikely to be successful. Rather, cities need more carefully targeted policies that address their particular socio-economic and physical realities. On the theme of policy, Oli Mould and

Roberta Comunian's contribution focuses on that of developing 'cultural quarters'; over the last two decades, these have been used by many local authorities across the United Kingdom in an attempt to redevelop and revitalise declining urban centres. They describe how in many cases visitor numbers remain lower than expected, and in some extreme examples flagship projects have been sold off or closed down. Framed within the wider debate as to the role of creativity in urban regeneration and the apparent contradiction between artistic merit and commercial viability, they argue that there is a need for a more practice-based, subjective account of the cultural quarter paradigm.

The neo-liberal economic development policies outlined in Mould and Comunian's chapter are almost ubiquitous in their emphasis on translating creativity into competitive outcomes. However, the context is often a neglected factor in such debates. To this end, Nick Clifton and Tony Macaulay consider what an appropriate policy agenda might be within what they refer to as a 'Post-Conflict' society, that is a place that has recently experienced significant levels of social unrest and/or political violence, which now has largely ceased but whose legacy remains. Using the illustrative case of Northern Ireland in the United Kingdom, they argue that the present policy that appears to consider social cohesion, tolerance and diversity largely as by-products of aspired-to economic success rather than potential contributory factors towards it represents a missed opportunity both in terms of attracting and retaining mobile creatives within Northern Ireland, and unleashing as yet untapped pools of creativity within its society. The chapter by Sophie Bennett, Steven McGuire and Rachel Rahman also considers creative workers in a particular context, in this case the rural. They address the issue as to why the presence of creatives in peripheral regions does not necessarily lead to economic development outcomes therein. Employing a survey of micro and small craft enterprises in Mid and West Wales, UK, they attribute this finding to the observed mismatch between government-led business development incentives, and the bohemian values of local enterprises. They suggest that policies formulated on the basis of an urban creative development model are therefore likely to have limited relevance in rural places, where creative employment is typically skewed towards art and craft activity.

Shifting the geographical focus to Europe, Montserrat Pareja-Eastaway and Marc Pradel i Miquel present a comparative analysis of four Spanish cities, Madrid, Barcelona, Bilbao and Valencia, exploring the issues of path dependency and policy transferability with regard to the creative economy. These cities have different historical paths to industrialisation and modernisation, which play out in combination with their own set of actors and economic traditions. Thus, these authors outline different forms of transition towards the creative economy. However, like a number of other Spanish cities, these four case-study cities developed ambitious policies and programmes to foster the creative economy in the context of economic expansion largely driven by real estate development. Now, in the context of the post-crisis recession, such initiatives need a critical reassessment. By shifting the policy focus from cities to regions, the chapter by Thomas Perrin discusses creative and cultural policies that are developed on a cross-border scale, via a comparative case study of the Pyrenees-Mediterranean 'Euroregion', located on the French-Spanish eastern border and the 'Greater Region' between Luxembourg, Germany, Belgium and France. He focuses on uses of culture, identity and creative resources in the strategies of territorial attractiveness and institutional capacity building. As a result, these dynamics emphasise the contribution of cultural policy to the construction of territoriality, and subsequently the contribution of Euroregions to the territorial and cultural construction of Europe. In this way he suggests that one of the main challenges of the 'Creative Euroregions' is to advocate European construction and cultural diversity, while preserving regional identities and sub-state prerogatives.

This special issue concludes with two chapters examining the geography of creativity in Germany. The chapter by Christoph Alfken, Tom Broekel and Rolf Sternberg contributes to the ongoing debate regarding the relative importance of economic and amenity-related factors for attracting talent, more specifically members of the creative class. Unlike many researchers in the field who have limited availability of cross-sectional data, they were able to employ panel data to address this question. This chapter explores the concentration of artists across 412 German regions over a 4-year period; amenity-related factors are largely found to fail to explain the agglomeration processes of artists, while in contrast their results clearly confirm the relevance of economic factors which are central in the literature on regional productions systems, local labour markets and externalities. Moreover, artists are shown to be a heterogeneous group as the relative importance of regional factors significantly differs between artist groupings (in this case visual artists, performing artists, musicians and writers). Finally, in research complementing that of Alfken et al., Jan Wedemeier provides an analysis of the impact of the wider creative sector (not just restricted to artists more also incorporating the broader creative class) on the total employment and on the creative sector's employment growth in Western German regions from 1977 to 2004. He finds that large shares of creative sector employment lead to an increase in the total employment of a region, but that this also reduces the growth rate of this employment group. As the former effect outweighs the latter, this means a convergence in creative professionals' employment between regions is observed. In contrast to Alfken et al., however, Wedemeier finds that amenities do play a role in explaining the attraction of creatives—albeit with regard to a narrow definition thereof—that is amenities proxied by the presence of bohemian occupations in the locality.

Concluding Remarks

Thus, some of the key issues raised within the contributions in this book are:

(1) How might we reconcile the notions of the cultural and the economic when looking at impact and expectations with regard to the development of the creative class and the creative industries across Europe? What is the relationship between creative individuals and creative cities within different European contexts and policies?
(2) How are creative workers and individuals shaping the dynamics of creative production and local and regional development? How do cultural and creative workers and firms share and support the image and cultural identities of cities, localities and regions? How can these creative people and activities be retained and become engaged citizens as well as fostering the visitor economy?
(3) What role does the concentration of creatives play at different geographical scales and contexts? For example, how do these concentrations work in small towns and rural contexts compared to the more traditional larger city perspectives?
(4) What is the role of local and regional policies and policy frameworks and what are the best practices/lessons emerging in different European contexts? Are there any geographical patterns emerging linked to national policy contexts (liberal, interventionist, federal, central states)?

Acknowledgements

The eight chapters featured in this book arose out of work originally presented (in its formative stages) at a number of 'Creative Regions' research seminars (www.creative-regions.org); these were co-organised by the three co-authors of this edited book and sponsored by the Regional Studies Association, to whom we are grateful for the support.

References

Andersen, K.V., Bugge, M.M., Hansen, H.K., Isaksen, A. and Raunio, M. (2010a) One size fits all? Applying the creative class thesis onto a Nordic context. *European Planning Studies*, 18(10): 1591–1609.

Andersen, K.V., Hansen, H.K., Isaksen, A. and Raunio, M. (2010b) Nordic city regions in the creative class debate: putting the creative class thesis to a test. *Industry & Innovation*, 17(2): 215–240.

Andres, L. and Chapain, C. (2013) The integration of cultural and creative industries into local and regional development strategies in Birmingham and Marseille: towards an inclusive and collaborative governance? *Regional Studies*, 47(2): 161–182.

Andres, L. and Chapain, C. (2015) Creative systems: a new integrated approach to understanding the complexity of cultural and creative industries in Eastern and Western countries. In Bryson, J. and Daniels, P. (Eds.), *The Handbook of Service Business*. Cheltenham: Edward Elgar, pp. 349–370.

Asheim, B. (2009) Guest editorial: introduction to the creative class in European city regions. *Economic Geography*, 85(4): 355–362.

Bakhshi, H., Hargreaves, I. and Mateos-Garcia, J. (2013) *A Manifesto for the Creative Economy*. London: NESTA.

Bell, D. and Jayne, M. (2010) The creative countryside: policy and practice in the UK rural cultural economy. *Journal of Rural Studies*, 26(3): 209–218.

Boland, P. (2014) The relationship between spatial planning and economic competitiveness: the 'path to economic nirvana' or a 'dangerous obsession'? *Environment and Planning A*, 46(4): 770–787.

Boschma, R. and Frisch, M. (2009) Creative class and regional growth: empirical evidence from seven European countries. *Economic Geography*, 85(4): 391–423.

Braun, E. and Lavanga, M. (2007) *An International Comparative Quickscan into National Policies for Creative Industries*. Rotterdam: Euricur.

Brenner, N., Peck, J. and Theodore, N. (2012) Towards deep neoliberalization. In Künkel, J. and Mayer, M. (Eds.), *Neoliberal Urbanism and Its Discontents*. London: Palgrave Macmillan, pp. 27–45.

CEBR. (2013) *The contribution of the arts and culture to the national economy*. A Report for Arts Council England and the National Museum Directors' Council. London: Centre for Economics and Business Research.

Chapain, C. and Comunian, R. (2010) Enabling and inhibiting the creative economy: the role of the local and regional dimensions in England. *Regional Studies*, 44(6): 717–734.

Chapain, C., Cooke, P., De Propris, L., MacNeill, S. and Mateos-Garcia, J. (2010) *Creative clusters and innovation: Putting creativity on the map*. London: NESTA.

Chapain, C., Clifton, N. and Comunian, R. (2013) Understanding creative regions: bridging the gap between global discourses and regional and national contexts. *Regional Studies*, 47(2): 131–134.

Chapain, C. and Hargreaves, I. (2016) Citizenship in the creative economy. In Hargreaves, I. and Hartley, J. (Eds.), *The Creative Citizen Unbound: How Social Media and DIY Culture Contribute to Democracy, Communities and the Creative Economy*. Bristol: Policy Press.

Clifton, N. (2008) The 'creative class' in the UK: an initial analysis. *Geografiska Annaler Series B: Human Geography*, 90(1): 63–82.

Clifton, N. (2014) Towards a holistic understanding of county of origin effects? Branding of the region, branding from the region. *Journal of Destination Marketing & Management*, 3(2): 122–132.

Clifton, N., Cooke, P. and Hansen, H.K. (2013) Towards a reconciliation of the 'context-less' with the 'space-less'? The creative class across varieties of capitalism: new evidence from Sweden and the UK. *Regional Studies*, 47(2): 201–215.

Clifton, N. and Macaulay, T. (2015) Creativity, cohesion and the 'post-conflict' society: a policy agenda (Illustrated from the case of Northern Ireland). *European Planning Studies*, 23(12): 2370–2389.

Comunian, R., Chapain, C. and Clifton, N. (2010) Location, location, location: exploring the complex relationship between creative industries and place. *Creative Industries Journal*, 3(1): 5–10.

Comunian, R., Chapain, C. and Clifton, N. (2014) Creative industries & creative policies: a European perspective? *City, Culture and Society*, 5(2): 51–53.

Comunian, R. (2011) Rethinking the creative city: the role of complexity, networks and interactions in the urban creative economy. *Urban Studies,* 48: 1157–1179.

Comunian, R., Gilmore, A. and Jacobi, S. (2015) Higher education and the creative economy: creative graduates, knowledge transfer and regional impact debates. *Geography Compass,* 9: 371–383.

Comunian, R. and Jacobi, S. (2015) Chapter 8: Resilience, creative careers and creative spaces: bridging vulnerable artist's livelihoods and adaptive urban change. In Pinto, H. (Ed.), *Resilient Territories: Innovation and Creativity for New Modes of Regional Development.* Cambridge: Cambridge Scholars.

Comunian, R. and Mould, O. (2014) The weakest link: creative industries, flagship cultural projects and regeneration. *City, Culture and Society,* 5: 65–74.

Council of European Union (EU). (2007) *Contribution of the cultural and creative sectors to the achievement of the Lisbon objectives—Adoption of the Council conclusions.* Introductory note. Cult 29, 9021/07, Brussels 8 May 2007.

Creative Europe. (2013) The European Union programme for the cultural and creative sectors. 2014–2010. Available online at: http://ec.europa.eu/programmes/creative-europe/documents/creative-europe-flyer_web_en.pdf [Accessed on 15 February 2016].

Department for Media Culture and Sport (DCMS). (1998) *Creative Industries Mapping Document.* London: DCMS.

Department for Media Culture and Sport (DCMS). (2000) *Creative Industries: The Regional Dimension.* The report of the Regional Issues Working Group. London: DCMS.

Department for Media Culture and Sport (DCMS). (2010) *Creative Industries Economic Estimates.* Technical note, February. London: DCMS.

Department for Media Culture and Sport (DCMS). (2015a) *Creative Industries Economic Estimates.* London: DCMS.

Department for Media Culture and Sport (DCMS). (2015b) *Creative Industries: Focus on Employment.* Detailed tables by Creative Industries group. London: DCMS.

ERICARTS. (2010) Study on the contribution of culture to local and regional development. Evidence from the structural funds. Final report. Sevenoaks, Kent: Centre for Strategy and Evaluation Services.

European Cluster Observatory. (2013) Creative industries analysis of industry-specific framework conditions relevant for the development of world-class clusters. Available online at: http://www.clusterobservatory.eu/index.html#!view=documents;mode=one;sort=name;uid=1b5a1d43-1eb4-42c0-b1fa-ca136d5551e2;id= [Accessed on 16 February 2016].

European Commission (EC). (1998) *Culture, the Cultural Industries and Employment in Commission Staff Working Paper Document Sec (98) 837.* Brussels: EC.

European Commission (EC). (2010) *Green Paper: Unlocking the Potential of Cultural and Creative Industries.* COM (183), Brussels: EC.

European Parliament (EP). (1999) Cultural industries and employment in the countries of the European Union. Summary. Education and Culture Series EDUC 104A. Available online at: http://www.europarl.europa.eu/workingpapers/educ/104aensum_en.htm [Accessed on 16 February 2016].

European Parliament (EP). (2013) European cultural and creative sectors as sources of economic growth and jobs. European Parliament resolution of 12 September 2013 on promoting the European cultural and creative sectors as sources of economic growth and jobs (2012/2302(INI)). Available online at: http://www.europarl.europa.eu/sides/getDoc.do?pubRef=-//EP//NONSGML+TA+P7-TA-2013-0368+0+DOC+PDF+V0//EN [Accessed on 15 February 2015].

European Union (EU). (2012) Policy handbook on how to strategically use the EU support programmes, including structural funds, to foster the potential of culture for local, regional and national development and the spill-over effects on the wider economy? Working Group of EU Member States Experts (Open Method of Coordination) on Cultural and Creative Industries, April. Available online at: http://ec.europa.eu/culture/library/publications/cci-policy-handbook_en.pdf [Accessed on 15 February 2016].

Evans, G. (2009) Creative cities, creative spaces and urban policy. *Urban Studies,* 46: 1003–1040.

Fleming, T. (2015) Cultural and creative spillovers in Europe. Report on a preliminary evidence review. Available online at: http://www.artscouncil.org.uk/advice-and-guidance/browse-advice-and-guidance/cultural-and-creative-spillovers-europe [Accessed on 16 February 2016].

Florida, R. (2002) *The Rise of the Creative Class.* New York; Basic Books.

Gibson, C. (2012) *Creativity in Peripheral Places: Redefining the Creative Industries.* London: Routledge.

Hall, P. (2000) Creative Cities and Economic Development. *Urban Studies,* 37(4): 639–649.

Hansen, H.K. and Niedomysl, T. (2009) Migrations of the creative class: evidence from Sweden. *Journal of Economic Geography,* 9(2): 191–206.

Hartley, J., Potts, J., Cunningham, S., Flew, T., Keane, M. and Banks, J. (2013) *Key Concepts in the Creative Industries*. London: Sage.

Haughton, G., Allmendinger, P. and Oosterlynck, A. (2013) Space of neoliberal experimentation: soft spaces, postpolitics, and neoliberal governmentality. *Environment and Planning A*, 45(1): 217–234.

Huggins, R. and Clifton, N. (2011) Competitiveness, creativity, and place-based development. *Environment and Planning A*, 43(6): 1341–1362.

Jayne, M. (2005) Creative industries: the regional dimension? *Environment & Planning C: Government & Policy*, 23: 537–556.

KEA. (2006) The economy of culture in Europe. Available online at: http://ec.europa.eu/culture/library/studies/cultural-economy_en.pdf [Accessed on 15 February 2016]. Brussels: European Commission.

Ketels, C. and Protsiv, S. (2014) European Cluster Panorama 2014. Prepared for the European Cluster Observatory. Available online at: http://ec.europa.eu/growth/smes/cluster/observatory/cluster-mapping-services/cluster-mapping/cluster-panorama/index_en.htm [Accessed on 8 January 2016].

McGranahan, D.A, Wojan, T.R. Lambert, D.M. (2011) The rural growth trifecta: outdoor amenities, creative class and entrepreneurial context. *Journal of Economic Geography*, 11(3): 529–557.

Martin-Brelot, H., Grossetti, M., Eckert, D., Gritsai, O. and Kovács, Z. (2010) The spatial mobility of the creative class: a European perspective. *International Journal of Urban and Regional Research*, 34(4): 854–870.

Matarosso, F. (1997) *Use or Ornament? The Social Impact of Participation in the Arts*. Stroud: Comedia.

Musterd, S. and Gritsai, O. (2013) The creative knowledge city in Europe: structural conditions and urban policy strategies for competitive cities. *European Urban and Regional Studies*, (20): 343–359.

Musterd, S. and Kovacs, Z. (Eds.). (2013) *Place Making and Policies for Competitive Cities*. Chichester: Wiley & Sons.

NESTA. (2015) *Creative Economy Employment in the EU and UK: A Comparative Analysis*. London: NESTA.

Oakley, K. (2004) Not So Cool Britannia: The Role of the Creative Industries in Economic Development. *International Journal of Cultural Studies*, 7(1): 67–77.

Peck J. (2005) Struggling with the creative class. *International Journal of Urban and Regional Research*, 29(4): 740–770.

Perez Monclus, R. (2015) Public banking for the cultural sector: financial instruments and the new financial intermediaries. *International Review of Social Research*, 5: 88–101.

Power, D. (2011) *Priority Sector Report: Creative and Cultural Industries*. European Cluster Observatory, Europa Innova Paper N. 16, Brussels: EC.

Richards, G. and Wilson, J. (2007) The creative turn in regeneration: creative spaces, spectacles and tourism in cities. In Smith, M.K. (Ed.), *Tourism, Culture and Regeneration,* Wallingford: CABI, pp. 12–24.

Rozentale, I. and Lavanga, M. (2014) The "universal" characteristics of creative industries revisited: the case of Riga. *City, Culture and Society*, 5(2): 55–64.

Sager, T. (2011) Neo-liberal urban planning policies: a literature survey 1990–2010. *Progress in Planning*, 76(4): 147–199.

Slee, B., Hopkins, J. and Vellinga, N. (2015) Could the creative class be a factor in Scottish rural development? *Scottish Affairs*, 24(2): 207–226.

Smith, C. (1998) *Creative Britain*. London: Faber & Faber.

Stryjakiewicz, T., Gritsai, O., Dainov, E. and Egedy, T. (2013) Addressing the Legacy of Post-Socialist Cities in East Central Europe. In S. Musterd and Z. Kovács (Eds.), *Place-making and Policies for Competitive Cities*. New York: Wiley.

Stryjakiewicz, T., Stachowiak, K., Męczyński, M. (2012) Editorial. *Quaestiones Geographicae*, 31(4): 5–7.

Suwala, L. (2010) The role of EU regional policy in driving creative regions. *Regions Magazine*, 277(1) 11–13.

TERA. (2014) The economic contribution of the creative industries to EU GDP and employment. Evolution 2008–2011. Available online at: http://www.teraconsultants.fr/en/issues/The-Economic-Contribution-of-the-Creative-Industries-to-EU-in-GDP-and-Employment [Accessed on 21 December 2014].

United Nations (UN). (2013) *Creative Economy Report 2013. Special Edition. Widening Local Development Pathways*. Geneva and New York: UN.

Home from Home? Locational Choices of International "Creative Class" Workers

JULIE BROWN

School of Performance and Cultural Industries, University of Leeds, Leeds, UK

ABSTRACT *This paper focuses on the international migration dynamics of the highly skilled "creative class". To date, little research has been undertaken to provide an in-depth understanding of the underlying reasons behind the movements of these workers. By providing a micro-level, qualitative analysis of the motivations, experiences and migration trajectories of a sub-group of these workers, namely "creative Bohemians", this paper offers a perspective that is currently lacking in the literature. These individuals are considered to be particularly attracted by diverse and open urban milieus, as well as being instrumental in creating the type of urban environment that attracts other members of the "creative class". Birmingham, UK, was chosen as an example of a European city emulating "creative city" policies and being potentially well-placed to attract international talent due to its culturally diverse population and reputation for "tolerance". Findings call for a more nuanced understanding of the factors associated with both the attraction and retention of international talent, as it is clear that migration decisions depend on factors other than simply "quality of place" or diversity and tolerance. Policies focusing on subjective concepts of place attractiveness are thus unlikely to be successful. Instead, cities need carefully targeted policies that address their particular socio-economic and physical realities.*

Introduction

Much has been written in recent academic and policy literature about the competitive imperative for cities to attract and retain high levels of "human capital" (Turok, 2009; Musterd & Murie, 2010). Despite potentially greater international mobility throughout the EU, coupled with the claim that the "creative class"—that is, workers who are highly educated and talented—are individually and collectively highly mobile, moving frequently in search of urban "quality of place" (Florida, 2002a), only limited, mostly quantitative research has been undertaken to provide an understanding of the factors associated with the movements of these workers.

The existing literature on highly skilled migration has tended to focus on intra-company, corporate transfers of "elite" workers (Scott, 2006b)—but it is now accepted that the nature and reasons for highly skilled migration are far more complex. As Ryan and Mulholland (2014) and others (e.g. Conradson and Latham, 2005; Kennedy, 2008) note, there is an acknowledgement of the need for more research in this area. Further, skilled migration has historically been limited to world cities (e.g. Beaverstock, 2005; Nagel, 2005; Scott, 2006b; Ryan & Mulholland, 2014), and much of the literature examines migration to these locations. Second-tier European cities have received very little attention to date, but many are emulating "creative city" policies and are attempting to compete to attract international talent, although they often lack the physical and socio-cultural conditions deemed attractive to the "creative class" (Houston *et al.*, 2008; Brown *et al.*, 2013). Finally, while there is recognition that the heterogeneity of highly skilled migration is increasing, very little attention has been devoted to understanding the motivations or experiences of "creative class" migrants (Hansen & Niedomysl, 2009; Syrett & Sepulveda, 2011). There is a lack of knowledge of their reasons for migrating; whether or not they prefer locations with specific attributes; the importance of factors such as "diversity" or "tolerance" and their experiences after migration, particularly relations with the host society and existing migrant communities. Also, as the "creative class" is hypothesized to be hyper-mobile, whether or not these migrants tend to move frequently.

As a first step in addressing these issues, the overarching aim of this paper is to assess the findings from qualitative, in-depth interviews conducted with highly skilled "creative class" migrants to provide a micro-level analysis of their motivations, experiences and migration trajectories. The aim is to provide a perspective on these individual's decision-making that is currently lacking in the literature. Birmingham, UK, was chosen as an example of a second-tier European city emulating "creative city" policies as a critical component in its ongoing regeneration. The role of international migrants in this process has, however, been largely disregarded in city-level policy-making to date, despite the city being well-placed within the UK to attract international talent due to its culturally diverse population and reputation for tolerance (Brown *et al.*, 2007). It thus makes a particularly interesting case study.

The paper begins by expanding on the "creative class" concept and notions of hyper-mobility as well as the perceived significance of certain physical and social attributes—including population "diversity"—in attracting and retaining international talent; theories of, and trends in, skilled migration in Europe are then introduced. Next, the history of migration to Birmingham is contextualized, and policy designed to attract "creative class" workers briefly addressed. Research methods are then outlined and the main qualitative findings presented. The paper concludes with a discussion of the implications of the research findings for Florida's "creative class" thesis in the context of second-tier European cities and some recommendations for urban development policy in light of these findings.

Attracting the "Creative Class"? Amenities, Diversity and Tolerance

A new "creative class" (Florida, 2002a, 2005a, 2005b) comprising a hyper-mobile army of highly talented workers is, we are told, moving around the world in search of places of excellence—they "possess the means, resources and inclination to seek out and move to locations where they can leverage their talents" (Florida, 2005a, p. 79). The claim is that regional economic growth is now powered by these people, as they bring new innovations and skills to the cities fortunate enough to appeal to them (Florida, 2002a, 2002b, 2005a, 2005b). Leading cities, it is argued, are moving further ahead in the competitiveness stakes due to their ability to provide the "quality of place" attributes emphasized by Florida and others (e.g. Clark *et al.*, 2002; Kloosterman, 2013) as essential preconditions for attracting the inflow of this creative talent: they are rich in authentic cultural experiences, including a vibrant "street-level" culture; offer a wide range of high quality arts, recreational and leisure amenities (including nightlife and theatres and music venues); have varied and abundant (semi) public "third places" for social interaction and for people to meet (such as cafes and bookstores) and have attractive and varied urban living environments (Florida, 2002a).

Moreover, Florida argues that the "creative class"; "prefer places that are diverse, tolerant and open to new ideas" (Florida, 2002a, p. 223). Creative people are often characterized as individualists with alternative lifestyle preferences and non-conformist behaviours. This is particularly the case for those in Florida's (2002a) "super-creative core"—and especially the creative "bohemians", who include writers, poets, musicians, designers, actors, sculptors, singers, photographers, dancers, choreographers, painters and figurative artists, conductors, directors and composers—that is, workers who "fully engage in the creative process" (Florida, 2002a, p. 69) and who are posited to be particularly attracted to such environments (Florida, 2002b; see also Boschma & Fritsch, 2007). Florida describes social "diversity" as heterogeneity in terms of ethnicity, sexuality and lifestyle, and "tolerance" as a form of social openness that includes a willingness to accept new people and embrace different ways of thinking, that is, "low barriers to entry for people" (Florida & Tinagli, 2004, p. 12). He argues that "[d]iversity increases the odds that a place will attract different types of people with different skill sets and ideas" (Florida, 2002a, p. 249), while tolerance "is critical for the ability of a region or nation to attract and mobilize creative talent" (Florida & Tinagli, 2004, p. 25).

The argument is that cities, which can make themselves "global talent magnets" (Florida, 2005a, p. 10) through a combination of these physical and social factors, will outperform those which remain homogeneous, mono-cultural and less open to the outside. But despite popularity in policy circles, Florida's ideas concerning the "creative class" have engendered much critical debate (e.g. Peck, 2005; Markusen, 2006; Scott, 2006a; Storper & Manville, 2006; Hoyman & Faricy, 2009; Musterd & Murie, 2010). In particular, the assumed "hyper-mobility" has been questioned; as has the claim that highly skilled individuals choose to move to (or from) specific (urban) places simply because of their aesthetic, cultural or recreational qualities. The role of population "diversity" and "tolerance" in attracting talent also remains largely unsubstantiated.

Of particular relevance to this paper, Florida introduced the concept of competition for the "creative class" within the context of mainly quantitative correlation measures and indexes conducted within the US.[1] Research undertaken in Europe indicates that different socio-cultural and political structures; language differences; different education, health and welfare systems; and limits set by legislation on employing migrants, all make movement between countries potentially less frequent than might otherwise be expected (Nathan, 2007; Houston *et al.*, 2008; Hansen *et al.*, 2009; Hansen & Niedomysl, 2009; Musterd & Murie, 2010).

Further, as Hansen and Niedomysl (2009, p. 193) state, there has been an almost total lack of studies assessing the primary "push" and "pull" mechanisms behind the migration of the "creative class". Exceedingly, little qualitative research has been conducted to determine why highly skilled migrants choose to locate in specific places or the extent to which urban "quality of place" factors influence, or not, these decisions. Significantly, Florida argues that neighbourhoods which are "seething with the interplay of cultures and ideas" (Florida, 2002a, p. 227) act as catalysts for creativity. But, as also highlighted by Syrett and Sepulveda (2011, p. 494, emphasis in original) "the extent to which cultural diversity does produce creativity and innovation within cities, and *how it* does this, remains curiously underspecified and under-researched".

Similarly, Florida does not directly address the more thorny issues of increased urban population "diversity", including the challenges in relation to socio-economic inclusion and exclusion and community cohesion and tension, or the effects these might have on the (continued) attractiveness of certain locations for "creative class" workers, who may choose to move elsewhere if they do not feel welcomed (Syrett & Sepulveda, 2011).

Highly Skilled Migration in Europe: Drivers and Trends

The last decades have seen trans-national migration in Europe that both exceeds and differs from earlier population movements. Marked changes have been seen in the scale of migration flows; the origins and destinations of migrants; migration channels and types of flows and motivation(s) for migration (Vertovec, 2006, 2007). The result is greater diversity within already established cosmopolitan cities and increasingly diverse populations in places where past populations have been more homogenous (Syrett & Sepulveda, 2011, p. 488). Many cities are now characterized by "super-diversity" (Vertovec, 2007, p. 1024) in terms of ethnicity, language(s), religious tradition, regional and local identities, cultural values and practices (Vertovec, 2006).

Highly skilled migration, in particular, has been gaining relative importance in European migration flows since the 1980s (Scott, 2006b). More liberalized immigration policies in many EU countries have led Richard Florida to surmise that "the US' advantage seems to be shifting" as EU countries are able to more effectively attract and retain global talent (Florida & Tinagli, 2004, p. 6). As Bailey and Boyle (2004, p. 233) point out, however, "social, cultural and political structures remain which make movement between [European] countries less 'free' than may be imagined" (see also Martin-Brelot *et al.*, 2010).

Until recently, highly skilled migration mainly consisted of "elites"—trans-national company executives from developed countries who were seconded via their organizations for time-limited durations to mainly first-tier, "global" cities around the world, and who represented a fairly homogeneous socio-cultural group. The associated literature often assumes the notion of "nomadic workers", remaining in one location for only a short duration, and that of a "frictionless mobility characterized by the absence of any kind of meaningful encounter or incorporation in the host society" (Smith & Favell, 2006, p. 15). Integration, for example, was not generally considered an issue. Due to the removal of barriers for labour migration within the EU, coupled with the stronger support for student mobility within the EU and globally, the socio-economic background and the motives and means of skilled trans-national migration have diversified (Conradson & Latham, 2005; Scott, 2006b).

A small but growing literature suggests that a variety of motivations other than purely economic ones may be important in highly skilled migration. According to Scott (2006b), new skilled migrant groups that include "young professionals" who stay on in the host country as new graduates or migrate at the start of their careers; "international Bohemians" who move to enjoy cultural amenities; and "assimilation-settlers" who marry a partner in the host country, have gained rapidly in importance but have received little in the way of research attention. Ryan and Mulholland (2014, p. 587) found that opportunities for learning English, experiencing a new culture and simply "having an adventure" featured in the migratory strategies of highly skilled French migrants in London (see also Conradson & Latham, 2005). It has been suggested that migration is used to accumulate "cultural capital" and as "a route towards distinction" (Scott, 2006b, p. 1123). Nonetheless, as Ryan and Mulholland (2014) note, this may not be the case, as skills and experiences gained in one context may not be transferrable to another (see also Nagel, 2005). Regardless, as also documented by Ryan and Mulholland (2014), there has been a lack of research on the full range of contemporary highly skilled migratory movements.

A number of researchers now consider that "movement" or "mobility" may be more appropriate when considering highly skilled migration, characterized by patterns of circulation, and temporary, frequent and non-permanent moves (Koser & Salt, 1997; Favell *et al.*, 2011). What is meant by "permanent" and "temporary" migration is, however, not straightforward: "permanent" migration often occurs following periods of "temporary" migration. Also, the initial intention of temporary migration may be transformed into permanent migration and "vice versa" depending on a number of factors including migrants' initial experiences in the host country. As discussed by Baláz *et al.* (2004), temporary migration of young graduates may satisfy their desire for new experiences and boost marketable skills in their domestic labour market, negating the need for permanent migration. Alternatively, temporary migration may provide enhanced knowledge and self-confidence, thereby facilitating further migration. Ryan and Mulholland (2014) found strong evidence that the fluid migratory trajectories and motivations of graduates were associated with a particular life stage, that is, young, single and childless, and they gradually become more "emplaced" with career and family commitments, but, rather than a permanent settlement versus mobility binary, they suggest "a continuum of emplacement whereby migrants gradually extend their stay, while at the same time keeping future options open" (Ryan & Mulholland, 2014, p. 587).

Birmingham—A City of Migrants

Since its assumed position as the "workshop of the world" during the Industrial Revolution, Birmingham has attracted large numbers of international migrant workers (see Brown *et al.*, 2007). Today, the city has one of the most diverse populations in the UK, second only to certain inner areas of London: 32.0% of the population has a non-White background. Resonant with its long history of migration from New Commonwealth countries, Pakistani (9.7%) is the largest minority group in the city, followed by Indian (5.8%) and Black Caribbean (4.0%).[2] The percentage of Birmingham residents born outside the UK is also markedly higher at 20.3% compared with 11.6% nationally ONS (2011a).

Similar to most UK cities, Birmingham has seen marked changes in the nature of migration over the past 10–15 years: immigration has exceeded emigration for the first time; there has also been a significant diversification in countries of origin and reasons for migration, to include asylum seekers and refugees from areas including the Balkans, the Middle East and Africa. Since 2004, there has been an influx of new economic migrants from Accession 8 (A8) countries, particularly from Poland (Green et al., 2007). Student flows also form a major part of international migration movements to and from Birmingham: numbers of foreign students studying at Higher Education Institutions in the city increased by 42.0% from 2002, to 13,280 in 2009/2010 (BCC, 2011). While non-UK nationals now account for some 4.9% of regional employment (Green et al., 2007, p. 10), they represent a diverse profile. Although there are some "migrant-dense" professional sectors such as Health and Social Welfare, there has been a trend towards a greater concentration of more recent migrant workers—particularly "A8" migrants—in less skilled occupations, particularly in Manufacturing and Operatives and Elementary Occupations (Green et al., 2007, p. 11&52).

Birmingham has had a difficult post-industrial transition. Following waves of decline, more than two-thirds of manufacturing jobs were lost between 1978 and 2002. High levels of unemployment and social and urban deprivation resulted. Since the early 1990s there has been a steady growth in service sector employment, but the city faces a number of significant restructuring challenges including a continued reliance on low-skilled manufacturing and a lack of a resident skilled workforce (BCC, 2012; Parkinson, 2007). The low level of demand for higher level skills from the region's private sector has also had a significant impact on both the retention and attraction of graduates and other "knowledge sector" workers (WMRO, 2009).

The city has long used "culture" as a policy tool to change perceptions and increase its attractiveness for inwards investment. Initiatives have included "flagship" cultural developments (such as Symphony Hall, the International Conference Centre and, most recently, the new library of Birmingham); support for mainstream cultural organizations (including the City of Birmingham Symphony Orchestra and Birmingham Royal Ballet); and events to animate spaces (such as the annual Artsfest, the largest free arts festival in the UK). The city centre has undergone a series of major physical regeneration initiatives, including the re-making of central areas for new economic and cultural activities (such as Brindleyplace, which hosts IKON Gallery; The Mailbox, which houses the BBC; and the new Bullring shopping centre); and the promotion of "city apartment living" in previously industrial inner-city areas (such as the Jewellery Quarter) in an attempt to bring young professionals to live and work in the city centre (Barber & Hall, 2008). Nevertheless, Birmingham still poses a challenging physical and social environment in which to attract international talent (Brown et al., 2007).

Against this background, the creative industries have been utilized as a policy tool by key public agencies for more than a decade—for their own economic impact as well as their ability to generate "quality of place" and boost the economy by attracting other highly skilled workers to the city (Brown et al., 2010). Estimates[3] indicate the creative industries account for around 18,720 jobs, or 3.9% of the city's employment (lower than the 5.1% of UK employment), with Visual Arts & Design being the fastest growing sector (BOP, 2009). This is more people than are directly employed in the construction, vehicle manufacture or financial intermediation sectors in the city. Birmingham has just under a fifth (19.4%) of all creative employment in the eight English core cities. As a percentage of all employment within the city, however, Birmingham ranks behind Bristol, Manchester, Leeds and Newcastle (BOP, 2009).

The role of skilled migrants in this process has, however, been largely disregarded in city-level policy-making to date, despite Birmingham being potentially well-placed within the UK to attract and retain international talent, due to its existing population diversity and its reputation for tolerance (Brown *et al.*, 2007). For example, culture and the creative industries run through several key strands of the new, 20-year city centre masterplanning document. But while it is acknowledged that the city centre is "not sufficiently diverse in terms of its cultural facilities, heritage, retail offer and services especially for young and ethnic minority groups" (BCC, 2010, p. 11), notably absent are acknowledgements of more fundamental issues associated with attracting international talent, including social and community relations of new and existing ethnic groups; spatial segregation and resultant socio-economic inequalities.

Research Methods

This paper draws upon data derived from in-depth, semi-structured interviews undertaken in September 2008 with 10 "creative class" migrants living and working in Birmingham. Interviewees were all part of Florida's "super-creative core"—the creative "bohemians", that is, workers who "fully engage in the creative process" (Florida, 2002a, p. 69). These individuals are considered to be particularly attracted by a diverse and open milieu, as well as being instrumental in creating the type of urban environment that attracts other members of the "creative class" (Florida, 2002b; see also Boschma & Fritsch, 2007). As such, the location choices of these individuals were judged to be important for the study.

Interviewees were selected using the following criteria: (1) Using the UK DCMS Creative Industries definition, they were working in the "Music and Visual & Performing Arts" sector (SIC07 90.01 Performing arts; SIC07 90.02 Support activities to performing arts; SIC07 90.03 Artistic creation; SIC07 90.04 Operation of arts facilities; and SIC07 59.20 Sound recording and music publishing activities); (2) they were working in a creative role, that is, not in administration; (3) As a proxy for "human capital", they were educated to at least degree level or an equivalent vocational-level qualification; (4) they had been resident in Birmingham for a minimum of 6 months and a maximum of 10 years and (5) they were self-initiated movers, that is, none were corporate transferees or had moved with parents.

There is no city-level database of firms or organizations where international migrants are working. Interviewees were therefore recruited using personal industry contacts and thereafter "snowball" techniques were used to identify suitable candidates. In such a convenience sample, it was not possible to control for nationality or to select interviewees proportional to the regional migrant profile. Similarly, it was not possible to control for gender or age. The demographic profile of interviewees is summarized in Table 1.

Interview duration was on average around 45 minutes. Key themes covered were the same for all interviews and included open questions about reasons for migration; factors important in attracting migrants to Birmingham; experiences of living and working in Birmingham, including relations with the host society and other migrant communities; intended duration of stay before arriving in Birmingham, whether these plans had changed and why; and future migration plans. Interviews were all recorded and transcribed "ver batim". NVIVO software was used to organize findings according to the topics detailed earlier.

Table 1. Profile of interviewees

Interviewee	Job title	Nationality	Gender	Age
C1	Audience Development Manager	Indian	F	29
C2	Freelance Artist	Swedish	F	30
C3	Freelance Animator	Greek	M	29
C4	Freelance Artist	Taiwanese	F	33
C5	Art Curator	Australian	F	31
C6	Freelance Musician	Kurdish	M	31
C7	Communications Manager	Indian	M	29
C8	Music director	Australian	M	36
C9	Freelance Visual Artist	Polish	F	29
C10	Freelance Visual Artist	Polish	F	27

Findings: Migrants' Motivations, Experiences and Trajectories

As already discussed, there is a lack of knowledge of the factors associated with the international movement of the "creative class"—their reasons for migrating; whether or not they prefer locations with specific attributes; the importance of factors such as "diversity" or "tolerance"; and their experiences after migration, particularly relations with the host society and other migrant communities. Also, as the "creative class" is hypothesized to be hyper-mobile, whether or not these migrants tend to move frequently. In this section, the main results from the qualitative interviews addressing these issues are presented.

1. *Does Place Attractiveness Matter? Why Skilled Migrants Move to Birmingham*

No evidence was found to support the claim that "creative class" migrants are drawn to places because of a particular set of urban amenities (Florida, 2002a, 2005a, 2005b). Serendipity played a leading role in decisions to move to Birmingham, supporting other research carried out in the region (Green *et al.*, 2007). Indeed, "quality of place" factors were seldom mentioned, thus appearing to be much less influential than the literature may suggest.

Personal developmental opportunities associated with international travel and the idea of exploring another culture or developing an international angle to their creative practice were key migration factors for several interviewees (C3, C4, C5 and C8). It was clear, however, that there was no specific desire to move to Birmingham:

> I mean the main reason was really to get out of Taiwan and to see the world and develop my career as a more international artist I suppose [...] to break through that sort of international market at the time I felt like I needed to develop my knowledge of international markets. (C4)
> ... it was more the idea of coming to a different culture that I wanted to explore rather than the specific area. (C3)

Educational opportunities in creative arts programmes not available in migrants' home countries were also primary attractors, and 6 of the 10 interviewed (C1, C2, C3, C4, C9 and C10) had initially moved to the West Midlands for this reason. Studies indicate that students who spend periods in education abroad are more likely to undertake further migration during their careers (Salt, 1997; Santacreu *et al.*, 2009). Indeed, two interviewees who came to the region for short-term work placements with arts organizations arranged by their home universities both returned to work in the creative sector after graduating. Social networks formed during the initial work placement partly influenced their decision to return, but the potential to find creative-sector employment was also influential:

> I found it quite, well, relatively easy to find employment in creative industry which is, it was for me surprising because I was sure, I'm still sure that if I stayed in Poland I wouldn't be given so many opportunities and chances to do, you know, do what I'm, really stay with my occupation rather than try to do something completely different and basically just earn money. (C9)

Indeed, the initial links developed while studying in the region, both with creative-sector organizations and with peers—some of whom were already working in the local creative sector—were vital for enabling migrants to become quickly networked into the local creative "scene". Placements, internships and voluntary work were key routes and ways into further creative employment that strongly influenced decisions to stay in Birmingham after graduating:

> ...as soon as I start my MA and I meet people from the MA—some people older than me that were already working in the region, and suddenly you are in a network of artists that the references into the City of Birmingham in terms of cultural events and art events are happening more often and more often and then you start getting more clued up to the idea of coming here and seeing what's happening. (C3)
> I was put in touch with an organisation called XXXX who are a South Asian arts development agency and I was doing my internship with them, and that's how I kind of went into the arts....So I did my internship with XXXX and then and stayed and worked for them for a year. (C1)

Again, interviewees pointed out that the choice of Birmingham was largely unplanned:

> I would be honest, it wasn't a conscious choice as such, it was the fact that I moved here [Birmingham] with my first job, well my internship, really. (C1)

Similarly, two interviewees who were already living and working elsewhere in the UK had both re-located purely because of specific job/career opportunities. One had been travelling in Europe and was living in London when offered a "dream job" with a major Birmingham arts organization:

> I lived in London, as most Australians do, on people's floors and I lived in Italy for a little bit and in Germany for a little bit and got some work in London which was really great and that work actually led directly to an interview opportunity, which got me a job here in Birmingham [...] Honestly, I hadn't really thought of moving to Birmingham until I was aware of the job. (C8)

For those looking at alternative locations within the UK, most had considered London, but living expenses were considered prohibitive. Thus, similar to other European research (e.g.

Boyle, 2006; Houston et al., 2008; Hansen & Niedomysl, 2009), these findings question whether amenities and place attractiveness are the key determinants of location choice.

2. Birmingham as "Cultural Melting Pot": How Attractive is Diversity and Tolerance?

Another fundamental premise of the "creative class" thesis is that location choice is strongly influenced by high levels of population "diversity", that is, talent is drawn towards socially and culturally mixed places where anyone from any background, race, ethnicity, gender, or sexual orientation can easily "plug in" (Florida, 2002a). Again, little evidence was found to support this claim. Nonetheless, migrants valued Birmingham's "diverse" and "tolerant" culture, which was regarded as a positive aspect in their experiences of living and working in the city.

Most interviewees reported that they knew very little, if anything, about Birmingham before deciding to move there. For some, the city was known merely as the second largest in the UK, and was chosen because of its size; for others, Birmingham was "just a name" (C10). The perception that several had acquired from colleagues, friends, literature, the internet and the Media prior to arrival was largely negative—a grey, post-industrial city with high unemployment and crime levels and social problems associated with the extreme diversity of the population:

> Well, I think before I moved here I had a lot of negative press about Birmingham, it was, like, oh my God, you know, you're going to get shot and whatever. (C1)

Those who had already experienced life in the region during periods of study or work placements were more likely to comment positively:

> I knew about it [population diversity] after my first visit which was a year before I decided to move and I knew it was encouraging in terms of, I knew that my accent would not seem strange because you have so many strange accents around. So yes definitely it was helping that you did not feel like an outsider, because everybody seems to be from somewhere else. (C10)

Following arrival, most related the feeling of being accepted and the openness to other cultures, resonating with Florida's (2002a, 2005a, 2005b) ideas around "tolerance", although the importance was downplayed by some:

> I found out that people here, because they [are] used to live and work with foreigners and refugees, asylum seekers, now they are more friendly here and we are not a stranger anymore. (C6)
>
> I think the fact that it's multicultural helped as well, being, you know, somebody who's not from this country. You do feel more accepted, I guess, though it wasn't such a big factor, I don't think. (C1)

None had encountered discrimination or racism or any of the social integration problems associated with some lower skilled migrants living in more migrant-dense areas in the city (see Karner & Parker, 2011). In general, interviewees did not actively frequent these areas of the city, however. Preferences for residential locations, for example, were for the city's "urban villages" (Edgbaston, Moseley, Kings Heath), gentrifying "middle-class" areas populated by professionals and students. These areas were attractive for their mix of local (independent) and 'niche' shops, restaurants and cafes. Only one interviewee (C6) mentioned the importance of living in within a country of origin ethnic community.

Interviewees living in less affluent inner-city neighbourhoods had not chosen these because of their "diversity", rather the choice was housing affordability and a central location near work or transport links. Indeed, one interviewee reported feeling uncomfortable about her inner-city neighbourhood:

> ...it is very scary to go out on a Sunday and there is no one outside, you just wonder what's wrong or is there something not quite right [...] There are kind of a few gangs of youths that scare me pretty much—but they have never caused any trouble to me, but I have seen them cause trouble to others though. (C2)

There were mixed feelings about the integration of different migrant groups. A couple of interviewees (C2 and C8) commented negatively about spatial segregation:

> Despite the fact that it is ethnically diverse, I think that it's—and despite me finding many positive things about that—in certain areas, at the same time, I think that it's quite segregated and you know where you can find the wealthy whites, the working class whites, the Pakistanis, the Hindus, so and that's something I never liked. (C8)

Nonetheless, "diversity" appears to have been a positive factor for creative-sector employment. One interviewee (C7) had experienced racism in the media sector in London and had moved to Birmingham specifically because it widened access to job opportunities. Again, this resonates with Florida's ideas around "low entry barriers for human capital" (Florida & Tinagli, 2004, p. 12):

> Wherever I was working in London, basically, different media organisations, I was being typecast either to cover Asian stories or because I worked in PR agencies also, you know, handling Asian clients, and one of the things I noticed about Birmingham, was that a large amount of ethnic population was working in mainstream media, which I wanted to do [...] so, yeah, that was one of the reasons I moved to Birmingham it's quite ethnically diverse but also it's quite integrated. (C7)

A freelance visual artist (C3) indicated that multiculturalism brought an added dimension to his work:

> here in Birmingham it's [the cultural diversity] a very visible thing, it's very if you want, 'in your face' as well and that I admire because for me the way I understand it is that people are proud about it and people from different communities and different culture are proud to know that Birmingham has a multicultural, has a multicultural environment, community, everything and that gives, as an artist it's very interesting to go and integrate into that community. (C3)

Integration into some artistic fields was more challenging, however. A professional musician (C3) found that his qualifications were not recognized in the UK, and he was only able to continue his music career through his entrepreneurial abilities, by pulling together a group of other migrant musicians to develop an outlet for their musical talents. Significantly, living in Birmingham had enabled him to work with musicians from many different nationalities and to draw on a variety of musical traditions to produce new hybrid musical creations which he felt was highly positive and would not be possible elsewhere:

> I maybe know about 30 musicians here in Birmingham and they are from different nationalities, different backgrounds [...] now we have got another band which I am the coordinator of this band, it is called XXXX—we are about eight or nine different nationalities in one band [...] without the band, we couldn't work together and now because all of us we want to work in the music area and we have to come together and work together and when you work together you make a relationship. (C6)

Finally, while cultural "diversity" was mentioned as an attractive element of city life by most interviewees, this was mainly experienced in relation to specific "cultural consumption" opportunities: the different international cuisines available; the abundance of ethnic food shops; the different cultures that were represented in festivals, traditional and modern music and dance productions as well as art exhibitions and cinema were all mentioned positively and often. Again, there was generally very limited contact and interaction with existing migrant communities and neighbourhoods, however. Social networks, for example, generally revolved around work and other creative professionals and people of similar "social capital" (see next section). Interviewees also typically frequented "establishment" cultural venues in or near the city centre (e.g. IKON; Midlands Arts Centre; Symphony Hall; the Rep Theatre; Drum Theatre), or spent time in their own neighbourhoods. Thus rather than breaking down barriers, it could be argued that highly skilled migration reinforces existing divisions (Peck, 2005).

3. Should I Stay, or Should I Go? Mapping Migration Trajectories

The hyper-mobility of the "creative class" (Florida, 2002a, 2005a, 2005b) was the final element to be explored. A complex mix of factors associated with personal and professional network formation, labour market characteristics and related employment and career opportunities primarily influenced migration trajectories. Although a desire for new challenges and perceived "quality of place" elsewhere influenced some, rather than "creative class", "life stage" and career may explain this migration tendency.

Most migrants were ambivalent about how long they intended to live and work in Birmingham before they arrived, but none saw it as a long-term or permanent move. As one interviewee stated; "I came here with an idea to leave" (C9). Some intended returning home immediately after finishing their studies; a few were going to try out a job or see what professional development opportunities there were in Birmingham and what living in the city was like; others saw Birmingham as a "starting point" before moving to London:

> Initially, when I took this position, it was interim post for 3 months and basically, for me, that 3 months was the testing ground...testing Birmingham, like, can I live here? (C7)
> I was just going to try it out and see how it goes. I didn't have any set length of time, but I think in the back of my head, you know, thinking about it and I'd always thought I'd move to London at some point, though I didn't, you know, I didn't know when. (C1)

Migratory trajectories did, however, alter over time. Several had stayed in Birmingham much longer than they initially intended. Most stated "work and people" (C8) as the main reasons they had remained. Job satisfaction and close links with the creative and cultural sector in Birmingham were also factors:

> I think it's the job—it's job satisfaction and I'm closely associated with the culture industry over here. So, yeah, that's what's basically keeping me here. It's quite fun. (C7)

Several (C1, C2, C4 and C8) had met UK partners or spouses while studying or working in the city, which made any immediate further migration unlikely:

> It's different now of course because, well, I'm married now and I have to consider my partner as the reason to stay, although he doesn't mind going back to Taiwan, but I think we just want to see whether we can actually build something here. (C4)

As interviewees became more socially "emplaced" (Scott, 2006b) within personal networks as well as the creative arts community in Birmingham, this inhibited further migration (see also Ryan & Mulholland, 2014). The importance of high quality social networks for gaining work and for career development in the creative sector is widely acknowledged (see Watson, 2012). Migrants all reported access to strong and generally inclusive professional networks, which were important for retention, echoing findings by Borén and Young (2013). The city size (large but not too large) and relatively less-well developed creative sector in Birmingham were seen as beneficial in this regard. In comparison with London, for example, interviewees stated that these networks formed more easily and it took less time for people to be recognized professionally:

> ...in terms of the art community it's more close, you feel like you've made a lot of friends as artists and that's probably something I can't imagine in London because if you go to private views every night you see different people in London but here, because the art community is still quite small, you get to know people quite well. (C4)

These networks existed for more than the strategic reasons outlined by Blair (2009). Work colleagues often also became close friends, and there was a complex intertwining of professional and social networks which tied people to the city:

> with my small group of friends, two of whom still live around the corner from us, even though we have moved a lot [in Birmingham], we are very steeped—they have been in Birmingham for probably an additional 5 years on top of me—very steeped into the kind of arts community [...] They were colleagues of mine at XXXX, but we spend a lot of time with them and just gradually widened our circle of friends. (C8)
> ...because the whole cultural scene is quite closely intertwined with each other, you know, we work a lot with the Birmingham REP, Symphony Hall team, you know...the Hippodrome, Audience Central and all these people, so it was pretty fast and I made a good circle [of friends], so I liked it here... (C7)

Significantly, a number of "push" factors related to lack of perceived or actual job and career opportunities contributed to migrants considering a further move. These findings support other research on the vital importance of "thick labour markets" for attracting as well as retaining creative talent, especially freelancers who migrate to places that offer wider opportunities rather than for specific firm-based jobs (Storper & Scott, 2009; Hracs & Stolarick, 2011). In particular, the draw of London as a world city and global creative capital was mentioned often:

> Well, I think it really depends because we can see how it's developing in terms of our own career and because the more I do here, the more I feel like I belong here, but then at the same time, like all young artists, we're still looking at London and thinking whether I should go to London or not. (C4)

Other weaknesses discussed included a lack of a strong client base; high competition for a very limited number of artistic commissions; a proliferation of very short-term contracts and little national exposure of Birmingham-based arts. Some felt that their career ambitions were constrained:

> The opportunities there are in Birmingham, they're very limited after a certain level, there's a full stop to that and you can't go anywhere, you know? (C7)

The creative vibrancy of Birmingham was also questioned. Some were critical of the support for the creative sector in Birmingham, and saw this declining:

> ...Birmingham it was quite up and coming for a while, a couple of years ago, but now it's kind of a lot of artist led spaces closed down and there's not really much in terms of, not many gallery spaces, not many studio spaces and it just feels like you need to kind of do it yourself. Which is fine, but if there is not much else going on, it's not, there's no infrastructure or not enough infrastructure. (C9)
> ...making money seems to be the priority for the city council or to host promotional events for the city. No organic development seems to be supported or appreciated by the city council. (C2)

The external perception that working as a creative professional in Birmingham was somehow "second rate" was also a "push" factor—some interviewees thought that remaining in the city would harm their careers:

> ...if I go anywhere else in the UK and say I live in Birmingham, people ask me why, why you are an artist and you live in Birmingham, because they don't see Birmingham as a city where creative industries are developed. (C10)

Longer term, most were still "open to" the possibility of further moves. A general desire for "new challenges" was expressed by some:

> I do, at some point fairly soon, actually, want to move out, but, I mean, there isn't anything pushing me, there's nothing about the city that's pushing me out of there, as such, I just feel that I'm ready for other challenges [...] I mean, to be honest, I think, you know, the more I live it, I like it better, but I don't see myself just staying here for, you know, for the rest of my life or anything. (C1)

Resonating with Florida's (2002a) "quality of place", a desire to experience life and work in other cities which were regarded as culturally "more vibrant" and more "cosmopolitan" or which offered a "better lifestyle" (more relaxed way of life; better weather; better social environment) or a more attractive physical environment was expressed. These possibilities were largely speculative, and included mainly international cities (Berlin, Paris, Chicago, New York and Melbourne). Only Bristol and London were mentioned as alternatives within the UK. The feeling was that these moves would also be temporary, however, an experience, before moving somewhere more permanent.

This tendency for further migration may relate more to "life stage" and career stage than a particular "creative class" migration tendency, however. None of the interviewees had children, so their motilities were seemingly less hindered for further moves. For example, several (C2, C4, C5 and C8) indicated that they would consider re-locating back home permanently when starting a family. Furthermore, career trajectories were also at a formative stage and more fluid, demanding a certain degree of mobility for further development, and international locations were seen as a way of fulfilling this. Ryan and Mulholland (2014) similarly found that "life-stage" issues significantly influenced the mobility of highly skilled migrants in London.

Discussion and Conclusions

The presence of a diverse, vibrant, culturally cosmopolitan urban environment is increasingly regarded as a key, distinctive and competitive requirement for cities wishing to attract (and retain) the hyper-mobile "creative class" (Florida, 2002a, 2005a, 2005b; Musterd & Murie, 2010). Much recent UK and European urban policy has focused on developing the tools necessary for cities to achieve this, and a proliferation of "creative city" strategies have emerged, focused on developing urban "quality of place". At the same time, only limited—and mainly quantitative—research has been undertaken to provide an understanding of the factors associated with the location choices of these workers. This paper is a first step towards a better understanding of the migration dynamics of the "creative class". The focus has been on a qualitative analysis of the motivations, experiences and migration trajectories of "creative Bohemians" working in the Music and Visual & Performing Arts sectors in Birmingham, UK.

Rather than urban "quality of place" (Florida, 2002a, 2005a, 2005b), migration for these individuals was motivated primarily by factors related to higher education and personal and career development opportunities as well as creative employment within the city. Thus, while the "creative class" may be attracted to cities such as London, Paris, Amsterdam or New York because of "quality of place", these findings challenge the idea that international talent might be attracted to second-tier cities purely because of a set of urban amenities. Rather, they support findings from a number of other recent studies (e.g. Houston et al., 2008; Hansen & Niedomysl, 2009; Storper & Scott, 2009; Borén & Young, 2013) demonstrating that jobs, far more than amenities, govern these decisions. Indeed, these findings question whether the attraction power of specific urban amenities deserves to be highlighted in urban development policy for such cities.

Similarly, little evidence was found to support claims that location choice is strongly influenced by high levels of population "diversity"—migrants were largely unaware of Birmingham's culturally diverse population or reputation for tolerance before moving there. Again, these findings substantiate other UK-based research (e.g. Nathan, 2007). Nonetheless, socio-cultural aspects did play some role. Similar to findings by Houston *et al.* (2008) migrants valued the "tolerant" and "diverse" culture in Birmingham, which were seen as positive factors in experiences of both living and working in the city. Resonating with Florida's ideas around "low entry barriers for human capital" (Florida & Tinagli, 2004, p. 12), this appeared to offer advantages by opening up opportunities in "mainstream" creative occupations. There was also some (limited) indication that the mix of different cultures and influences in the city enabled artistic innovation and facilitated new "inter-cultural" products (see also Ghilardi, 2005). Further research is needed to understand how commonplace this tendency is in the creative industries more widely and how this leads, or not, to the types of innovation and knowledge flows identified by Florida (and others) as precursors to economic prosperity.

Nonetheless, "diversity" was mainly experienced in relation to "cultural consumption" opportunities and there was limited contact and interaction with existing migrant neighbourhoods and communities. Social networks, for example, generally revolved around work and other creative professionals and people of similar "social capital" and interviewees typically frequented "establishment" cultural venues in or near the city centre, or spent time in their own neighbourhoods. Thus rather than breaking down barriers, it could be argued that highly skilled migration may reinforce existing divisions (Peck, 2005).

Similar to findings by Ryan and Mulholland (2014, p. 587), rather than a permanent settlement versus high-mobility binary, migrants gradually extended their stay, while keeping their future options open. Although initial moves to Birmingham were considered temporary, migrants quickly became socially "emplaced" (Scott, 2006b). Several had met their partner or spouse while studying or working in the city, which made immediate further migration unlikely. Access to strong and generally inclusive professional networks—often developed during study—positively influenced retention, echoing findings by Borén and Young (2013). Significantly, these networks existed for more than the strategic reasons outlined by Blair (2009): work colleagues often became close friends, and there was a complex intertwining of the professional and social. It is unclear how typical this pattern of network formation is. City size and hierarchy and the extent and/or growth stage of the creative sector may be crucial, but these issues have received almost no attention in the "creative class" literature (Borén & Young, 2013) and deserve further attention.

Significantly, a number of "push" factors associated with a lack of perceived or actual job and career opportunities contributed to migrants considering a further move. The creative vibrancy of Birmingham and local-level support for the sector were also questioned. These findings substantiate other research on the vital importance of "thick labour markets" for attracting as well as retaining creative talent, especially freelance creative workers who migrate to places that offer wider opportunities rather than for specific firm-based jobs (Hracs & Stolarick, 2011; Storper & Scott, 2009). In particular, the draw of London as a world city and global creative capital was mentioned often. Cities such as Birmingham may easily lose the skills and innovation capacity they are attempting to build up if they do not address these issues, and there may be very little policymakers can do in terms of "place attractiveness" to mitigate against the departure of the "creative class".

Nonetheless, a desire for "new challenges" or experiencing life and work in other cities which were regarded as culturally "more vibrant" and more "cosmopolitan" or which offered a "better lifestyle" were also expressed. This may relate more to "life stage" and career stage than a particular "creative class" migration tendency, however. Interviewees were all in their 20s or early 30s, recently graduated and none had children, so their mobility was seemingly less hindered. Several, for example, indicated that they would consider relocating back home when starting a family. Ryan and Mulholland (2014) likewise found that "life stage" significantly influenced the mobility of the highly skilled migrants they interviewed in London. Boyle (2006) found that while Dublin was attractive to younger migrants, it was less attractive when thinking of starting a family. Certain cities may therefore only be "attractive" to migrants at certain points in their lives. Furthermore, career trajectories were at a formative and more fluid stage, demanding a certain degree of mobility for further development, and international locations were seen as a way of fulfilling this. This resonates with the existing literature on motives for highly skilled migration (see Scott, 2006b). Also, Markusen (2006) found that occupational characteristics (e.g. high levels of self-employment) made creatives more "footloose" rather than a desire for "quality of place". Further research is needed to explore whether these findings are applicable to other demographics of the "creative class".

In sum, these initial findings call for a more nuanced understanding of the factors associated with the both the attraction and retention of international "creative class" workers as it is clear that migration decisions depend on a far more complex mixing of factors rather than simply "quality of place" and that what is key to attraction may also differ from that of retention. Hracs and Stolarick (2011), for example, have developed a three-stage model of locational expectations, satisfaction and mobility which offers potential.

The prolific spread of urban policies based on "creative city" strategies has been criticized on a number of accounts. Many are poorly adjusted to the specificities of particular urban contexts (Musterd & Murie, 2010) and often they are "narrowly fixated on a particular vision of a diverse city" (Syrett & Sepulveda, 2011, p. 499). As Peck observes, policies which focus on creating attractive, sanitized, middle-class environments and utilizing culture for "consumption-oriented place-promotion" (Peck, 2005, p. 761) risk further segregation within already segregated cities. Landry (2008) additionally notes that creativity may suffer if existing ethnic groups withdraw into their own cultures as a defence against change.

Instead, carefully targeted policies that address the socio-economic, cultural and physical realities of cities are required (Houston *et al.*, 2008; Musterd & Murie, 2010). This includes recognition that international talent is attracted by more than abstract concepts of place attractiveness. Rather, policies are required to ensure access to a diversity of creative labour market opportunities both to attract and retain talent in the longer term. Localized creative infrastructures are also vital, and the significance of accessible and inclusive local creative networks cannot be overlooked. As Borén and Young (2013, p. 206) indicate, "How these networks operate [...] has a variety of impacts on artists' mobility and also has implications for the degree to which cities offer low entry barriers to those in 'creative' occupations."

At the same time, the "problematic issues" of policy aimed at attracting a high-skilled international workforce need to be addressed: increased spatial inequalities, segregation and socio-economic exclusion of lower skilled host and migrant communities are often the unintended consequences. As Ghilardi (2005, p. 5) notes "urban policy needs to move beyond the orthodoxy of 'multiculturalism' which [...] accentuates difference and even separation, to 'interculturalism' in which the interaction of cultures and communities becomes a driver of innovation and growth". This is seldom seen in UK urban policy, however, which often lacks joined-up thinking and a comprehensive approach to economic development and spatial and community planning. New approaches to the design of contemporary urban living space that allow for cultural mixing and social integration are required. But before cities re-design themselves in order to reap the "diversity dividend" (Syrett & Sepulveda, 2011), further qualitative research is needed to better understand the real needs, attitudes and preferences that influence the locational choices of highly skilled migrants and how relationships with existing communities can be strengthened and made conducive to cross-cultural knowledge exchanges that lead both to wider economic gains and that also support and enhance the creation of culturally rich and socially just cities.

Acknowledgements

This research forms part of a larger EU project—ACRE (Accommodating Creative Knowledge: Competitiveness of European Metropolitan Regions within the Enlarged Union). The author gratefully acknowledges discussions with various ACRE researchers throughout the project. The author would also like to thank Prof. Calvin Taylor, for helpful comments on a draft version of the paper and the insightful comments of the anonymous reviewer.

Disclosure statement

No potential conflict of interest was reported by the author.

Funding

This work was supported by the Sixth Framework Programme of the EU [grant number 028270].

Notes

1. Florida and Tinagli (2004) focussed their European analysis at the national level.
2. ONS (2011b). Adapted from Table EE1.
3. Accurately assessing that the size of the creative industries is notoriously difficult, and the data and statistical issues well documented (see UIS, 2009).

References

Bailey, A. & Boyle, P. (2004) Untying and retying family migration in the New Europe, *Journal of Ethnic and Migration Studies*, 30(2), pp. 229–241.
Baláz, V., Williams, A. M. & Kollár, K. (2004) Temporary versus permanent youth brain drain: Economic implications, *International Migration*, 42(4), pp. 3–34.
Barber, A. & Hall, S. (2008) Birmingham: Whose urban renaissance? Regeneration as a response to economic restructuring, *Policy Studies*, 29(3), pp. 281–292.
Beaverstock, J. (2005) Transnational elites in the city: British highly-skilled intercompany transferees in New York city's financial district, *Journal of Ethnic and Migration Studies*, 31(2), pp. 245–268.
Birmingham City Council (BCC) (2010) *Birmingham Big City Plan*. Birmingham: BCC.
Birmingham City Council (BCC) (2011) *Demographic Briefing 2011/04*. Birmingham: BCC.
Birmingham City Council (BCC) (2012) *Closing the Skills Gap*. Birmingham: BCC.
Blair, H. (2009) Active networking: Action, social structure and the process of networking, in: A. McKinlay & C. Smith (Eds) *Creative Labour: Working in the Creative Industries*, pp. 116–134 (Basingstoke: Palgrave Macmillan).

Borén, T. & Young, C. (2013) The migration dynamics of the "creative class": Evidence from a study of artists in Stockholm, Sweden, *Annals of the Association of American Geographers*, 103(1), pp. 195–210.

Boschma, R. & Fritsch, M. (2007) *Creative Class and Regional Growth—Empirical Evidence from Eight European Countries*. Jena Economic Research Papers, 2007-066.

Boyle, M. (2006) Culture in the rise of tiger economies: Scottish expatriates in Dublin and the "creative class" thesis, *International Journal of Urban and Regional Research*, 30(2), pp. 403–426.

Brown, J., Chapain, C., Murie, A., Barber, A., Gibney, J. & Lutz, J. (2007) *From City of a Thousand Trades to City of a Thousand Ideas: Birmingham, UK* ACRE Report 2.3 (Amsterdam: AMIDST).

Brown, J., Lutz, J., Gibney, J., Barber, A., Chapain, C., Murie, A. & Lee, P. (2010) *Policies and Strategies for the Creative Knowledge Economy in Birmingham and the West Midlands Region* ACRE Report 10.3 (Amsterdam: AISSR).

Brown, J., Murphy, D. & Pradel, M. (2013) Capitalising on position: Policies for competitive capital and non-capital cities, in: S. Musterd & Z. Kovacs (Eds) *Future Policy Directions for Creative Cities: Debates and Challenges*, pp. 59–76 (London: Wiley Blackwell).

Burns Owens Partnership Consulting (BOP) (2009) *Why the Creative Industries Matter to Birmingham: An Analysis of the City's Creative Economy* (Birmingham: CBPB).

Clark, T. N., Lloyd, R., Wong, K. K., & Jain, P. (2002) Amenities drive urban growth, *Journal of Urban Affairs*, 24(5), pp. 493–515.

Conradson, D., & Latham, A. (2005) Friendship, networks and trans-nationality in a world city: Antipodean trans-migrants in London, *Journal of Ethnic and Migration Studies*, 31(2), pp. 287–305.

Favell, A., Recchi, E., Kuhn, T., Solgaard Jensen, J. & Klein, J. (2011) *The Europeanisation of everyday life, cross-border practices and transnational identifications among EU and third-country citizens*. EUCROSS Working paper # 1.

Florida, R. (2002a) *The Rise of the Creative Class* (New York: Basic Books).

Florida, R. (2002b) Bohemia and economic geography, *Journal of Economic Geography*, 2(1), pp. 55–71.

Florida, R. (2005a) *The Flight of the Creative Class* (New York: Harper Business).

Florida, R. (2005b) *Cities and the Creative Class* (New York: Routledge).

Florida, R. & Tinagli, I. (2004) *Europe in the Creative Age* (London: Demos).

Ghilardi, L. (2005) *Intercultural City: Making the Most of Diversity* (London: Comedia).

Green, A. E., Owen, D. & Jones, P. (2007) *The Economic Impact of Migrant Workers in the West Midlands* (Birmingham: LSC and AWM).

Hansen, H. & Niedomysl, T. (2009) Migration of the creative class: Evidence from Sweden, *Journal of Economic Geography*, 9(2), pp. 191–206.

Hansen, H., Asheim, B. & Vang, J. (2009) The European creative class and regional development: How relevant is Florida's theory for Europe? in: L. Kong and J. O'Connor (Eds) *Creative Economies, Creative Cities: Asian-European Perspectives*, pp. 99–120 (Dordrecht: Springer).

Houston, D., Findlay, A., Harrison, R. & Mason, C. (2008) Will attracting the "creative class" boost economic growth in old industrial regions? A case study of Scotland, *Geografiska Annaler: Series B, Human Geography*, 90(2), pp. 133–149.

Hoyman, M. & Faricy, C. (2009) It takes a village: A test of the creative class, social capital and human capital theories, *Urban Affairs Review*, 44(3), pp. 311–333.

Hracs, B. & Stolarick, K. (2011) *Satisfaction Guaranteed? Talent Mobility and Regional Satisfaction* (Toronto: Martin Prosperity Institute, University of Toronto).

Karner, C. & Parker, D. (2011) Conviviality and conflict: Pluralism, resilience and hope in inner-city Birmingham, *Journal of Ethnic and Migration Studies*, 37(3), pp. 355–372.

Kennedy, P. (2008) The construction of trans-social European Networks and the neutralisation of borders: Skilled EU migrants in Manchester—Reconstituting social and national belonging, *Space and Polity*, 12(1), pp. 119–133.

Kloosterman, R. C. (2013) Cultural amenities: Large and small, mainstream and niche—A conceptual framework for cultural planning in an age of austerity. *European Planning Studies*, 22(12), pp. 2510–2525.

Koser, K., & Salt, J. (1997) The geography of highly skilled international migration, *Population, Space and Place*, 4(3), pp. 285–303.

Landry, C. (2008) *The Creative City: A Toolkit for Urban Innovators*, 2nd ed. (London: Earthscan).

Markusen, A. (2006) Urban development and the politics of a creative class: Evidence from a study of artists, *Environment and Planning A*, 38(10), pp. 1921–1940.

Martin-Brelot, H., Grossetti, M., Eckert, D., Gritsai, O., & Kovács, Z. (2010) The spatial mobility of the 'creative class': A European perspective, *International Journal of Urban and Regional Research*, 34(4), pp. 854–870.

Musterd, S. & Murie, A. (Eds) (2010) *Making Competitive Cities* (Oxford: Wiley Blackwell).

Nagel, C. (2005) Skilled migration in global cities from 'other' perspectives: British Arabs, identity politics, and local embededdness, *Geoforum*, 36(2), pp. 197–210.

Nathan, M. (2007) The wrong stuff. Creative class theory and economic performance in UK cities, *Canadian Journal of Regional Science*, 30(3), pp. 433–450.

ONS (2011a) *Migration Statistics Quarterly Report*, No. 8, pp. 18–19.

ONS (2011b) *Population Estimates by Ethnic Group Rel. 8.*

Parkinson, M. (2007) *The Visioning Study for Birmingham City Centre Masterplan* (Liverpool: John Moore's University).

Peck, J. (2005) Struggling with creative class, *International Journal of Urban and Regional Research*, 29(4), pp. 740–770.

Ryan, L. & Mulholland, J. (2014) Trading places: French highly skilled migrants negotiating mobility and settlement in London, *Ethnic and Migration Studies*, 40(4), pp. 584–600.

Salt, J. (1997) *International Movements of the Highly Skilled* (Paris: OECD).

Santacreu, O., Baldoni, E. & Albert, M. C. (2009) Deciding to move: Migration projects in an integrating Europe, in: E. Recchi and A. Favell (Eds) *Pioneers of European Integration*, pp. 52–71 (Cheltenham: Edward Elgar).

Scott, A. J. (2006a) Creative cities: Conceptual issues and policy questions, *Journal of Urban Affairs*, 28(1), pp. 1–17.

Scott, S. (2006b) The social morphology of skilled migration: The case of the British middle class in Paris, *Journal of Ethnic and Migration Studies*, 32(7), pp. 1105–1129.

Smith, M. P. & Favell, A. (Eds) (2006) *The Human Face of Global Capital* (New Brunswick: Transaction Publishers).

Storper, M. & Manville, M. (2006) Behaviour, preference and cities: Urban theory and urban resurgence, *Urban Studies*, 43(8), pp. 1247–1274.

Storper, M. & Scott, A. J. (2009) Rethinking human capital, creativity and urban growth, *Journal of Economic Geography*, 9(2), pp. 147–167.

Syrett, S., & Sepulveda, L. (2011) Population diversity and urban economic development, *Environment and Planning A*, 43(2), pp. 487–504.

Turok, I. (2009) The distinctive city: Pitfalls in the pursuit of differentiating advantage, *Environment and Planning A*, 41(1), pp. 13–30.

UIS (2009) *Framework for Cultural Statistics Handbook* (Montreal: UIS).

Vertovec, S. (2006) *The emergence of super-diversity in Britain*. ESRC Centre on Migration, Policy and Society WP-06-25.

Vertovec, S. (2007) Super-diversity and its implications, *Ethnic and Racial Studies*, 29(6), pp. 1024–54.

Watson, A. (2012) Sociological perspectives on the economic geography of projects: The case of project-based working in the creative industries, *Geography Compass*, 6(10), pp. 617–631.

West Midlands Regional Observatory (WMRO) (2009) *State of the Region Dialogue—The Region's Knowledge Economy: Interim Report*. Birmingham: WMRO.

Hung, Drawn and Cultural Quartered: Rethinking Cultural Quarter Development Policy in the UK

OLI MOULD* & ROBERTA COMUNIAN**

*Department of Geography, Royal Holloway, University of London, Egham, UK, **Culture, Media and Creative Industries, Kings College London, London, UK

ABSTRACT *Throughout the last two decades, cultural quarters have been used by many local councils across the UK as attempts to redevelop and revitalize declining urban centres. Cities have spent millions of pounds developing cultural quarter policies, justified by the prevailing rhetoric of culture revitalizing the local economy and the creation of a "cultural milieu" that stimulates creative industry activity. However, in many cases in the UK, visitor numbers remain lower than expected, and in some cases, flagship projects have been sold off or closed down. High rents force out small and freelance creative industry actors, and (non-commercial) artistic interventions are strictly policed. Forming part of the wider debate on the political circumscription of the creativity paradigm, this paper argues that cultural quarters have been viewed within a predominately economistic, dichotomous and simplistic framework. This paper argues that there is a need for a more practiced-based, subjective account of cultural quarters that goes beyond such a traditional framework to include more deleterious practices such as community impoverishment, precariousness and short-termism.*

Introduction

Cultural quarters (CQs) have emerged in the policy imaginary and rhetoric of the last two decades as tools for urban and economic regeneration across many UK cities and towns. Since the first "experimental" and (sometimes) informal interventions in the 1980s in cities such as Sheffield and Manchester, they have slowly become a structured, planned and formalized practice hailed as a solution to many socio-economic problems affecting UK cities before and after the recent recession. However, the literature analysing these interventions is polarized between promotional "how-to manuals" (Landry, 2006; Montgomery, 2008; Roodhouse, 2006) and critical case studies (Christophers, 2008; Evans, 2009;

McCarthy, 2005; Moss, 2002; Porter & Barber, 2007; Shorthouse, 2004). It can be argued also that from the rapid growth of the economic discourses of creative industries and creative cities, attention towards CQs has increased exponentially. Indeed, as Oakley (2004, p. 68) noted, "no region of the country, whatever its industrial base, human capital stock, scale or history is safe from the need for a 'creative hub' or 'cultural quarter'". Nearly 10 years hence, this has proved the case as more cities develop CQs justified by, or linked to, a cultural regenerative paradigm. However, to date, while there has been literature that has identified the broader dynamics and consequences of these interventions on the local scale, far less attention has tried to systematize the forces and powers which drive the development of CQs across the UK, and hence couch these within the wider narratives of neoliberal urban development theories. Moreover, the role of culture within a CQ as more than a consumption or production determinant has yet to be addressed holistically. This paper then highlights these apparent lacunas and offers a viewpoint that could be utilized critically in future work to begin addressing these issues. To do this, the paper first offers a critical review of the literature and the development of the concepts and ideas around CQs, considering its connections with other literature on politically co-opted creativity themes, such as creative clusters and creative cities. Then, considering the key neoliberal forces and power relations behind the development of CQs, the paper proposes a move beyond a dualistic, instrumental and traditional framework of CQ development, to a more subjective, practice-based account of the incumbent processes that have deleterious consequences.

To this end, the rest of the paper is structured into two main parts. First, we critically engage with the economically deterministic concept of the CQ and its role in the neoliberal development of cities, with particular emphasis on the political and economistic valorization of "culture" within CQs as part of a consumption or production dialectic. We also consider the hype surrounding CQ policy and its establishment as a new tool for urban governance structures in UK. In particular, we highlight some key neoliberal characteristics of this new management of urban space. In the second part, we consider the importance of understanding the issues of differentiated cultural values and stakeholders through a more inclusive, less instrumental account of CQs that considers some of the problematic processes that a CQ engenders—namely community impoverishment, precariousness and short-termism. Finally, we draw conclusions from these loose categories in relation to the traditional framework presented in the first part. In particular, we argue that the result of the proliferation of a standardized CQ "template" has a deleterious effect on the spaces of local and differentiated cultural expression and creative commons, questioning how "cultural" CQs actually are.

The Economic Determinism of Cultural Quarters

Before outlining the literature, it is pertinent to clarify what a CQ actually is, as there is an extensive literature on CQs, with varying (and sometimes ambiguous) definitions (see McCarthy, 2005; Porter & Barber, 2007; Roodhouse, 2006, Shorthouse, 2004). The concept's origin is linked to the development of locally based cultural industry policies in a few UK cities during the 1980s, namely Sheffield, Manchester and London. The emergence of new cultural scenes particularly clustered around often disused areas of these post-industrial cities was seen as a great opportunity to maximize on the growth in consumption of cultural goods and experiences, which also encompassed the potential to re-design and re-develop declining urban spaces (Brown *et al.*, 2000). However, since these first works on cultural industry clusters and artists' reuse of declining urban areas emerged, further connotations and arguments have been added to refine, define and classify the emergence and development of CQs within policy and the local government vernacular. First—influenced by the DCMS' definition of the "Creative Industries" drawn up in 1998—there has been a shift from the term "cultural quarter" to "creative quarters" and "creative hubs" (see Evans, 2009, Oakley, 2004). This reflects the wider shift of the urban policy lexicon towards "creativity", which has been utilized more readily on the global stage (see Peck, 2005). Second, influenced by the literature on industrial clusters *a lá* Porter, some urban governments and policy institutions have instead talked of cultural districts and cultural clusters (Pratt, 2004). In both these augmentations of the initial CQ articulation from the 1980s, they have used prevailing political economy narratives to couple CQ development to the economic regeneration of cities. In the former, they are linked to the benefits of creativity and innovation, while in the latter, the economic advantages of agglomeration and local linkages are emphasized. However, in both cases, the broad definition of a clustering of cultural and creative activities remains relatively constant.

Some authors have tried to identify and classify the various definitional characteristics of CQs. Santagata (2002) proposed a classification based on the type of cultural goods and services supplied and the kind of knowledge, that is generated and protected within the agglomeration. He distinguishes between cultural districts that are industrial, institutional, museum or metropolitan. The first two are based around the production of creative goods (either from an industrial base or from an institutional framework). The other two are based on the clustering of traditional cultural institutions such as museums or other forms of cultural consumption centres such as cinemas and theatres. Institutions (public or private) play a key role in the historical establishment and development of cultural districts and therefore also in their classification. Legnér and Ponzini (2009) offer a geographical classification of the range of activities across cultural clusters, cultural districts and CQs, suggesting that the varying policy frameworks (i.e. bottom-up versus top-down) allow for a distinction between clusters or quarters; with clusters being more "bottom-up", and quarters being more "top-down". Such a simplistic binary, however, can obfuscate the often complex and institutionally varied process of CQ formation. Therefore, given the diverse range of terms and nuanced definitions, different political and urban institutions (and indeed some academic literature) adopt the terms interchangeably.

While reviewing these definitions and classifications is a viable starting point to discuss the development of CQ policy in the UK, it is also important to note that often CQs (or creative clusters) have been considered as planning interventions, but lack an investigation of the institutional power and subjective contestations behind these activities. Moreover, the effect of the narrowly defined application of "culture", as well as the role of smaller (economic and non-economic) cultural producers have been problematized. Furthermore, while in most of this literature there is an assumption that the production and consumption of culture come together in these spaces, very little attention has been placed on the real connections and supply-chain relations between consumption and production in CQs. In fact, if we look at the literature and case studies (for an overview see Chapain & Comunian, 2010), there seems to be a general assumption that creative clusters place a stronger emphasis on economic production (Crewe, 1996; Ettlinger, 2003), which catalyses policy and public intervention. On the other hand, if talking about CQs specifically, then the emphasis is on consumption. Cultural producers are present in CQ rhetoric, however, they are often seen as secondary to the creation of a flagship institution (see Comunian & Mould, 2014; Evans, 2009; Mommaas, 2004; Pratt, 2008). While in policy documents and rhetoric, there is a clear aspiration for the integration of a consumption/production dynamic, the actualities of such integration have not been sufficiently interrogated. Literature has tended to focus either on the networks of productions, or the role of cultural consumption and the visitors' economy (Shaw *et al.*, 2004), creating a further dualistic premise in CQ characterization.

A more general critique of culture-led urban regeneration is that it follows a neoliberal agenda (see McGuigan, 2005). CQs have not been immune to such an agenda given the array of descriptive accounts of CQ formation, often purported by those involved in the private consultancy institutions hired to initiate and promote them. Montgomery (2003, 2008) for example, outlines a detailed prescription for a successful CQ. Among a detailed list of consumption and creative industry production facilities, he argues that cultural activity in a CQ "should include production (making objects, goods, products and providing services) as well as cultural consumption (people going to shows visiting venues and galleries)" (Montgomery, 2003, p. 296). The emphasis here (as has been also noted previously to be in the academic literature) is on the importance of production and consumption to the success of a CQ, as the former creates wealth and profit and the latter is the means by which it can proliferate. There is then a sense that a CQ is inherently a vehicle for wealth generation and urban redevelopment, or at least that is the primary, central function. Social engagement and community-orientated cultural activity often are lower on the agenda unless bonded to a profit-making operation.

The spread of the CQ across the UK speaks to the fact that urban regeneration discourse determines cultural activities along economistic and instrumental lines. By means of promoting particular urban locations, culture is being further promoted as a "place making" tool, one that can be integrated into marketing strategies and used to attract tourists and other externalized capital resources. As such, the clamour to construct these CQs inevitably leads to the emancipation of privately formulated CQ "models" which in turn, produces the "serial replication" of CQs across the country (McCarthy, 2005). Posited against the backdrop of the recent financial crisis and the onset of the coalition-led policy of austerity, the desire to spend money more efficiently only exacerbates inexpensive "tool kit" CQs models, further creating homogenous urban landscapes under the rubric of the CQ as they are "copied and pasted" across UK towns and cities.

These identifiable "models" of CQs are evidenced through the material used to promote them. Montgomery (2008) for example suggests that there is a triumvirate of characteristics critical to the success of a CQ. They are "activity", "built form" and "meaning". Activity covers a range of cultural and creative economic characteristics, from "the strength of small firm economy" to the "presence of an evening economy" (Montgomery, 2008, p. 309). Second, the built form of the CQ must contain "fine grained urban morphology" and an (undetermined) "amount and quality of public space" (Montgomery, 2008). In analysing the built form of a CQ, he suggests that

> In the more successful quarters this design ethos is carried through into architecture (modern, but contextual in that it sits within a street pattern), interior design (zinc, blonde wood, brushed steel, white wall) and even the lighting of important streets and spaces (ambient,

architectural and signature lighting, as well as functional). All of these reinforce a place's identity as modern and innovative. (Montgomery, 2008, p. 307–308)

Essentially, there is a suggestion CQs need very specific architectural styles and use particular materials that represent the contemporary working environments of the modern economy. While aiming to promote some original design-led style, the unreflexive take up of this approach has produced standardized spaces, with strong corporate aesthetics (Julier 2005). Finally, the CQ has to have meaning, which Montgomery (2008, p. 310, original emphasis) argues centres around its culture, as "culture after all 'is' meaning". However, what this "meaning" purports to is chronically under-developed.

Landry (2006) and Roodhouse (2006) also forward a premise of the CQ as a catalyst for urban change, one based on prescriptive processes, or in other words, a "model of best practice". These (often quite detailed) prescriptions of CQs are of course not a derivative from the local urban council, but from the architects, construction companies and interior design firms that are part of what Wilson (2004) describes as variegated systems and processes of space-mobilizing constructions. The networks of private companies, in negotiation with the commissioning councils will pinpoint the built form that is seen to be conducive to cultural and creative industry production. But in doing so, homogenized office spaces and replicated "incubator" spaces proliferate within CQs, narrowing the resource base for those cultural activities that do not conform or require these very specific (and often expensive) urban spaces.

As well as the presence of "incubator spaces", CQ "models" will often (in many UK cases) centre on a "flagship" development (Comunian & Mould, 2014). Often a large-scale cultural institution such as a museum, art gallery, major performance centre or cinema is built in the targeted locale with projected large visitor numbers and the promise of auxiliary and related cultural production businesses and institutions. Classic examples often cited within the literature include the Tate Modern in London (Newman & Smith, 2000), the Guggenheim Museum in Bilbao (Plaza *et al.*, 2009) and the Sage in Gateshead (Miles, 2005). These large-scale developments are, however, standalone instances of culture-led urban development, whereas more recent CQ initiatives have sought to use flagship developments as part of a wider strategy of urban renewal. The co-locational presence of these large purpose-built cultural institutions can create schisms with local cultural production. Indeed, as Newman and Smith (2000, p. 22) argue

> the land-value impacts of large venues and sites of cultural consumption work against small and marginal cultural enterprises [...] building up the image of a cultural quarter may itself encourage high-value uses and thus operate against small-firm relocation and start-ups.

Given the overall preponderance of economically deterministic characteristics of CQs (that can be linked to a neoliberal agenda of culture-led urban development (Peck, 2005)) that this section highlights, it is clear that there is a heavy reliance on CQ characterization as an economically and politically charged narrative. However, the fundamental question remains somewhat unexamined, namely where is the "culture" within these CQs? Are CQs forever to be characterized as neoliberal urban regeneration schemes yoked to a production–consumption definitional nexus? This paper goes on to ask if there is a more progressive account with which to understand CQs as part of the urban fabric. The next section therefore identifies and details the existing framework of CQ that is based on economically deterministic characteristics. It then offers an alternative view that takes into account a suite of deleterious practices that are not captured by such a framework. Our aim is to highlight how these processes and institutions of small-scale cultural production, local engagement and/or long-term community development, while differentiated (perhaps marginal) from mainstream CQ discourse can be included in a more subjective, practice-based account of CQs.

From Dualistic to Differentiated CQs

We have seen in the previous section, how many classifications of CQs have been concerned with the mapping of different outputs, economic models and forms of CQs. Rather than considering levels of diversity in the nature of the cultural products or size of the cluster, we want to capture the alternative dimensions of a CQ by considering issues of differentiated cultural practices that are not immediately economistic.

Combining the critical and analytical review of the existing literature in the previous section with a brief but thorough analysis of all the policy literature on CQs in the UK,[1] it becomes clear that there is a tendency of local councils and urban promoters to oversimplify the concept of culture within CQ to an economic imperative. More specifically, however, such analysis identifies three main types of CQ; one based on a large cultural flagship institution as the main driver of growth; another based on the creation of functional and rentable "incubator spaces" for creative and cultural production and the third based on boutique and/or chain store retail developments. This triumvirate model mirrors the broad production–consumption spectrum by which CQs are characterized in the literature discussed in the previous section. The further analysis of the policy literature identified the key stakeholders involved in the development of CQs as locally sourced (existing small businesses, charities and/or cooperatives) and therefore the CQ develops organically (i.e. bottom-up) versus a CQ that is developed via policy intervention from "above" by a city council and/or national government in partnership with private companies (top-down) (also see Legnér & Ponzini, 2009).

Such an instrumentalist typology has a symbiotic relational existence with the development of CQs. In other words, the more such a model is perpetuated, the more systematic and replicative CQs become. As has been mentioned in the previous section, this overtly economistic and neoliberal framework leaves little space (if any) for the exploration of the issue of where the "cultural" is within the CQ narrative. As such, we offer a tentative alternative viewpoint, one which moves away from the frameworks of the current (academic and policy) literature which has the outcome of creating a putative instrumentalism along prescribed economistic lines. Such a viewpoint is not concerned with the creation of an alternative framework, but with the emancipation of the under-represented cultural and social characteristics that are affected by the development of a CQ. To do so requires not only a focus on how they are constructed (and the public-private institutional nexus it entails), but also on identifying those processes and people that are affected, but not already recognized, be they local residents, small-scale cultural workers or users in the longer term that are not yet articulable. We argue that there is a need to focus less on frameworks and how they coerce CQ development to fit into a particular typology of design (i.e. a replicable, economically mobile model *a la* Montgomery (2008)) and more on the practices and processes of those who build, use and are affected by CQs. Then we can begin to realize a more nuanced view of CQ development—one that "makes room" for the cultural, social and community-orientated practices "as well as" the more economic neoliberal processes that build the CQs in the first instance.

In order to position such a view, it is useful to identity three "processes" that are embroiled within CQs development, but are often under-represented or "hidden" in current frameworks and evaluative methods. These processes we have articulated as "community impoverishment", "precariousness" and "short-termism". The initiators of CQs have been well-versed above, and their public-private constitution problematized (Christophers, 2008; Evans, 2009; Julier, 2005; McCarthy, 2005). So, we are proposing that these processes need to be brought into a qualitatively constituted viewpoint of a CQ that does not rest on an economistic and instrumental framework. We of course realize that isolating such processes is, in itself, an instrumental process and can risk mirroring the very thing that we are looking to transcend. However, we see this very much as a starting point of inquiry, rather than a peremptory classification to be rigorously followed. It is therefore merely a humble "step in the right direction", and have used such delineatory categories purely for the purposes of clarity.

Community Impoverishment

There is often an entrenched incommensurable dichotomy in policy interventions and CQ development; they seem to cater either for tourists or for the local population, with the economic determinism prioritizing the former to the social detriment of the latter (Christophers, 2008; Evans, 2009; Mommaas, 2004). As we have already seen, this paradigm sees the promotion of a globalized consumption culture that homogenizes, and can cause a location to lose "cultural individuality" (Bailey *et al.*, 2004). Such urban regeneration processes aim to offer the widest choice of cultural consumption and production opportunities, instead of rediscovering a sense of place, history and belonging; a process which is linked to a larger on-going debate on who should be the target for cultural development of cities (see Zukin, 1985). Such a trend to cater to visitors rather than embark upon more complicated and socially inflected procedures to cater for local communities means local services suffer from lack of funding, and are often displaced (Donald & Morrow, 2003). As such, an oversupply of tourist-orientated retail and leisure functions (cafés, nightclubs, restaurants, cinemas, etc.) coexist with a lack of community facilities or social services. Therefore, a more socially inclusive CQ ideology needs to address such concerns. Purely commercial concerns need to be counter-balanced by non-economic, non-profitable services.

A concrete example of community impoverishment can be seen with the case of MediaCityUK in Salford. As a CQ, it is perhaps one of the most controversial given the national (and some international) (in)famous exposure garnered during the planning, construction and first few years of operation (Christophers, 2008). The financial backing of the project (estimated to be nearly £1bn) was almost exclusively from private sources (with one real estate company the sole backer), creating a CQ (combined with the wider development of Salford Quays) that while politically and nationally foregrounded is privately managed and resourced (Mould, 2014).

The area is characterized by highly privatized and corporatized aesthetics, with high-rise buildings housing business space and luxury accommodation, both of which come at premium rental rates. The area has been characterized as economically uneven (Christophers, 2008), with highly deprived wards surrounding the relative luxury of

MediaCityUK, moreover, the council has had to divert funds from social services to cater to MediaCityUK's auxiliary services. For example, Salford Council spent £330,000 on a bus service between Salford Crescent Bus station and MediaCityUK. Such an endeavour is questionable given the expense and lack of funds the council has for more fundamental social services, and that it has seen large budget cuts through the national government's austerity programme. The more general critique of the impoverishment of MediaCityUK and the wider Salford Quays area as a CQ has also pointed towards the lack of engagement with existing cultural infrastructure and creative community initiatives, characterizing the overt "top-down" narrative. An example includes the demolition of "Graffiti Palace", a stretch of wall along the Orsdall canal which has been replaced with commercial developments linked to MediaCityUK. Also, the Secret Gardens Festival in 2012 was an attempt to directly engage the local residents with MediaCityUK via creative and digital technologies, yet other than the celebratory event itself, there has been no sustained collaborations (Haywood & McArdle, 2012). The perceived lack of community and local-level engagement serves therefore to ossify the view of the predominately economic priorities of the CQ as an urban locale, and the defenestration of community-level social offerings.

The area then is very much a CQ characterized by high-end production, consumption and a lack of local community cultural intentness. In essence then, any cultural provisions are very much of a professionalized, corporate nature that is utilized for distinct financial rewards in retail and leisure consumption on the one hand, and the production of cultural goods (although mainly media, television and advertising artefacts) on the other. MediaCityUK then presents a specific perspective that mirrors many other privately-led CQ developments in the UK (and indeed internationally) in that it is dependent on the commercial exploitation of creativity and the impoverishing effects on local social provisioning that it inevitably entails.

Precariousness

From the vast array of political documentation on CQs, it is clear that often public policy makers and urban promoters will equate "culture" with commercial institutions and flagship developments, that is something that can be built and consumed. During the CQ planning process then, while large cultural institutions, cultural partnerships and investors find easy access to committee and planning discussions, this is often not the case for local creative industry firms, freelancers and practitioners. As such, the physical spaces are not designed with such production in mind. As the cultural and creative sector is populated mainly by small and medium size companies, freelancers and sole-traders (Mould *et al.*, 2013), it is almost impossible for the voices and needs of the sector to be heard or to play a role in shaping CQ development. Therefore it is critical that any articulation of a CQ needs to redress this imbalance, and start to incorporate the "grass-roots" cultural enterprises. These small firms and their workers (mainly freelance, part-time or interns) are often characterized as "precarious labour" (Bain and McLean, 2013, Gill and Pratt, 2008; Hracs, 2009; McAuliffe, 2012, Ross, 2008). Such precariousness, rather than being guarded against by large-scale creative and cultural industry institutions, is instead glorified through the creativity paradigm. For example, the recent trend of pop-up urbanism seems to glorify the precariousness of creative/retail work, celebrating the innovative and agile nature of such work. However, the realities are that the large majority of creative industry workers live subsistence lifestyles and struggle for new work (Banks and Hesmondhalgh, 2009). Incubator spaces, temporary work spaces and the like are often part of a CQ provision, but if their rents are affordable, they are only so for the short-term. After a certain time period of residency, the subsidized rents are taken away and if the incumbents have not progressed to fully-fledged profitable companies, then it is difficult for them to stay, and so the cycle of nomadism starts again. Such a view, if taken in isolation risks festishizing local, small-scale production as a panacea for the problems inherent in the CQ process. But instead of posting them as the rightful end users of CQs, there is a more pressing need for the CQ development process to be more sensitive to their (often non-economic) needs and to recognize that precariousness is a fundamental part of creative and cultural work.

Such an example of the precariousness engendered by CQs can be seen in the Ouseburn area, located one mile from the East of Newcastle city. From the 1970s, Ouseburn was declared an Industrial Improvement Area (the first in the Newcastle area) in response to changes in government policy aiming to revive derelict areas through industrial policy. Alongside a co-operative that was formed by existing businesses, a formalized Trust (called the Ouseburn Trust) was set up in 1996 primarily because of fears that the prevailing urban development being undertaken by real estate developers could threaten the remaining Victorian heritage in the Ouseburn area (Bailey *et al.*, 2004, Gonzalez & Vigar, 2010).

Despite the presence of the Trust and a desire from incumbents to maintain its unique productive capacity, Ouseburn highlights how a creeping formalized CQ development policy can catalyse precariousness within the creative workforce. Previously, Ouseburn had remained distinctly rooted in the working-class context of the area. Indeed, the role of the Ouseburn Trust was very much seen as an asset to the preservation of such socialities within the local community, something that was shared by the incumbent local artists, and cultural and creative producers who had been there since its inception in 1982 (Comunian, 2011). However, this approach soon had negative repercussions as the area was marginalized in reference to the broader cultural development of the city, in particular in relation to the mainstream culture-led regeneration taking place on the Quayside because of the distinct lack of sustained profit-making (and therefore rent-paying) practices of the resident businesses. At the marketing and promotional levels, the Newcastle-Gateshead Initiative developed the first CQ map of the city. In it, five CQs were included: the Quayside, Grainger Town, the Haymarket, Chinatown and Jesmond, but no mention was given to the Ouseburn Valley which had the largest co-location of artists and creative practitioners in the area at the time. Nevertheless, a creative production cluster, however large, if uncoupled to a cultural consumerist aesthetic, will increasingly not be in keeping with the political economic rhetoric of what a CQ should be. With the refurbishment of the Grade II listed building at 30 Lime Street and the establishment of a new flagship cultural institution (the "Seven Stories" national centre of Children's Book opened in 2005), there has been a growing attention towards integrating visitors' experiences and attraction. But they are introduced at the expense of the incumbent local producers who are seeing their rents increase because of it and are subsequently displaced. Overall, the grass-roots development of Ouseburn Valley was strongly linked to the affordable working space that it has offered to local artists and craft people, and the establishment of the Trust has allowed local businesses and local artists to resist the rise of rents that comes with property speculation. However, the pressure from local and national government agendas towards attracting more economic investment and growth to the area has been overwhelming, and many properties have been given over to more commercialized and corporatized cultural consumption activities. This is increasing the precarious working conditions of creative workers in the Ouseburn Valley, and the push towards favouring economically driven creative activities rather than amateur artists or precarious workers is eradicating the area's distinctiveness and creating a more "identikit" CQ.

Short-termism

The third process of "short-termism" is perhaps universally applicable to the broader problems of neoliberal capitalist and political agency. When looking at CQ strategies and proposals, there is a clear tendency of planners and developers to adopt a short-term perspective (what has been widely been seen as "short-termism" (Carley, 2000)), and a systemic quality is seen that directly affects the other two processes. In other words, short-termism fuels the economic imperative to prioritize commercial services, often with the involvement of "outside" companies and private investors, over investment in local services and amenities. It also implies that investment and support are directed to starting the CQ (for instance with initial funding available for start-up companies) but very little in the way of support or guidance after the first few years, and so we see precariousness increase. Furthermore, this also supports a new form of competition amongst cities and CQs, where capital attraction strategies and localized advantage might move/attract new companies (but only for a very short period of time). As Gray (2009, p. 19) argues, "it assumes that every city can win in the battle for talent and growth. Creativity scripts, however, are better understood as 'zero-sum' urban strategies constituted within the context of uneven urban growth patterns". However contrarily, some arguments within the literature suggest that investing in 'grass-roots' creative industries can prove to be more beneficial; "the development of a viable indigenous sector is crucial to providing a long-term basis for employment in the industry" (Coe, 2000, p. 392). More than this though, if CQ formulation engages with local non-economic community production "as well as" small-scale industry producers, it can be more inclusive and "culturally robust", in that it is not predicated upon a narrow set of homogenous commercialized cultural provisions that can move on very quickly. But a fix on short-term boosterism negates such a view.

Take for example Sheffield's CQ, which was one of the first to be developed in the UK. It was predicated on a pre-existing cultural vibrancy (particularly a thriving music scene) which led to the development of the National Centre for Popular Music (NCPM) in Sheffield. Forwarded as a millennium project, construction was completed in 1998 and it officially opened in March 1999. Sheffield council commissioned the NCPM, drawing on lottery funding in an attempt "reassert the local within global cultural flows" (Brown *et al.*, 2000, p. 440). Costing £15 million to build, the NCPM hoped to attract half a million visitors per year according to the promotional material. With poor visitor numbers and a failed £2 million re-launch as a live music venue, it was bought by Sheffield Hallam University in 2003 and is now their Student Union building. The positioning of the NCPM in Sheffield's CQ was a deliberate ploy to stimulate the local creative industry community and complement the vibrant music industry within Sheffield with a flagship institution (Brown *et al.*, 2000). However, despite the relative success of the surrounding incubator spaces and the vibrancy created by the adjacent university, the low level of visitor numbers was not enough to maintain the centre economically, and hence it had no other option but to shut down.

The failure of the NCPM and the subsequent reuse of the building as Sheffield Hallam University's Student Union, purports to a number of different issues, but notably, the high levels of intervention from the council during its implementation in the 1980s (including the NCPM and infrastructure upgrading) were due to the desire for short-term job creation at a time of severe deindustrialization in the city. Sheffield's CQ is still suffering as a relic of an overtly production-focused interventionist short-term strategy, lacking the leisure and "mixed" economy features (Moss, 2002), as well as the social and local cultural sensitivity that would retain users and residents. However, these perceived problems of Sheffield's CQ emanate from its comparison with subsequent CQs featuring a mixed economy *a la* the Montgomery (2008) model. Despite the failure of the NCPM, the area remains relatively productive in terms of its cultural industry activity, for example business spaces such as the Workstation have high occupancy levels and there are graduate employment links with the adjacent Sheffield Hallam University. However, the CQ is not the "national" hub that it has hoped to be in the original remit as it remains an area predominantly devoted to production rather than consumption of cultural products, therefore adhering to the traditional models of CQ development.

Conclusions

Looking at the extensive literature on CQ, we could argue that much has been learnt about the development of CQ in UK in the last decades. However, looking more closely, we see homogenously designed urban spaces, failed flagships projects and the boom of private consultancy firms offering CQ design services, and the uncritical and unreflexive take-up of CQ as a neoliberalized "model" of urban renewal across the UK. As has been argued throughout this paper, this has been achieved through a predominately traditional typological framework that is yoked to a perceived production–consumption and top-down–bottom-up axis. We have argued that more needs to be understood about the nuances and exact practices of CQ development that cannot be so easily identified as part of a production or consumption paradigm. While the discussion and analysis in this paper are more of an introduction and marker towards a more critical engagement with CQs, we have attempted to offer a more holistic and culturally sensitive reading of CQ development that takes into account local communities, the effect on cultural work and the long-term (non-economic) goals. These are of course arbitrary groupings of practices to be sure, and other more nuanced and specific cultural and social idiosyncrasies could be articulated. But what they represent (and what we want to purport) is a move away from pragmatic instrumentalism to a focus on the (often deleterious) practices of those affected by CQs, as this is what is needed to fully appreciate the full impact of CQ development in any given area.

Without these subjectivities being referenced, there will always be one big question that remains: who are CQs for? It seems obvious that commercial and economic power plays a key role in shaping the profile and nature of CQs, which means that small-scale creative and cultural producers, and local needs and long-term goals are regularly squeezed out of the discussion. The role played by developers and rent value cannot be underestimated and can completely change the configuration of CQs (as is the case in Salford, with MediaCityUK being built and financed by one large property company (Christophers, 2008)). We have focussed on three processes that we have seen as immediately obvious in terms of their non-consideration in CQ development. However, what our discussions demonstrate is that they are three articulations of a multifaceted, complex neoliberalized process. Community impoverishment and precariousness are inevitable consequences of a short-term agenda, which comes as part of the package of contemporary CQ development. While consultants tend to promote the re-design and embellishment of public spaces for CQs, these actions only lead towards the attraction of outside investors and large commercial entities that will empty the CQs of any locally incumbent producers who cannot afford the new rental spaces, and marginalize existing communities through the up-scaling of the housing stock and other gentrifying activities. Furthermore, it seems obvious that in recent developments, the market-driven end of the creative industries (media, software and design) is being favoured rather than the more artistic and often less economically viable sectors (craft, performing arts and visual arts). The former are now more profitable sectors, but they are populated by larger companies that fed on short-term locational incentives that are offered by CQs. This causes an even greater clamour for short-term "boosts" that such companies can provide and hence propagates even more community impoverishment and precariousness. It is therefore timely to begin to question the validity of such a CQ policy; a question which we have begun to pose throughout this paper. But such an inquisitive viewpoint risks a fetishization of local and community-based actors if they are posited as a panacea for the ills of commercial, neoliberalized CQ development. Our arguments though, have pointed to the fact that such a focus on localized, non-economic, community activity should simply be included into the development discussions rather than marginalized.

The paper argues for the need to take into account what Healey (2006) calls the "relational complexity" of local dynamics in the governance and planning processes of CQs, because there is a difficult balancing act needed between cultural consumption, cultural production and fostering a cultural (non-economic) milieu. We have argued throughout this paper that to date, the balance is far too skewed in favour of the first of these. Thinking about these narratives together as a suite of inter-connected and often conflicting processes, rather than as part of a dichotomous cultural–production/top-down–bottom-up framework can help to deconstruct a rhetoric "fast-urban policy" fuelled by a very narrow, and economically determined view of creativity and culture (Peck, 2005) which has dominated CQ policy to date. Rather than taking for granted that large cultural investments and CQs help local creative industries and the local community, it is important to consider what kind of tangible benefits they can provide and verify and evaluate if these benefits are tangibly felt, rather than just theoretically forwarded (Comunian & Mould, 2014).

The key question of what kind of culture is promoted and fostered in CQ development also needs further investigation. We have deliberately avoided the definitional quagmire of the term "culture" (with all its multidisciplinary understandings) as it is far beyond the remit of this paper. But, from our introductory analysis of CQs, it is clear that many of them promote a culture of pure production and/or consumption, by either the institutional public culture (especially in flagship projects) or the leisure, retail and entertainment consumption culture. While enjoying restaurants and cafes can be described as a cultural experience—if CQs are to engender the political rhetoric of improving the local cultural commons, CQs need a substantial shift in their planning mantra. CQs pay very little attention to the role played by subcultures, informal scenes, community creative initiatives and general creative freedom of expression. Spaces tend to be highly regulated, securitized and often sanitized to cater to outside visitors and shoppers rather than communities sharing values and community cultural practices. The diversity and heterogeneity of cultures is often ignored—the culture of a CQ is hence too narrow, and economically deterministic. It is time to really explore what kind of culture we want in a CQ.

Disclosure statement

No potential conflict of interest was reported by the authors.

Note

1. Which has been mapped at http://goo.gl/maps/1j6K

References

Bailey, C., Miles, S. & Stark, P. (2004) Culture-led urban regeneration and the revitalisation of identities in Newcastle, Gateshead and the North East of England, *International Journal of Cultural Policy*, 10(1), pp. 47–65.
Bain, A. & McLean, H. (2013) The artistic precariat. *Cambridge Journal of Regions, Economy and Society*, 6(1), pp. 93–111.
Banks, M. & Hesmondhalgh, D. (2009) Looking for work in creative industries policy. *International journal of cultural policy*, 15(4), pp. 415–430.
Brown, A., O'Connor, J. & Cohen, S. (2000) Local music policies within a global music industry: Cultural quarters in Manchester and Sheffield, *Geoforum*, 31(4), pp. 437–451.
Carley, M. (2000) Urban partnerships, governance and the regeneration of Britain's cities, *International Planning Studies*, 5(3), pp. 273–297.
Chapain, C. A. & Comunian, R. (2010) Enabling and inhibiting the creative economy: The role of the local and regional dimensions in England, *Regional Studies*, 44(6), pp. 717–734.
Christophers, B. (2008) The BBC, the creative class, and neoliberal urbanism in the north of England, *Environment and Planning A*, 40(10), pp. 2313–2329.
Coe, N. M. (2000) The view from out west: Embeddedness, inter-personal relations and the development of an indigenous film industry in Vancouver, *Geoforum*, 31(4), pp. 391–407.
Comunian, R. (2011) Rethinking the creative city: The Role of complexity, networks and interactions in the urban creative economy, *Urban Studies*, 48(6), pp. 1157–1179.
Comunian, R. & Mould, O. (2014) The weakest link: Creative industries, flagship cultural projects and regeneration, *City, Culture and Society*, 5(2), pp. 65–74.
Crewe, L. (1996) Material culture: Embedded firms, organizational networks and the local economic development of a fashion quarter, *Regional Studies*, 30(3), pp. 257–272.
DCMS (1998) *Creative Industries Mapping Document* (London: Department for Culture, Media and Sport).
Donald, B. & Morrow, D. (2003) *Competing for Talent: Implications for Social and Cultural Policy in Canadian City-Regions* (Hull: Strategic Research and Analysis (SRA)).
Ettlinger, N. (2003) Cultural economic geography and a relational and micro-space approach to trusts, rationalities, networks and change in collaborative workplaces, *Journal of Economic Geography*, 3(2), pp. 145–171.
Evans, G. (2009) Creative cities, creative spaces and urban policy, *Urban Studies*, 46(5–6), pp. 1003–1040.
Gill, R. & Pratt, A. (2008) In the social factory? Immaterial labour, precariousness and cultural work. *Theory, Culture & Society*, 25(7–8), pp. 1–30.
Gonzalez, S. & Vigar, G. (2010) The ouseburn trust in newcastle: A struggle to innovate in the context of a weak local state', in: F. Moulaert F. Martinelli E. Swyngedouw & S. Gonzalez (Eds) *Can Neighbourhoods Save the City? Community Development and Social Innovation*, pp. 128–140 (Abington: Routledge).
Gray, N. (2009) Glasgow's merchant city: An artist led property strategy, *Variant*, 34, pp. 14–19.
Haywood, P., & McArdle, K. (2012) The secret gardens festival of mass narrative. [Show/Exhibition]
Healey, P. (2006) Relational complexity and the imaginative power of strategic spatial planning, *European Planning Studies*, 14(4), pp. 525–546.

Hracs, B. J. (2009) Beyond Bohemia: Geographies of everyday creativity for musicians in Toronto, in: T. Edensor, D. Leslie, S. Millington & N. Rantisi (Eds) *Spaces of Vernacular Creativity: Rethinking the Cultural Economy*, pp. 75–88. London: Routledge.
Julier, G. (2005) Urban designscapes and the production of aesthetic consent, *Urban Studies*, 42(5/6), pp. 869–887.
Landry, C. (2006) *The Art of City-making* (London: Earthscan).
Legnér, M. & Ponzini, D. (Eds) (2009) *Cultural Quarters and Urban Transformation: International Perspectives* (Klintehamn: Gotlandica Förlag).
McAuliffe, C. (2012) Graffiti or street art? Negotiating the moral geographies of the creative city, *Journal of Urban Affairs*, 34(2), pp. 189–206.
McCarthy, J. (2005) Promoting image and identity in 'Cultural Quarters': The case of Dundee, *Local Economy*, 20(3), pp. 280–293.
McGuigan, J. (2005) Neo-liberalism, culture and policy, *International Journal of Cultural Policy*, 11(3), pp. 229–241.
Miles, S. (2005) 'Our Tyne': Iconic regeneration and the revitalisation of identity in Newcastle Gateshead, *Urban Studies*, 42(5–6), pp. 913–926.
Mommaas, H. (2004) Cultural clusters and post-industrial city: Towards the remapping of urban cultural policy, *Urban Studies*, 41(3), pp. 507–532.
Montgomery, J. (2003) Cultural quarters as mechanisms for urban regeneration. Part 1: Conceptualising cultural quarters, *Planning Practice & Research*, 18(4), pp. 293–306.
Montgomery, J. (2008) *The New Wealth of Cities. City Dynamics and the Fifth Wave* (Burlington, VA: Ashgate).
Moss, L. (2002) Sheffield's cultural industries quarter 20 years on: What can be learned from a pioneering example? *International Journal of Cultural Policy*, 8(2), pp. 211–219.
Mould, O. (2014) 'Mediating creative cities: The role of planned media cities in the geographies of creative industry activity', in: B. Derruder, S. Conventz, A. Thierstein & F. Witlox (Eds) *Hub Cities in the Knowledge Economy: Seaports, Airports, Brainports*, pp. 163–180. Basingstoke: Ashgate.
Mould, O., Vorley, T. & Liu, K. (2013) 'Invisible creativity? Highlighting the hidden impact of freelancing in London's creative industries', *European Planning Studies*, doi:10.1080/09654313.2013.790587
Newman, P. & Smith, I. (2000) Cultural production, place and politics on the south bank of the Thames, *International Journal of Urban and Regional Research*, 24(1), pp. 9–24.
Oakley, K. (2004) Not so cool Britannia: The role of the creative industries in economic development, *International Journal of Cultural Studies*, 7(1), pp. 67–77.
Peck, J. (2005) Struggling with the creative class, *International Journal of Urban and Regional Research*, 29, pp. 740–770.
Plaza, B., Tironi, M. & Haarich, S. N. (2009) Bilbao's art scene and the "Guggenheim effect" revisited, *European Planning Studies*, 17(11), pp. 1711–1729.
Porter, L. & Barber, A. (2007) Planning the cultural quarter in Birmingham's eastside, *European Planning Studies*, 15(10), pp. 1327–1348.
Pratt, A. (2008) Creative cities: The cultural industries and the creative class, *Geografiska Annaler: Series B, Human Geography*, 90(2), pp. 107–117.
Pratt, A. C. (2004) Creative clusters: Towards the governance of the creative industries production system? *Media International Australia*, (112), pp. 50–66.
Roodhouse, S. (2006) *Cultural Quarters: Principles and Practice* (Bristol: Intellect).
Ross, A. (2008) The new geography of work power to the precarious? *Theory, Culture & Society*, 25(7–8), pp. 31–49.
Santagata, W. (2002) Cultural districts, property rights and sustainable economic growth, *International Journal of Urban and Regional Research*, 26(1), pp. 9–23.
Shaw, S., Bagwell, S. & Karmowska, J. (2004) Ethnoscapes as spectacle: Reimaging multicultural districts as new destinations for leisure and tourism consumption, *Urban Studies*, 41(10), pp. 1983–2000.
Shorthose, J. (2004) The engineered and the vernacular in cultural quarter development, *Capital & Class*, 84, pp. 159–178.
Wilson, D. (2004) Toward a contingent urban neoliberalism, *Urban Geography*, 25(8), pp. 771–783.
Zukin, S. (1985) *Loft Living: Culture and Capital in the Urban Change* (New Brunswick: Rutgers University Press).

Creativity, Cohesion and the 'Post-conflict' Society: A Policy Agenda (Illustrated from the Case of Northern Ireland)

NICK CLIFTON* & TONY MACAULAY**

*Cardiff School of Management, Cardiff Metropolitan University, Cardiff, UK, **Macaulay Associates Network, Belfast, Northern Ireland

ABSTRACT *The intertwining of economic crises and political violence has been an ongoing narrative for Northern Ireland over the past four decades. However, with the end of 'The Troubles' and the transition to what has been termed a 'post-conflict' society (i.e. one in which the violence has largely ceased but its legacy remains), what is an appropriate agenda for economic development? To this end, we consider the current context in Northern Ireland in terms of cohesion, diversity and inclusion, and the implications therein of present policies. The geography of creative individuals within Northern Ireland is reviewed, and found to be particularly polarized within Belfast. That the highest areas of present deprivation are typically found in those most affected by past conflict suggests failures of policy since the 'Good Friday' Agreement of 1998. If economic growth, tolerance and diversity are linked, then all stakeholders must address these issues. Northern Ireland should neither be seen as a 'normal' lagging region nor one into which a standard neo-liberal development agenda can be transplanted free of context. At present, social cohesion appears to be regarded as an outcome of economic prosperity rather than as a factor that might actually drive it.*

1. Introduction

The previous decade and a half has seen a growing focus on the role of creativity in fostering economic development, with the emergence of concepts such as creative industries, creative economy and the creative class (Chapain, Clifton, & Comunian, 2013). The underlying assumption is that these industries—and the firms and individuals that comprise them—are highly innovative and are thus the new motor of economic growth. Consequently, they are placed by many policy-makers across Europe at the heart of their national innovation and economic development agendas (Comunian, Chapain, & Clifton, 2014), within a broader adoption of a neo-liberal (Sager, 2011) policy-making orthodoxy. Context matters in the successful nurturing of creativity and its translation into sustainable economic outcomes (Clifton, Cooke, & Hansen, 2013; Huggins & Clifton, 2011); however, this very success can have the effect of countering the social cohesion and diversity that is said to underpin creativity and the locational choices of creative people. Such potential complications are typically disregarded in simplistic adoptions of this neo-liberal development agenda (Boland, 2014; Nagle, 2009).

So if it is true that the most economically successful places are those which are characterized by tolerance, diversity, creativity and social cohesion, how might the various stakeholders in societies with particular challenges in these areas—and indeed ones that have experienced high levels of social division and/or actual conflict—respond with regard to social and economic policy? In order to address this question, we consider the case of Northern Ireland—a 'post-conflict' society. The term post-conflict can appropriately be applied in the case of Northern Ireland because, although the majority of the political violence has ceased, the historical conflict is clearly not resolved in the sense that neither side has demonstrably 'won'. Thus, rather than being placed in the largely arbitrary states of being 'in conflict' or 'at peace', as Brown, Langer, & Stewart (2011) suggest 'post conflict' societies should be seen as lying along a continuum of transition—in which at any given time the direction of travel is not necessarily always from the former to the latter.

Although Northern Ireland has become a more diverse society in recent years, the size of the minority ethnic and religious communities is still much smaller than many other European countries. Northern Ireland remains a predominantly white and Christian society, albeit a deeply divided one. However, there is evidence of a significant level of intolerance towards even this relatively limited level of ethnic and religious diversity. This is unsurprising in a post-conflict and divided society in which there have been generations of acceptance of fear and mistrust of the 'other side'.

Crucially, with regard to policy-making, tolerance and inclusion appear to be regarded as an *outcome* of a strong economy, rather than being among the *drivers* of prosperity in Northern Ireland. Moreover, The Programme for Government document (Office of the First Minister and Deputy First Minister [OFMDFM], 2011) makes no substantive mention of migration, diversity or ethnic minorities. Thus, the approach has essentially been to address problems created by migration in the 'stand-alone' spheres of service provision and so on, rather than to develop a long-term policy on migration as an opportunity within the knowledge-based sectors of the economy. Moreover, we suggest that the failure to adequately join up the social cohesion policy agenda with the economic development and innovation one has allowed the presence of an untapped reservoir of indigenous creativity within Northern Ireland to persist. This is particularly prescient for those areas most affected by the legacy of the conflict, where the danger is that social division, related to but distinct from the sectarian division, will take root.

The paper thus proceeds as follows: the section below provides an overview of the economy and context of Northern Ireland; there then follows a discussion of the policy-making framework with specific reference to economic development issues. We then move on to an overview of the geography of creativity in Northern Ireland and Belfast in particular, and consideration of how Belfast performs as an 'open' city. The current context in Northern Ireland in terms of diversity and social cohesion is then considered in some detail, before attention is turned to the implications thereof for current government policies. Finally, we speculate on the unique challenges faced in developing creativity in Northern Ireland, the broader implications for other post-conflict societies and potentially fruitful avenues for further research.

2. Northern Ireland: Economy and Context—An Overview

While attention over the last four decades has typically focused on the sectarian conflict, the ongoing weakness of its economy is such that Gaffikin and Morrissey (2001a) have described it as Northern Ireland's 'other crisis'. Northern Ireland is the smallest region of the UK with a population of 1.8 million (thus around 3% of UK population) and 2% of its gross value added (GVA). As in other peripheral regions of the UK, the heavy industries which underpinned Northern Ireland's economy began to decline in the period following the First World War, with this relatively highly paid employment not adequately replaced for many decades if indeed at all. The inward investment that did begin to flow into Northern Ireland during the 1960s was itself victim of the subsequent oil shocks of the 1970s (Gaffikin, McEldowney, Morrissey, & Sterrett, 2001). Unsurprisingly, this has provided the region with a legacy of socio-economic problems, many of which persist to the present day. Average earnings are approximately 90% of UK average and there are relatively higher levels of economic inactivity, similar to those of other post-industrial regions of the UK (Brooksbank, Clifton, Jones-Evans, & Pickernell, 2001; Pickernell, 2011).[1] Northern Ireland also has the youngest demographic of the UK regions, with 21% of the population under the age of 16. Unlike some other peripheral regions of the UK however, systematic under-investment during the period of the Thatcher government in the early 1980s cannot be highlighted as a causal factor; as Gaffikin and Morrissey (2001a) note, during this period there were relatively high levels of spending and industrial development in Northern Ireland. However, the legacy of this is manifested in a subsidy culture, and a labour market in which high-skilled workers are often taken up by the public sector.

With over 300,000 inhabitants and a greater metropolitan area population of approximately 700,000, Belfast is the driver of the Northern Ireland economy, and thus its performance is influential for the prosperity of the region as a whole. Belfast was essentially a market town up until the early 1800s, after which rapid expansion followed in the first half of the nineteenth century, driven largely by the textile industry (Bronte et al., 2015). A second industrial revolution then followed from the mid-1850s, based on shipbuilding and associated trades. Belfast was thus the only industrial city on the island of Ireland, with the British Empire and its associated access to markets playing a key role in this. Now the city possesses nearly a third of all service-sector jobs in the region, with half of Northern Ireland's high-tech manufacturing jobs, three-fifths of information and communications technology (ICT) and related jobs, and two-thirds of creative media and arts jobs located in Belfast (Oxford Economics, 2011).

The distinguishing factor between Northern Ireland and other 'lagging' regions of the UK, however, has been the intertwining of economic crises and political violence, which have served to reinforce each other over the course of the previous four decades

(Gaffikin et al., 2001). Northern Ireland was for many years the scene of a violent and bitter ethno-political conflict—known as 'The Troubles'—between nationalists (predominantly Roman Catholic and seeking unification with the Republic of Ireland) and unionists (predominantly Protestant and intent on maintaining Northern Ireland as part of the UK) (Mesev, Shirlow, & Downs, 2009). The Troubles are typically viewed as beginning in the late 1960s and generally considered to have ended with the 'Good Friday' Agreement of 1998.

The conflict has had a direct impact on the prosperity of Northern Ireland as one would expect—research into the financial cost of the divided society by Deloitte (2007) put the cost of this divide at around £1.5 billion per annum. This included policing and security costs, and expenditure on social housing inflated by an estimated £24 million due to issues such as dual provision. The report also estimated that an absence of civil unrest could realize in excess of £3 million from savings on roads and public transport. It also identified a range of potential savings by greater collaboration across the schools sectors of between £15.9 million and £79.6 million per year. Lost opportunities were also quantified in terms of lost jobs (27,600 from 1983 to 2000), investment (£225 million) and the impact on tourism (£1461 million at 2006 prices). Significant though these direct costs have been, it is argued in this paper that the less-tangible impacts of a divided society are potentially even more serious in the long run.

Since 1999, Northern Ireland has possessed devolved governance within the UK via the Northern Ireland Assembly. However, the legacy of nearly four decades of conflict persists, and sporadic violence has been ongoing (Shirlow, 2006a). In terms of the direct impact on the labour market, evidence from the Equality Commission for Northern Ireland has shown a decline in the overall level of religious segregation. However, less-tangible 'chill factors' remain influential (Shirlow, 2006b)—essentially the avoidance of places of employment due to fears relating to hostility and personal safety.

3. The Policy-making Context

With regard to economic development policy specifically, one of the first acts under devolution in Northern Ireland was the creation of the InvestNI development agency, drawing together the activities of the previous disaggregated development agencies (Cooke & Clifton, 2005). This would appear to have offered an opportunity to 'join-up' development priorities and indeed better connect them with the broader needs of the territory, but this has been something of a missed opportunity. The lead was taken from the model adopted by *Enterprise Ireland*, including instruments such as university incubators, spin-out firms, venture capital, exacting technology customers, supply chains, cluster-building programmes, science park facilities and science entrepreneurship support. Thus, the priority was to engage fully with the knowledge economy. Such initiatives can be interpreted in the context of a broader shift towards neo-liberal policy-making as orthodoxy, exemplified by a focus on growth and the benchmarking of competitiveness (Boland, 2014) via policies focused on competitive bidding (quasi-markets and partnership working), attracting potential 'customers' (companies, tourists, mobile knowledge workers), urban planning involving spaces for consumption, recreation, cultural events, nightlife and artistic districts, plus high-quality residential areas (Sager, 2011). The case has indeed been made by a number of authors for such an agenda pervading policy-making in Northern Ireland, and in particular its association with the transition towards a post-conflict society

(Horgan, 2006; Nagle, 2009; O'Hearn, 2008), with the Programme for Government 2011–2015 (OFMDFM, 2011) highlighting the Northern Ireland Executive's 'top priority' as the economy, although such statements are hardly unique of course. Moreover, Boland (2014) notes that a belief in free-market policies as the key route towards peace and reconciliation is to be found across the political spectrum in Northern Ireland. This then is essentially the 'fix the economy and society will follow' view—with the neo-liberal policy-making route seen as the best bet with which to achieve the former goal. There are, however, complications that are specific to Northern Ireland, namely ethno-sectarian resource competition post-devolution, and the higher than average dependency on state transfers (Boland, 2014; Murtagh & Shirlow, 2012).

Produced in the immediate aftermath of devolution, Strategy 2010 (Department of Economic Development, 1999) had ambitious targets for closing the gap between Northern Ireland and the UK. For example, GDP per head (80% of the UK level in 1998) was targeted to increase to 90% by 2010; similarly a business start-up rate of 31 per 10,000 adult population was to rise to 40. However, despite some relative improvements in areas such as skill levels, the performance gap remains largely intact and indeed wider in a number of areas. This broader picture can be seen in Table 1, which shows regional data from the UK Competitiveness Index (Huggins et al., 2014); the pattern is one of diverging performance within the UK with only three regions—London, South East and East of England—scoring over 100. That this gap has widened between 2006 and 2014 suggests that the global crisis has exacerbated already significant regional disparities in the UK. With specific regard to Northern Ireland, it remains at number 10 in the rankings albeit further away from the UK average than it was in 2006 (as is the case for most of the non-core UK regions). Similarly, Northern Ireland remains well below the UK averages for share of knowledge-based businesses and share of businesses engaged in exporting (Huggins & Thompson, 2010).

In their report, Oxford Economics (2014) refers to Northern Ireland as an 'economy in transition'; having come through the globally driven recession of 2008–2012, they identify a more internal set of drivers for the following five years or so—UK government policy, historic weaknesses of the Northern Ireland economy but also its future demographics. In other words, the underlying weaknesses of the economy remain, and these will need to be addressed in more innovative ways if progress is to be made (which chimes with issues we address in this paper). Although beyond the remit for which it was commissioned of course, it is still significant that the report makes no mention of the parallel social challenges involved in realising Northern Ireland's future as a post-conflict society. This issue is not unique to the work of Oxford Economics; in their discussion of Strategy 2010, Gaffikin and Morrissey (2001a) suggest that building competitiveness needs to go beyond a narrow focus on economic growth—rather a more nuanced understanding of what is required should include networking, social capital and inclusive government institutions. Thus, with specific reference to Northern Ireland, they state that "... it is contended that social cohesion and reconciliation, within the region and between the states in Ireland, have also to be at the core of the [competitiveness] agenda" (Gaffikin and Morrissey 2001a, p. 4). We argue in this paper that a decade and a half later this is an issue that still needs addressing, and one which remains neglected in the policy discourse.

As outlined above, a neo-liberal policy-making development agenda pervades the regions and nations of the UK and despite its unique set of circumstances, Northern Ireland is also home to such a consensus. Regions have become more open to competition

Table 1. UK Regional Competitiveness Index 2006–2014.

Rank	Region	2014 index score	2006 index score	Change in rank 2006–2014
1	London	128.32	113.9	0
2	South East	117.98	110.5	0
3	East of England	104.82	106.0	0
4	South West	97.68	94.9	+1
5	North West	95.41	92.3	+3
6	Scotland	93.59	94.2	0
7	East Midlands	92.13	96.1	−3
8	West Midlands	88.43	92.7	−1
9	Wales	84.22	86.7	+2
10	Northern Ireland	83.53	88.0	0
11	North East	82.88	84.2	+1
12	Yorkshire and the Humber	80.57	90.5	−3
	UK	100.00	100.00	–

Source: Derived from Huggins, Izushi, Prokop, & Thompson (2014).

from elsewhere, hence the increased emphasis on competitiveness, and there has therefore been an increasing focus on the importance of creativity in fostering economic development with the emergence of concepts such as creative industries, creative economy and the creative class (Chapain et al., 2013). In particular, the creative class thesis (Florida, 2002) suggests that the ability to attract and retain creativity and to be open to diverse groups of people of different ethnic, racial and lifestyle groups can provide distinct advantages to regions able to foster such environments. Northern Ireland clearly faces particular challenges here, which have largely been ignored within the neo-liberal consensus—or more to the point assumed to be solvable by economic success itself. However, there is increasing evidence that for realising creativity context matters (Boschma & Frisch, 2009; Clifton et al, 2013; Comunian et al., 2014; Martin-Brelot, Grossetti, M., Eckert, D., Gritsai, O., & Kovács, 2010) and that society and business are deeply intertwined at the cultural level (Clifton et al., 2011). Moreover, the policy climate plays an important role in the degree to which creativity is successfully translated (or not) into economic outcomes at the local level (Huggins & Clifton, 2011).

A decade earlier, Gaffikin and Morrissey (2001b) posed the key question as to what extent development in Northern Ireland would depend on effecting reconciliation within civic society; they argued that the twinning of the regeneration and reconciliation processes would be essential in the long term, but what they were not explicitly considering was the more direct relationship between society and economy implied by a creativity-based model of development where 'softer' factors play an important role in providing the right climate for innovation as the motor of economic growth. This is particularly pertinent for Northern Ireland given its low innovation base (Roper, 2009).

4. The Geography of Creativity in Northern Ireland, Belfast as an 'Open' City

In this section, we provide an overview of the geography of creativity in Northern Ireland, and within Belfast, using data on 'creative core' occupations as the best proxy indicator available (for a full account of the data and methods employed in associated research on creativity in the UK, see Clifton, 2008; 2013). Attention is then turned to how Belfast performs as city which is open to talent and creativity, via a range of comparative quality of place indicators derived from data generated by the British Council (see below for details). Additional factors specifically related to tolerance and social cohesion are then discussed in the following section.

Figure 1 shows the concentration of creative core occupations across the 26 Local Government Districts in Northern Ireland.[2] At this level of geography, there are relatively few outliers to be observed; the districts of Strabane, Limavady Ballymoney (listed west to east) are the areas of lowest concentration, that is, below 8.33% of the labour force. Conversely, Belfast has a relatively high concentration of creative core occupations, but not outstandingly so. Castlereagh to the immediate southeast of Belfast has the highest level of concentration; it should be kept in mind that these statistics are residence-based (i.e. as opposed to those collected by workplace location), meaning a significant number of these are likely to reflect employment in Belfast's knowledge-based economy.

When the spatial units are changed to Parliamentary Districts (of which there are 18—see Figure 2), most of the variation that was visible in Figure 1 disappears around the Northern Ireland average of approximately 10% of the labour force. However, what does begin to emerge is the polarisation that is apparent within Belfast itself, with the

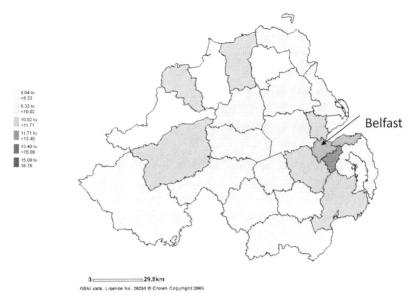

Figure 1. Creative core occupations by Local Government Districts in Northern Ireland (percentage of labour force).
Source: Generated using Census data from Northern Ireland Statistics and Research Agency.

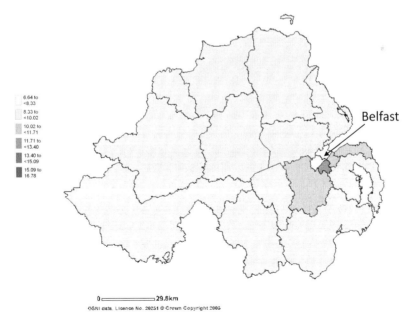

Figure 2. Creative core occupations by parliamentary constituencies in Northern Ireland (percentage of labour force).
Source: Generated using Census data from Northern Ireland Statistics and Research Agency.

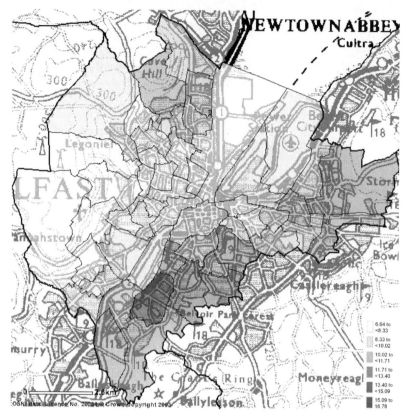

Figure 3. Creative core occupations by electoral wards in Belfast (percentage of labour force).
Source: Generated using Census data from Northern Ireland Statistics and Research Agency.

highest levels of creative core occupations in Northern Ireland (South Belfast) but also the lowest within the region (West Belfast) in close proximity. This is shown in more detail using ward-level data in Figure 3. This confirms what Shirlow (2013) has described as the 'four cities' model of Belfast, with the West of the city as nationalist, catholic and largely working class, the South affluent and politically moderate, North Belfast being contested, while East Belfast has a mixture of affluence and poverty. Thus, Shirlow sees Belfast now as much as a socially divided city as a purely politically or religiously segregated one. That said, Shirlow (2006b) also identified fewer than 20% of the population of Belfast (which is shared roughly 50/50 between Catholics and Protestants) as living within areas that can genuinely be described as mixed.

Figures 1–3 have focused on Northern Ireland (and Belfast) internally, regarding the distribution of its creative core of knowledge workers; Figure 4 focuses on another important aspect of a successful creative economy—how open it is to the outside world. There are various ways that such a notion might be captured (Clifton & Cooke, 2009; Florida, 2002), but here we have chosen to use data generated by the British Council and made available via their OPENCities Project. This has the advantage of providing a comprehensive set of indicators—themselves each comprising a number of underlying

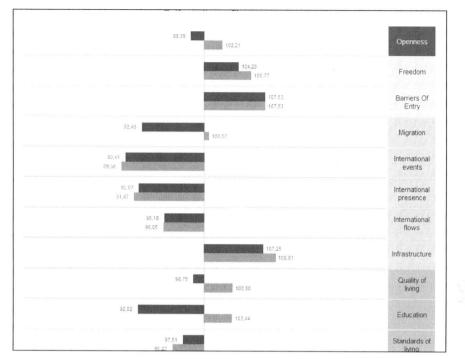

Figure 4. Belfast profile—measuring the 'openness' of the city.
Source: Generated using data from British Council OPENCities Project.

variables—which are comparable across 26 cities from different continents.[3] Thus in the figure, the centre line represents a normalized score of 100, that is, the average across all the cities in the database, with data shown for Belfast itself and for a comparator group of other UK 'provincial' cities.

From this analysis, Belfast is shown overall to be less open than its counterparts. Within this, the areas of Migration, Quality of Living and Education are of particular concern. The Migration figure reflects both the presence of international populations in the city, but also public attitudes towards ethnic diversity. Belfast scores well below the average, while the UK comparator group is on a par with this figure. Quality of Living assesses employment possibilities, rates of violent crime and also access to medical services. The quality of life of the international population in the city also depends on public attitudes towards people from another cultural/religious background, hence the inclusion of data on levels of trust towards those of different religions and nationalities. The historical context means it is unsurprising that Belfast ranks below average here, but given its significance for future prosperity, this is a key area that needs to be addressed. Similarly so with regard to Education, the measure refers to the choice of good-quality education opportunities in the city at all levels—including higher education and the presence of international schools—and the presence of international students in the city's universities. Ranking well below the average (and even further behind the UK comparator group) is thus a major cause for concern and one that merits significant effort to address—something that present policy is ill-equipped to do, as discussed below.

5. Diversity, Tolerance and Social Cohesion

Although Northern Ireland has become an increasingly diverse society in recent years (Wallace, McAreavey, & Atkin, 2013), the size of the minority ethnic and religious communities is still much smaller than many other European countries.[4] Northern Ireland remains a predominantly white and Christian, albeit with a deep divide down the middle. However, research into racism experienced by minority ethnic groups alongside police statistics on reported racially motivated hate crime suggests that there is a significant level of intolerance towards even this relatively limited level of ethnic and religious diversity. For example, survey research by the Department of Employment and Learning Northern Ireland (2007) showed high levels of perceived prejudice towards migrant workers in Northern Ireland; 24% of respondents thought that people were very prejudiced towards migrant workers, with 60% stating that people in Northern Ireland are 'fairly prejudiced'. Perhaps most worryingly, younger people were more likely to be prejudiced than were older respondents. In the late 2000s, there were some highly publicized attacks in which minorities (the majority Roma and Polish people) were displaced from their homes and, as Knox (2011) has noted, the reputation of Northern Ireland in terms of race relations was damaged. More positively, there is evidence to suggest that the increase in sectarian and hate crime has now been reversed (Nolan, 2012). Although the Good Friday Agreement requires public agencies to promote equality and 'good relations' between religious and minority ethnic communities, both policy and legislation on racial equality in Northern Ireland have lagged behind that in the rest of the UK (Wallace et al., 2013). The Race Relations (Northern Ireland) Order became law in 1997, 21 years after similar legislation in Great Britain, with the first Racial Equality Strategy published in 2005 (OFMDFM, 2005).

Much of this is unsurprising in a post-conflict and divided society. Where there have been generations of acceptance of fear and mistrust of the 'other side', it is not surprising that this intolerance towards the others who are different is transferred towards newcomers (Wahidin, 2012). Thus, there is evidence that those who are prejudiced against one group of people are likely also to be prejudiced towards other groups who are different (Wallace et al., 2013); research into legacy impacts of the conflict in Northern Ireland has identified fear and anger at the 'other community' as the dominant emotional response (Fay, Morrissey, Smyth, & Wong, 1999). Thus, social prejudice can become a mind-set, a way of thinking and an unchallenged cultural norm.

The community and voluntary sector (in partnership with statutory bodies or acting alone) has been identified as a critical conduit for many marginalized groups (McAreavey, 2010; McVeigh, 2006). However in spite of much hard work, sectarianism and segregation remain deeply embedded, and ethnic diversity poses further challenges. The policy drift in community relations over the past 10 years has resulted in slow progress in addressing what was already going to be a long-term process. Indeed as Nolan (2012) bluntly stated, there is no strategy for reconciliation and no real solution found for dealing with the past. Sectarianism, racism and intolerance not only damages people and communities, but it also projects a negative image overseas which results in Northern Ireland becoming less attractive to international investors and to newcomers and indeed potential returners. It may also hamper the efforts of firms seeking to export products outside the region (Clifton, 2014).

If economic growth comes with tolerance and diversity, then all stakeholders in Northern Ireland need to address these issues. Moreover, if the most successful places are typically those with greater social cohesion, then there is another equally big challenge to face. The places in Northern Ireland that have suffered most from the conflict are also those with the highest levels of multiple deprivation. These two factors are intertwined not just at the regional level, but also at the local one; Mesev et al. (2009) show that neighbourhoods with high levels of conflict-related deaths were those with the highest levels of segregation— but also deprivation. They were also more likely to be located near physical barriers, the so-called peace lines. Moreover, post-conflict, a negative predictor of reconciliation and forgiveness has been shown to be direct personal experiences of violence (Bakke, O'Loughlin, & Ward, 2009) —which supports the view that the challenges to overcome in interface areas are likely to be greater.

Thus, we can add on to the sectarian divide another layer of social divide. Inequalities in physical and mental health, educational attainment and employment are a reality for people living in the most highly segregated areas, interface communities and areas with continued tensions and violence. As an example of this, work undertaken by one of the authors (Macaulay, 2012) regarding a Good Relations (see OFMDFM, 2007) project in an interface area of Belfast highlighted the fact that while there was evidence of progress in indicators such as 'Level of Interface Violence', there was no progress whatsoever in the local service provision indicators relating to educational provision, employment opportunities, level of economic investment, youth provision, and healthcare facilities. As Shirlow (2013) highlights, the generation that took part in the conflict is experiencing ongoing health issues—both physical and mental, and the lack of a comprehensive health strategy to deal with this in the post-conflict society is a problem. These issues can be observed more broadly across what we might term Low Peace Impact Areas (Macaulay, 2010)— geographical areas where there has been low engagement in peacebuilding activities, few benefits from the peace process and a continued risk of instability and violence. Such areas are characterized by high levels of economic and social deprivation, embedded and unchallenged sectarian attitudes, and alienation from the political process and the government. They typically have a low uptake up of government-sponsored programmes and little meaningful cross-community contact or dialogue. Most fundamentally, there is insufficient local community leadership committed to a shared future. There is therefore an urgent need for substantive, innovative and long-term investment in Low Peace Impact Areas if social cohesion is to be built into Northern Ireland, and this is not just about social inequality of course. There is potentially a large reservoir of untapped creativity and talent in such areas; thus, alongside efforts to attract new talent into Northern Ireland, existing talent within Northern Ireland could be released.

6. Current Northern Ireland Executive Policies

6.1. *The Programme for Government*

The Programme for Government (OFMDFM, 2011) states that

A strong modern economy is built upon a healthy, well-educated population backed by high quality public services and a commitment to use prosperity as a means of tackling disadvantage. This, in turn, will lead to a tolerant, stable and inclusive society that has the skills necessary to attract investment and promote growth. (p. 28)

From this, it is clear that tolerance and inclusion are regarded as outcomes of a strong economy rather than among the drivers of prosperity. The Programme for Government also commits to finalize the Cohesion, Sharing and Integration Strategy (CSI) in order to "build a united community and improve community relations" (OFMDFM, 2011; p. 50). The CSI policy was first introduced by OFMDFM in January 2007; the slow progress in publishing the draft for consultation (OFMDFM, 2010) and the fact that it was broadly criticized as lacking ambition and specific actions (Wallace Consulting, 2011), and subsequent further delays in the publication of the policy, has resulted in a policy vacuum around community relations. The key commitments in the Programme for Government were to finalize the strategy and agree early actions in 2012/2013, achieve and review early milestones in 2013/2014 and to achieve the remaining milestones and review performance in 2014/2015. However, due to fundamental disagreements on the implementation and progress of CSI, it was eventually scrapped, and subsequently replaced with the less ambitious 'Together: Building a United Community' policy in 2013 (OFMDFM, 2013), which largely side-steps the major reconciliation issues involved in dealing with the past—parades and protests, cultural expression (i.e. flags and emblems and so on). Despite this agreement, progress remains slow.

The draft CSI Strategy did acknowledge a link between the impact of improving community relations and reducing poverty and building prosperity. However, tolerance, diversity and social cohesion are seen as underpinning rather than actively driving economic growth. A more ambitious and robust replacement of the CSI policy could contribute to improving diversity, tolerance and cohesion in a way that could more effectively contribute to growth. The Programme for Government does include a commitment to seek local agreement to reduce the number of 'peace walls'[5] and this is the one area where 'Together: Building a United Community' is arguably more robust than its predecessor, with the stated policy goal of dismantling the peace walls by 2023. This is the first time it has been government policy to work towards the removal of one of the most visible signs of division. There is thus at least an implicit recognition that interface barriers are a barrier to economic growth both within interface communities themselves, and also a barrier to positive international perceptions of Northern Ireland as a normal place to do business. The Programme for Government also includes priorities and commitments on shared education not least to ensure all children have the opportunity to participate in shared education programmes by 2015. This new commitment does show recognition of the costs of the divide in education, and collaboration in the curriculum through the Entitlement Framework (Department of Education Northern Ireland, 2010) has already resulted in a substantial increase in cross-sectoral collaboration. There has been a substantial growth in shared education initiatives throughout Northern Ireland since 2009. There are now around 300 schools working together in over 80 separate partnerships involving around 44,000 pupils. However, they are almost entirely short-term projects, funded by international donors, rather than the Department of Education. This raises obvious and important questions regarding long-term sustainability and change, and the fact remains that nearly half of Northern Ireland's children are still taught in schools where 95% or more of the pupils are of the same religion (Hansson, O'Connor Bones, & McCord, 2013). More generally, there is a significant body of research available demonstrating the benefits of integrated education with regard to attitudes towards those perceived as the 'other' (see, e.g. Hayes & McAllister, 2009; Hughes, 2011; Niens & Cairns, 2005). Kelman (2008) makes the point that ultimately reconciliation can only be achieved with the removal of the negation of 'the other' in people's identities. Thus, contact with, and trust of, members from other communities are likely to be key determinants of this process (Hewstone, Cairns, Voci, Hamberger, & Niens, 2006; Noor, Brown, & Prentice, 2008). Moreover, with regard to the potential advantages of achieving a more integrated society in the broader sense—that is, moving beyond resolving those social problems arising as a direct result of Northern Ireland's past—the Programme for Government has practically nothing to say. It also does not directly mention migration, diversity or ethnic minorities.[6]

6.2. Economic Strategy

The Economic Strategy for Northern Ireland (Department of Enterprise, Trade and Investment Northern Ireland, 2012) has the explicit overarching goal of improving the economic competitiveness of the Northern Ireland, as alluded to above. It also stresses the need to 'rebuild and rebalance' the economy in response to the economic downturn, with the longer term vision of creating an export-led globally competitive regional economy by 2030. Viewed in parallel with the Programme for Government, The Economic Strategy can be criticized for not including a sufficient array of direct actions to improve social cohesion and to reduce poverty and inequality. It does not consider the costs or impact of ongoing division as a restraining factor to growth, and does not consider tolerance, diversity and social cohesion as economic priorities in the way we propose them in this paper; indeed the only use of the word 'diversity' in the Economic Strategy relates to fuel diversity.

The Strategy commits to 'stimulate innovation, R&D and creativity so that we widen and deepen our export base' (p. 10) with the note that a specific strategy in this area is due to be launched in 2012 to underpin this key economic priority (p. 48). In actuality this was published in 2014, by which time the proposed Innovation, R&D and Creativity Strategy had become more narrowly the Innovation Strategy (Department of Enterprise, Trade and Investment Northern Ireland, 2014).[7] This document in turn sets out the desire that by 2025 Northern Ireland '... will be recognized as an innovation hub... which embraces creativity and innovation at all levels of society' (p. 7). We would suggest that promoting this culture of creativity and innovation is the context in which some of the ideas discussed in this paper could be further developed. Indeed, the 2012 Economic Strategy makes no mention of (in) migration; this is interesting given that as outlined earlier in this paper Northern Ireland appears to fare badly in its relative performance in this area. This in turn would seem to reflect the limited level of cultural/international diversity that exists therein. Migration to Northern Ireland has been characterized by relatively large numbers of Eastern European migrants, with higher a concentration in the manufacturing, food processing and construction sectors (Jarman & Byrne, 2007). Policy in the area has tended to focus on issues such as discrimination, service provision, and information and advice for migrants. Thus, the approach has been to address problems created by migration rather than to develop a long-term policy on migration as an opportunity as envisaged in the creative-class idea. As we have seen, the other factors where Northern Ireland scores relatively less well are quality of living and education. Again this would appear to confirm the need to address the problems of social cohesion highlighted earlier, and educational underachievement in particular. Ultimately, as Ferguson and Michaelsen (2013) have noted, the fact that those places most affected by a conflict that formally ended well over a decade ago largely remain the most deprived today suggests significant failures—from successive governments—to deal effectively with the legacy of conflict.

7. Further Reflections and Conclusions

The economy of Northern Ireland, like those of many other peripheral regions, has faced continued pressure to improve its relative performance in a global climate now characterized by the advent of global value chains and trans-national corporate networks. To this can be added all forms of mobile capital, including talent. The response—as elsewhere—has been to adopt the standard suite of neo-liberal development policies in a more or less off-the-shelf fashion, with relatively little deviation from this consensus across the political divide. In one sense, this is perhaps unsurprising, given the extent to which these ideas have become received wisdom amongst policy-makers, politicians and other stakeholders far beyond Northern Ireland.

There is of course one significant difference between Northern Ireland and the vast majority of other territories where such approaches to development have been implemented—namely a recent history that includes four decades of ethno-sectarian conflict, with all the associated legacy issues that implies. We make the case in this paper, therefore, that the particular challenges of the Northern Ireland context have not been sufficiently taken into account within the present policy landscape. Similarly, policy that essentially treats the territory as a 'normal' weaker region of the UK (as per a simplistic interpretation of Table 1 in isolation to context) is also unlikely to meet with success in the long run. There are of course potential dangers in arguing a 'special case' for any given region, but we would suggest that for Northern Ireland such an approach is justified. The two key challenges in Northern Ireland—the transition from past conflict and the need for economic renewal—have to date largely been tackled in distinct policy spheres. This approach can be implicitly summarized as: fix the economy first, and the other issues (decreased sectarianism, a more tolerant and cohesive society) will follow. As we have seen in the sections above, while there has been a raft of social policies in Northern Ireland, these are typically not joined up with economic imperatives and thus development policy and cohesion policy have not been sufficiently intertwined to maximize effectiveness. This has been brought to a head by the current paradigm of development, that is, a globalized knowledge economy in which creativity and innovation are the key drivers of prosperity, and thus the attraction, retention and harnessing of creatives are particular issues. Tolerance and social cohesion have an important role to play here—thus a simplistic adoption of neo-liberal development policy is inconsistent with the best interests of Northern Ireland in the long run. Given that many of those individuals receiving the highest levels of education ultimately migrate to high-tech/high-wage regions, retention is a particular issue; that is, the benefits of knowledge economy policies around education and skills are unlikely to be fully realized in the absence of social cohesion and high quality of place. This would suggest that a more integrated approach to development policy—which we have argued has been largely absent to date—is imperative. Indeed, without it, Northern Ireland (in general) and Belfast (in particular) will be unable to reposition themselves as genuinely progressive places, as per Shirlow (2006a). That said, as Nolan (2012, p. 10) has observed "a new, confident, and neutral urban culture has emerged" within Northern Ireland, albeit often in close proximity to areas of persistent deprivation. The key question then is to what extent can the people who are able to enjoy this culture—the restaurants, arts venues and so on—themselves demonstrate a degree of civic leadership? Shirlow (2013) highlights the danger that in being 'post-sectarian', these individuals may actually be less politically engaged per se; put bluntly if sectarians are the only people voting, then politics cannot move on from post-conflict debates.

As Leadbeater (1999) highlighted, collaboration is key for creativity, and effective collaboration requires social capital, which in turn implies trust. In many ways, Northern Ireland is a society with high levels of social capital—but this is problematic when related to deep division and thus social capital is strong but typically *sectarian* rather than *civic* in nature. In the language of Putman (1995), *bonding* social capital is high—what is lacking is the *bridging* social capital, and both are needed for balanced development (Cooke, Clifton, & Oleaga, 2005). Consequently, Northern Ireland does possess communities of high social cohesion, but ones which also have been essentially closed to outsiders or those who otherwise do not fit in. As Ellison, Shirlow, & Mulcahy (2012) noted, the conflict actually fostered close-knit communities within which anti-social behaviour was paradoxically seen as an affront to 'community values'—values which were enforced often by paramilitary organisations rather than by more 'normal' forms of government or policing. Thus, in one sense, the very notion of 'community' was viewed by the authorities as 'toxic'. A key challenge of the peace process, therefore, is to build the cross-community links while not completely undermining beneficial aspects of existing community cohesion.

This paper has revealed some potentially fruitful areas for further research; for example, our mapping of the creative core is residence-based, but also of interest are the 'day-time' concentrations—that is, where are these people actually employed—and how open (or not) are these places? More detailed quantitative analysis of the Census data (possible if the Office for National Statistics extends its Workplace Zone output data to Northern Ireland as planned) could be revealing, particularly in combination with qualitative data (interviews) to gain a better understanding of individual trajectories and the drivers involved. We should also keep in mind that new forms of segregation might be emerging as the economy changes and working patterns evolve. For example, Shirlow (2006b) shows that firms with fewer than 25 employees are more likely to have polarized employment profiles—what might this mean for an employment model that features rising levels of free-lancing, co-working, and entrepreneurship? This might be an area in which lessons could be learned from other post-conflict places and/or those with an ongoing ethnic frontier—for example, the Balkans, Israel. Finally, given the implications for returners, new investors and potential migrants to Northern Ireland, an improved grasp of the wider destination-branding and place-marketing challenges by the relevant stakeholders is of high importance—that is, gaining a more holistic understanding of the projection of Northern Ireland to the outside world.

To conclude, Northern Ireland as a region and Belfast as a city have undergone dramatic changes over the past four decades, but still face challenges if they are to become places which can truly embrace a creative economy, and to ensure fair access to the economic opportunities thereof across all members of society. If this is to happen, we have argued in this paper that tolerance, diversity and social cohesion need to be placed much more within the mainstream of economic development policy in Northern Ireland, such that they are regarded as actual drivers of future economic growth, rather than as essentially at best by-products of it. The prevailing neo-liberal policy-making orthodoxy is unlikely to shift radically in the near future, but it can and should be adapted to a very particular set of circumstances—that is, that of a post-conflict society.

Acknowledgements

The genesis of this paper arose out the authors' contribution to a 'Masterclass' session organized by the Centre for Economic Empowerment at the Northern Ireland Council for Voluntary Action. We thank them for that invitation. We would also like to thank the two anonymous referees for their insightful comments on an earlier draft of this paper. The usual disclaimer applies.

Disclosure statement

No potential conflict of interest was reported by the authors.

Notes

1. Various data from http://www.ons.gov.uk (2013/2014).
2. These 26 units were merged into 11 new Local Government Districts as of 1 April 2015.
3. For full details of the methodology which employs data from Eurostat/Urban Audit, European Social Survey and OECD, commissioned by the British Council and developed by BAK Basel Economics Ltd, see http://www.opencities.eu/web/index.php?areas_en.
4. Data from the 2011 Census show that only around 1% of the population of Northern Ireland is of non-western foreign-born origin (the UK figure is around 6%). Belfast is 1.4%, and the highest electoral ward around 5%.
5. Barriers erected at urban interface areas designed to prevent inter-community violence.
6. The consultation on "Development of the Racial Equality Strategy for Northern Ireland 2014–2024" took place between June and October 2014. At the time of writing, the final strategy has still not been agreed.
7. There is a preceding strategy for the Creative Industries specifically (Department of Culture, Arts and Leisure Northern Ireland, 2008).

References

Bakke, K. M., O'Loughlin, J., & Ward, M. D. (2009). Reconciliation in conflict-affected societies: Multilevel modelling of individual and contextual factors in the North Caucasus of Russia. *Annals of the Association of American Geographers*, 99(5), 1012–1021. doi:10.1080/00045600903260622

Boland, P. (2014). The relationship between spatial planning and economic competitiveness: The 'path to economic nirvana' or a 'dangerous obsession'? *Environment and Planning A*, 46(4), 770–787. doi:10.1068/a4687

Boschma, R., & Frisch, M. (2009). Creative class and regional growth: Empirical Evidence from seven European countries. *Economic Geography*, 85(4), 391–423. doi:10.1111/j.1944-8287.2009.01048.x

Bronte, J., Connolly, A., Hanson, W., Liddy, A., & McGuiness, L. (2015). *Physicality of place-North Belfast: Spatial analysis + design strategy*. Retrieved from http://issuu.com/hans2568/docs/northbelfast.

Brooksbank, D., Clifton, N., Jones-Evans, D., & Pickernell, D. (2001). The end of the beginning? Welsh regional policy and objective one. *European Planning Studies, 9*(2), 255–274. doi:10.1080/09654310125540

Brown, G., Langer, A., & Stewart, F. (2011). *A typology of post-conflict environments* (CRPD Working Paper No. 1). Centre for Research on Peace and Development, University of Leuven.

Chapain, C., Clifton, N., & Comunian, R. (2013). Understanding creative regions: Bridging the gap between global discourses and regional and national contexts. *Regional Studies, 47*(2), 131–134. doi:10.1080/00343404.2013.746441

Clifton, N. (2008). The 'creative class' in the UK: An initial analysis. *Geografiska Annaler Series B. Human Geography, 90*(1), 63–82. doi:10.1111/j.1468-0467.2008.00276.x

Clifton, N., Gartner, S. & Rehfeld, D. (2011). Companies, cultures, and the region: Interactions and outcomes. *European Planning Studies, 19*(11), 1857–1864.

Clifton, N. (2013). Location, quality of place, and outcomes; applying the '3Ts' model to the UK. In F. Florida, B. Asheim, M. Gertler, & C. Mellander (Eds.), *The creative class goes global* (pp. 183–209). London: Routledge.

Clifton, N. (2014). Towards a holistic understanding of county of origin effects? Branding of the region, branding from the region. *Journal of Destination Marketing & Management, 3*(2), 122–132. doi:10.1016/j.jdmm.2014.02.003

Clifton, N., & Cooke, P. (2009). Knowledge workers and creativity in Europe and North America: A comparative review. *Creative Industries Journal, 2*(1), 73–89. doi:10.1386/cij.2.1.73/1

Clifton, N., Cooke, P., & Hansen, H. K. (2013). Towards a reconciliation of the 'context-less' with the 'space-less'? The creative class across varieties of capitalism: New evidence from Sweden and the UK. *Regional Studies, 47*(2), 201–215. doi:10.1080/00343404.2012.665991

Comunian, R., Chapain, C., & Clifton, N. (2014). Creative industries & creative policies: A European perspective? *City, Culture and Society, 5*(2), 51–53. doi:10.1016/j.ccs.2014.05.009

Cooke, P., & Clifton, N. (2005). Visionary, precautionary and constrained 'varieties of devolution' in the economic governance of the devolved UK territories. *Regional Studies, 39*(4), 437–451. doi:10.1080/00343400500128457

Cooke, P., Clifton, N., & Oleaga, M. (2005). Social capital, firm embeddedness and regional development. *Regional Studies, 39*(8), 1065–1077. doi:10.1080/00343400500328065

Deloitte (2007). *Research into the financial cost of the Northern Ireland divide*. Belfast: Author.

Department of Culture, Arts and Leisure Northern Ireland. (2008). *Strategic action plan: Creative industries in Northern Ireland*. Belfast: Northern Ireland Executive.

Department of Economic Development. (1999). *Strategy 2010: Report by the economic development strategy Review Steering Group*. Belfast: Northern Ireland Executive.

Department of Education Northern Ireland. (2010). *Delivering the entitlement framework*. Belfast: Northern Ireland Executive.

Department of Employment and Learning Northern Ireland. (2007). *Attitudes to migrant workers: Results from the Northern Ireland Ominbus survey*. Belfast: Northern Ireland Executive.

Department of Enterprise, Trade and Investment Northern Ireland. (2012). *Economic strategy for Northern Ireland*. Belfast: Northern Ireland Executive.

Department of Enterprise, Trade and Investment Northern Ireland. (2014). *Innovation strategy for Northern Ireland 2014–2025*. Belfast: Northern Ireland Executive.

Ellison, G., Shirlow, P., & Mulcahy, A. (2012). Responsible participation, community engagement and policing in transitional societies: Lessons from a local crime survey in Northern Ireland. *The Howard Journal of Criminal Justice, 51*(5), 488–502. doi:10.1111/j.1468-2311.2012.00738.x

Fay, M. T., Morrissey, M., Smyth, M., & Wong, T. (1999). *The cost of the troubles study: Report on the Northern Ireland survey—The experience and impact of the Troubles*. Derry: INCORE.

Ferguson, N. T. N., & Michaelsen, M. M. (2013). *The legacy of conflict: Regional deprivation and school performance in Northern Ireland* (IZA Discussion Paper No. 7489). Bonn: The Institute for the Study of Labor.

Florida, R. (2002). *The rise of the creative class: And how it is transforming work, leisure, community and everyday life*. New York, NY: Basic.

Gaffikin, F., McEldowney, M. Morrissey, M., & Sterrett, K. (2001). Northern Ireland: The development context. *Local Economy, 16*(1), 14–25. doi:10.1080/02690940010016985

Gaffikin, F., & Morrissey, M. (2001a). The other crisis: Restoring competitiveness to Northern Ireland's regional economy. *Local Economy, 16*(1), 26–37. doi:10.1080/02690940010016958

Gaffikin, F., & Morrissey, M. (2001b). Regional development: An integrated approach? *Local Economy, 16*(1), 63–71. doi:10.1080/026909401300050812

Hansson, U., O'Connor Bones, U., & McCord, J. (2013). *Integrated education: A review of policy and research evidence 1999–2012*, Report commissioned by the Integrated Education Fund.

Hayes, B. C., & Mcallister, I. (2009). Education as a mechanism for conflict resolution in Northern Ireland. *Oxford Review of Education, 35*(4), 437–450. doi:10.1080/03054980902957796

Hewstone, M., Cairns, E., Voci, A., Hamberger, J., & Niens, U. (2006). Intergroup contact, forgiveness, and experience of "the troubles" in Northern Ireland. *Journal of Social Issues, 62*(1), 99–120. doi:10.1111/j.1540-4560.2006.00441.x

Horgan, G. (2006). Devolution, direct rule and neo-liberal reconstruction in Northern Ireland. *Critical Social Policy, 26*(3), 656–668. doi:10.1177/0261018306065617

Huggins, R., & Clifton, N. (2011). Competitiveness, creativity, and place-based development. *Environment and Planning A, 43*(6), 1341–1362. doi:10.1068/a43559

Huggins, R., Izushi, H., Prokop, D., & Thompson, P. (2014). *The global competitiveness of regions*. London: Routledge.

Huggins, R., & Thompson, P. (2010). *UK Competitiveness Index 2010*. Cardiff: University of Wales Institute.

Hughes, J. (2011). Are separate schools divisive? A case study from Northern Ireland. *British Educational Research Journal, 37*(5), 829–850. doi:10.1080/01411926.2010.506943

Jarman, N., & Byrne, J. (2007). *New migrants and Belfast: An overview of the demographic context, social issues and trends*. Belfast: Institute for Conflict Research.

Kelman, H. C. (2008). Reconciliation from a social-psychological perspective. In A. Nadler, T. Malloy, & J. D. Fisher (Eds.), *Social psychology of intergroup reconciliation* (pp. 15–32). Oxford: Oxford University Press.

Knox, C. (2011). Tackling racism in Northern Ireland: 'The race hate capital of Europe'. *Journal of Social Policy, 40*(2), 387–412. doi:10.1017/S0047279410000620

Leadbeater, C. (1999). *Living on thin air: The new economy*. London: Viking.

Macaulay, T. (2010). *Concept paper: Low peace impact areas*. Belfast: International Fund for Ireland/Macaulay Associates Network.

Macaulay, T. (2012). *Summative evaluation report: Forthspring inter community group good relations project*. Belfast: Macaulay Associates Network.

Martin-Brelot, H., Grossetti, M., Eckert, D., Gritsai, O., & Kovács, Z. (2010). The spatial mobility of the creative class: A European perspective. *International Journal of Urban and Regional Research, 34*(4), 854–870. doi:10.1111/j.1468-2427.2010.00960.x

McAreavey, R. (2010). *Life as a stranger: The personal stories of migrants to Northern Ireland*. Belfast: Nuffield Foundation.

McVeigh, R. (2006). *Migrant workers and their families in Northern Ireland*. Belfast: Northern Ireland Congress of Trade Unions.

Mesev, V., Shirlow, P., & Downs, J. (2009). The geography of conflict and death in Belfast, Northern Ireland. *Annals of the Association of American Geographers, 99*(5), 893–903. doi:10.1080/00045600903260556

Murtagh, B., & Shirlow, P. (2012). Devolution and the politics of development in Northern Ireland. *Environment and Planning C: Government and Policy, 30*(1), 46–61. doi:10.1068/c10216r

Nagle, J. (2009). Sites of social centrality and segregation: Lefebvre in Belfast, a 'divided city'. *Antipode, 41*(2), 326–347. doi:10.1111/j.1467-8330.2009.00675.x

Niens, U., & Cairns, E. (2005). Lessons learnt: Peace education. *Theory into Practice, 44*(4), 337–344. doi:10.1207/s15430421tip4404_7

Nolan, P. (2012). *Northern Ireland peace monitoring report number one*. Belfast: Community Relations Council.

Noor, M., Brown, J. R., & Prentice, G. (2008). Precursors and mediators of intergroup reconciliation in Northern Ireland: a new model. *British Journal of Social Psychology, 47*(3), 481–495. doi:10.1348/014466607X238751

Office of the First Minister and Deputy First Minister. (2005). *A racial equality strategy for Northern Ireland 2005–2010*. Belfast: Northern Ireland Executive.

Office of the First Minister and Deputy First Minister. (2007). *A shared future and racial equality strategy good relations indicators baseline report*. Belfast: Northern Ireland Executive.

Office of the First Minister and Deputy First Minister. (2010). *Programme for cohesion, sharing and integration*. Belfast: Northern Ireland Executive.

Office of the First Minister and Deputy First Minister. (2011). *Programme for Government 2011–15*. Belfast: Northern Ireland Executive.

Office of the First Minister and Deputy First Minister. (2013). *Together: Building a united community*. Belfast: Northern Ireland Executive.

O'Hearn, D. (2008). How has the peace changed Northern Irish political Economy. *Ethnopolitics, 7*(1), 101–118. doi:10.1080/17449050701847202

Oxford Economics. (2011). *Research into the competitiveness of Belfast: Final report*. Belfast: Author.

Oxford Economics. (2014). *Northern Ireland economy in transition: Future drivers, challenges, impacts and issues for policy consideration*. Belfast: Author.

Pickernell, D. (2011). *Economic development policy in Wales since devolution: From despair to where? CEG papers in economic geography*. Cardiff: Centre for Economic Geography, School of Planning and Geography, Cardiff University.

Putman, R. (1995). Bowling alone: America's declining social capital. *Journal of Democracy, 6*(1), 65–78. doi:10.1353/jod.1995.0002

Roper, S. (2009). *Stepping forwards: Northern Ireland's innovation future*. London: NESTA.

Sager, T. (2011). Neo-liberal urban planning policies: A literature survey 1990–2010. *Progress in Planning, 76*(4), 147–199.

Shirlow, P. (2006a). Belfast: The 'post-conflict' city. *Space and Polity, 10*(2), 99–107. doi:10.1080/13562570600921451

Shirlow, P. (2006b). Measuring workforce segregation: Religious composition of private-sector employees at individual sites in Northern Ireland. *Environment and Planning A, 38*(8), 1545–1559. doi:10.1068/a3840

Shirlow, P. (2013, March 21). *Northern Ireland: From the crossroads to the roundabout, lecture given at the school of planning and geography*. Cardiff University, Innovation and Engagement Event Series.

Wahidin, A. (2012). Introduction to the special issue on 'the legacy of conflict and the impact on the Northern Irish criminal justice system'. *The Howard Journal of Criminal Justice, 51*(5), 437–441. doi:10.1111/j.1468-2311.2012.00734.x

Wallace, A., McAreavey, R., & Atkin, K. (2013). *Poverty and ethnicity in Northern Ireland: An evidence review*. York: Joseph Rowntree Foundation.

Wallace Consulting. (2011). *Programme for cohesion, sharing and integration: Consultation analysis*. Portadown: Author.

Living Hand to Mouth: Why the Bohemian Lifestyle Does Not Lead to Wealth Creation in Peripheral Regions?

SOPHIE BENNETT*, STEVEN McGUIRE* & RACHEL RAHMAN**

*School of Management and Business, Aberystwyth University, Aberystwyth, UK, **Psychology Department, Aberystwyth University, Aberystwyth, UK

ABSTRACT *Using demographic data from a study of micro and small business owners operating in the crafts industry in rural Mid and West Wales, this paper identifies a mismatch between government business incentives and the bohemian values of local enterprises. This is highlighted as a contributing factor to explain why creative organizations in Wales do not generate the regional economic wealth expected from those working within the creative industries. Chaston [2008. Small creative industry firms: A development dilemma?* Management Decision, *46(6), pp. 819–831] suggests that national policy relating to the economic development of regions is misguided because it is based on data collected in major cities. In periphery locations, many creative operations are concentrated in art and craft, yet little is currently known about these enterprises, and a limited amount of research has been conducted involving the craft sector in general. An initial investigation into micro and small craft enterprises is presented here, which indicates that although policy-makers view all creative firms as capable of economic development that will deliver growth and jobs [Oakley, 2011. In its own image: New labour and the cultural workforce,* Cultural Trends, *20(3–4), pp. 281–289], the type of creative firm attracted to the periphery regions of Mid and West Wales does not necessarily exhibit the type of growth anticipated from the creative industries sector.*

Introduction

Research into the issues surrounding regional economic disparities is growing in prominence. There remains a clear divide between the wealth of urban centralized areas and that of periphery regions despite the recent revisions in UK policy-making intended to minimize this (Morgan, 1996). Government strategies have become increasingly directed towards fostering local enterprise for community regeneration through creative innovation, yet rural locations such as Mid and West Wales continue to show high economic inactivity while at the same time showing strong levels of creative production (Econactive, 2010). This paper contributes to regional research that considers the type and impact of creative activity in small towns and rural areas by presenting demographic data from micro and small craft enterprises in Mid and West Wales which indicate that although these enterprises are sustainable, they do not necessarily demonstrate the growth potential anticipated from those operating in the creative industry sector.

This study supports research by Fillis (2006), Comunian (2009), McRobbie (2002) and Eikhof & Haunschild which suggests that those working within the traditional areas of creativity such as visual arts, craft or theatre demonstrate bohemian lifestyle values that are not necessarily commercially orientated. In contrast to the common notion of creativity and creative output described by Florida (2002) that occurs in urbanized areas and cities, the main creative players in the periphery region of Wales are micro-enterprises (Welsh Government, 2012b), many of whom are based in craft (Burns *et al.*, 2012). The owners or managers of these produce a low annual income for their creative work, yet regional strategies continue to implement profit-orientated policies in these areas. This mismatch between the craft enterprise in the periphery regions of Wales and the expectations of creative policy-makers for all creative subsectors is identified as an explanatory factor for the high creative output, but the low level of growth experienced in these areas.

An Overview of Regional Policy-making in Wales

For the past 20 years, the creative industries have been highlighted as being capable of fostering economic development to aid growth and employment. This has been encouraged by the work of eminent creativity researchers such as Florida (2002), whose study of the creative class and creative hubs emphasize a direct link between creativity and economic revival. The impact of this on policy-making can been seen at the global level in the formation of strategic groups such as the European Creative Industries Alliance, designed to better exploit the innovation potential of the creative industries (Creative Business, 2012); at the national level identified by the 2009 Labour government as one of the main facilitators to pull the UK out of the economic crisis; and at regional level through organizations such as Alliance Wales which has given prominence to the innovative small creative enterprise in the fast growth area of information and communication technology – ICT (Hargreaves, 2010).

The apparent growth potential of the creative industries and the associated policy-making strategies designed to foster such activity have been described, however, as a "one size fits all" approach (Oakley, 2011). A major criticism of this approach is that it applies the same expectation and evaluation criteria and implements the same business incentives to all subsectors despite the considerable variance in growth level displayed between them. This variance can be seen most prominently between the core creative activities that Chaston describes as "pure arts" and those involved in ICT. While industry-driven creativity such as ICT and new media has boomed, contributing towards the annual £60,800 billion GVA creative output in the early 2000s (DCMS, 2001), areas traditionally associated with the "pure arts" such as music, craft and visual arts can be seen to be underperforming, with a flat growth rate level (Comunian, 2009).

Evidence of this variance in creative potential is prominent in Wales where employment and participation in the creative industries are increasing at a far higher rate than economic regeneration. In 2009, the Office of National Statistics reported 36,000 employees in

Wales working in the area of arts and entertainment, which by 2011 had increased by 16% (Office for National Statistics, 2012). This shows a significant growth in creative areas, yet instead of also exhibiting significant expansion and profit increases, economic activity in Wales increased by just 2.2% within the same time-frame (Office for National Statistics, 2012).

A contributing factor to this low growth rate is the variance in creative output between urban and rural areas. In Wales, like other periphery regions, urbanized areas represent the minority of the population and therefore do not exhibit the same level of growth seen in the rest of the UK. Cities in Wales generate just 33% of the country's wealth, the lowest proportion in all UK nations (Welsh Government, 2012b) and achieve a low output of production in areas such as film, ICT and computer programming, the subsectors commonly found in urban areas and associated with the generation of wealth. Wales is characterized instead by its rural regions where the majority of creative output relates to low growth industries such as visual arts and craft (Econactive, 2010).

Participation in craft is a growing phenomenon across the UK (Scott, 2010) and is evidenced in the myriad of studios and galleries visible in small towns and villages. In Wales, it is one of the largest creative subsectors, with an estimated 3530 employees (Hargreaves, 2010); however, despite its popularity and prominence little attention has been paid to this area in regional research or in policy-making. Walters and Lawton Smith (2002) have called for government to recognize the importance of location-specific factors to the economies of peripheral regions, yet creative industry strategies remain centralized and favourable to urban areas and urban creativity. The 2004 Welsh Assembly Government Creative Industry Strategy (Hargreaves, 2010) identified the creative sector as one of the six strategically important sectors of the economy; yet policy-making focuses primarily on the exploitation of intellectual property despite the prominence of craft produce in periphery regions. Wales has invested £7 million into a creative Intellectual Property Fund to secure work for creative businesses (Hargreaves, 2010) focusing on licensing; there are no similar schemes for creative products such as craftwork.

Regional policy-making for the creative industries in Wales therefore appears misaligned. It pays little attention to the variance between the type of creative activity prevalent in urban and rural areas and therefore applies the same expectations and implements the same business incentives to all subsectors and all regions. Strategies are designed to foster urban creativity which demonstrates the high growth potential the creative sector has become synonymous with, yet the majority of creative output in regional areas is in craft, the sector that demonstrates little or no growth potential.

An Overview of the Attributes of Mid and West Wales

Mid and West Wales are made up predominantly of a network of small seaside towns and villages (Fuller-Love *et al.*, 2006) and exhibit many of the limiting characteristics of periphery regions including an outward migration of skilled labour (Fuller-Love *et al.*, 2006), aging population, high unemployment levels, limited technological resources and limited employment opportunities or industry cross fertilization. These regions are instead dependent upon urban conurbations in terms of resource allocation, infrastructure and the formation of policies for economic regeneration. As is the case for the majority of periphery areas, there is a failure to identify truly regional issues because regional planning guidance is a replica of national planning policy developed in urban areas (Hull, 2010).

In terms of employment, the Mid and West regions attract a high percentage of micro and small business investment. In these regions, enterprises tend to employ less than five people, the majority of whom are sole traders operating in locations that are remote from their own homes (Welsh Government, 2012c). The region displays a significantly high proportion of self-employed people in comparison to the rest of the country, exhibiting strong potential for small business creation and expansion (Day & Thomas, 2007). This type of industry accounts for 94.5% of all businesses in Wales and is responsible for 33.2% of private sector employment (Welsh Government, 2012c). In 2012, there were 13,960 micro-businesses operating in Powys, the second highest county for this type of output in the Country (Welsh Government, 2012c). The micro-business strategy for Wales (Welsh Government, 2012c) identifies these micro and small businesses as having the potential to maintain, improve and increase the contribution they make to the Welsh community if they are provided with access to finance, mentoring and simplified business regulations. This type of support has been provided and is evidenced in business incentives designed to encourage growth such as Start-up Grants (Business Connect Wales), Professional Development Apprenticeships (Go Wales) and the newly packaged Business Mentoring Service (Business Wales) to help employers and employees boost underactive local economies.

Wales displays a strong potential for small business creation (Haven-Tang & Jones, 2008) yet remains a periphery region in the full sense of the definition, with a GDP growth for 2012 forecast at just 0.7% (Office for National Statistics, 2012). Female activity rates remain at under 50% and are characterized by part time or casual employment (Day & Thomas, 2012). The Country's economic strategy detailed in the 2005 report "Wales: A Vibrant Economy" set clear objectives to nurture local industry and up-skill its workforce, thereby increasing average earnings to close the gap between its regional income and the rest of the UK (Jones & Sloane, 2007). This has done little, however, to help the trend for economic underperformance highlighted by Fuller-Love *et al.* (2006) which remains a reoccurring issue in rural areas, identified again by Haven-Tang and Jones (2008) in the downsizing of operations in Wales to run employee-free businesses.

A major barrier to economic progression has been identified as the limited access to resources to attract and retain the innovative and technological industry needed to generate economic wealth (Day & Thomas, 2007). While Wales displays a significant level of entrepreneurship in terms of business start-ups and the number of micro to small businesses operating in its periphery regions, the type of businesses within these locations does not demonstrate high levels of innovation. This has been highlighted as a major concern for Wales, and regional policy-makers have attempted to address this with innovation focused incentives such as computer software training programmes and other schemes outlined in the recently published Innovation Strategy (Welsh Assembly Government, 2012a).

The attitude of enterprise manager's in the peripheral areas of Wales has also been identified as a barrier to economic expansion, which appears to be adverse to facilitating growth. Fuller-Love *et al.* (2006) note that businesses based here often display an unresponsive attitude to change and some micro-businesses are reluctant to adopt ICT strategies due to the lack of time or a general suspicion of new technologies (Welsh Government, 2012a). Stough (2009) indicates that to remain competitive, regions must continually adjust to external market conditions and resource constraints, yet in an area where the population is change resistant there is little opportunity to compete.

The Mid and West Wales regions of Wales appear to attract micro and small business investment; however, this type of investment is not necessarily the type strategies aim to foster because it does not demonstrate the growth needed to generate regional wealth. Wales does not appear currently to have the resources, skills or managerial drive required to support the innovative creativity its business incentives seem to be encouraging; instead, it demonstrates a high level of involvement in low growth creative subsectors such as craft.

Craft Enterprises in Mid and West Wales

A cause for concern, which this paper takes the initial step towards addressing, is the lack of research undertaken involving the crafts industry in Wales, despite craft being one of the main creative sector employer in the area (Hargreaves, 2010). Comunian notes that there is a shortage of research to consider how the creative economy performs at a local level (2009). This has been highlighted by Hargreaves (2010) who identified a failure to map the creative industries in Wales which was raised again in the report from the Third Regional Studies Association research seminar (Winther & Hansen, 2012). The aforementioned report concluded that creativity does matter for urban and regional development, but that its impact varies according to geographical context; that is evidence which contrasts strongly with the "one size fits all" approach adopted by creative policy-making that is based on research in urban areas. Florida's influential work, focused on creative people within North American cities, has meant that inner cities are seen as edgy, cosmopolitan and creative (Collis *et al.*, 2010), while outer suburbs and rural areas are predominantly seen as non-creative. An ideal creative place, located within inner cities, has arisen from creative industries research and adopted associated strategies. Recent research into suburban creativity by Collis *et al.* (2010) and Lorenzen and Vaarst Andersen (2011) has brought attention to the creativity that flourishes in smaller cities, but there is still a distinct lack of research that considers the creative enterprise in rural periphery regions.

This is particularly true of those working within the area of craft. In his 2009 study of craft firms, Fillis presents four distinct orientations of owner/manager's operating within the industry throughout the UK (Figure 1): the *lifestyler*, who has chosen to work in this particular area because of the type of lifestyle involved; the business-orientated *entrepreneur*, who is willing to take risks and develop the firm; the *idealist*, who views craftwork not as a product but as a creative piece and the *late developer*, who enters the industry at a later stage of life, having previously engaged in non-creative employment. There remains a gap in studies undertaken focusing on craft and craftspeople in Wales however; with the exception of the currently unpublished work by McDermott, Venus, and Vincentelli, (2007) considering the motivation factors of women potters in Wales and the RIPPLE Producer Survey (1998) profiling small businesses in West Wales, the authors can find no other study involving micro and small craft enterprises specifically located in Wales.

This may, to some extent, explain the absence of the craftsperson in regional policy-making strategies. The 2012 review of the creative industries for the Welsh Assembly Government (Hargreaves, 2010) highlighted the need for governmental support in ICT

LIFESTYLER	ENTREPRENEUR
• Expansion of business not important • Unwilling to take many risks • Importance of quality of life • May or may not export; general reactive. • Unwilling to follow business and marketing philosophy and develop related skills.	• Risk taker • May or may not export; proactive • Most likely to embrace business and marketing philosophy in the longer term. • Realisation of importance of customer relationships/networking
IDEALIST	**LATE DEVELOPER**
• Risk taker • Unwilling to accept business and marketing philosophy • Dominance of 'Art for Art's sake' beliefs • May or may not export • Realisation of importance of establishing and building relationships and generating reputation. • Views self as artist rather than craftsperson	• Tends to come from non-creative background • Less motivated to expand business; less likely to export • Unlikely to accept new ideas • Believe in valuing own experience of business and life • Able to bring outside skills to the business • May find problems with accessing existing networks

Figure 1. Characteristics of the craft Enterprise Owner/Manager.
Source: Fillis (2009, p.141).

sectors while visual art and craft, along with subsectors such as theatre and publishing are identified only as "other creative industries". The number, type, lifestyle or motives of craft enterprises in Wales remain largely unknown; the Crafts Council does not hold a complete database for these, and the only indication of the variety of enterprises in Wales can be obtained from the various craft organizations and networks located throughout the area such as the Pembrokeshire Guild of Crafts and Ceredigion Craftmakers. Other arts organizations have databases specific to their needs and therefore do not show a true representation of the arts network in this region. For example, a report by Wavehill Consultancy, commissioned by Powys County Council, found that there are 1700 creative businesses within its borders; however, this includes all categories defined by the DCMI as creative; while the AXIS website lists contemporary artists by art form, rather than by region.

The absence of research or knowledge about the crafts industry in Wales means that a significant percentage of the workforce is underrepresented in regional planning. This is a significant issue, particularly as statistics suggest that sales and participation in the crafts sector are increasing (Barford, 2012). Further research is called for to investigate the craft industry in Wales. The aim of this paper is to build upon research by Fillis (2006, 2008, 2009) to investigate the demographic profile of the craftsperson in the rural regions of Wales. Given the socio-environmental context of Wales and the existence of a high level of creative output but low level of economic growth, the purpose is to identify who these people are, and in doing so, where the mismatch occurs between these enterprises and creative policy in Wales.

Research Approach

The research findings presented here form part of a larger project looking at the demographics, lifestyle and motivations of small to micro craft enterprises in the periphery regions of Mid and West Wales. The initial phase of this larger project is used as the basis for this study involving a demographic questionnaire survey. Results from the questionnaire present a profile of the craftsperson based in Mid and West Wales which is then discussed in relation to the bohemian lifestyle identified by Murger (1988) and in relation to creative policy-making in Wales.

Sample

The sample was identified on the basis of three criteria: by their profession as craftspeople or visual artists; their location in Mid and West Wales and their artistic product encompassing painting, illustration, photography, quilt making, jewellery, textiles and visual art. It is impossible to determine the population size due to lack of reliable statistical data involving this creative sector, however, enquiries made during this research involving arts organization in the area such as Ceredigion Craftmakers and Origin Dyfed, attendance at local craft fairs and online access to membership of social media sites for art and craft networks identified 297 craftspeople across Carmarthen, Ceredigion, Powys and Pembrokeshire. This provided the sample frame for the study.

Craftspeople in Mid Wales were identified using judgement and snowball sampling. Judgement sampling is not appropriate for research wishing to draw broad generalizations from the outcome (Kent, 2007); however, this was not the aim of the study which required judged targeting of a specific sample of crafts people in Mid and West Wales. The study also aimed at achieving a valid representation from this sample, and so having identified an initial target group, snowball sampling was then used to further expand the sample size. This mix of sampling is suitable for this study as it is often used for data sets that are homogenous and hard to locate (Bryman, 2008), and as it is a well-known fact that the arts world relies heavily on its connections and networks.

This study is particularly susceptible to systematic error because the authors have no way of identifying the true number of creative individuals working within Mid and West Wales; however, the data selection will involve individuals from organizations such as Ceredigion Craft Makers, Pembrokeshire Guild of Crafts, Origin Dyfed and Powys Arts Engine. These organizations represent the main hub of artistic activity in Ceredigion and the bordering counties; therefore, the risk of not obtaining a cross section of the artistic community can be reduced.

Data, Measures and Procedure

The preferred data collection method was questionnaires. A limitation of this method is that the average response rate is just 30%; however, the authors' connections with local arts organizations helped to ensure a reasonable rate of return.

The questionnaire was designed as part of a larger research project and the demographic section was used as the basis for this study. The full questionnaire consisted of 46 questions; only the demographic section of this questionnaire is relevant to the purpose of this research and is presented in this study. Ten structured questions in the demographic section of the questionnaire were used to allow data analysis to pin-point particular issues and enhance the comparability of data. Nominal scales were used to identify the recipients' beliefs while multiple-choice questions were used to aid identification and categorization. The full questionnaire took between 20 and 35 minutes to complete, and within this time the demographic section took between 4 and 10 minutes to complete. The questionnaire was designed to enable a basic analysis of the lifestyle of the craftsperson including their annual creative income bracket, how long they had lived in Wales, their type of creative work and the length of time they had been involved in their particular creative area. The eligibility of the respondents to take part was monitored using questions such as the area of creativity they worked in and the geographic location in which they were based. A pilot for the questionnaire was distributed to identify whether the layout and structure were clear and understandable and to confirm that questions were relevant to the sample population.

The final questionnaire was distributed with a covering letter which requested participation in the survey to build a profile of the craftsperson in Mid and West Wales. Questionnaires were sent by post; if a response was not received within three weeks, a letter was sent reminding people of the opportunity to participate in the research, and the questionnaire was included again in this second letter to increase the likelihood of a response. A final reminder of the opportunity to participate was sent again in three weeks with a suggested date for return. On return, questionnaires were given an identity code and data entered into SPSS. In total, 297 questionnaires were sent out, 105 questionnaires were returned and 65 of these matched the inclusion criteria. Responses from the 65 questionnaires matching the inclusion criteria based on location and type of creative work were produced and used to inform the results presented here.

Results and Discussion

The following trends were identified and help create a profile of the craftsperson based in Mid and West Wales.

The initial analysis considered the identity of the craftsperson to validate participant selection. In total, 47.7% of those involved in the study identified their work as craft, while a number of them described their work as visual art (32.3%) or as a combination of the two (20%). Those who identified their work as "other" were excluded from the results data as it was unclear if they work within the area of craft or visual art but do not identify with this description, or if the questionnaire was completed by someone other than the intended recipient.

The gender and age of the craftsperson in Wales were investigated to provide an indication of type of person involved in this creative work (Figure 2). The majority of those

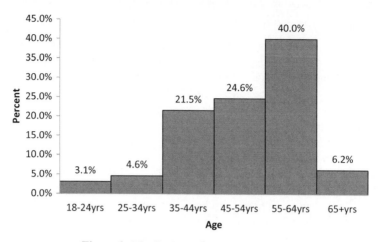

Figure 2. Distribution of age of craftsperson.

involved in the study were female (accounting for 68% of the sample). The average age of the craftsperson is between 55 and 64 years, representing 40% of the sample and is consistent with the aging population of periphery regions described by Haven-Tang and Jones (2008), who note that in Wales nearly 30% of the workforce is now over 45 years. Just 7.7% of the overall sample group are aged between 18 and 34 years, also characteristic of periphery regions. The migration of younger residents in these areas is highlighted by Day and Thomas (2007) as a significant barrier to business growth, while the high ratio of aging workers and female participation in craft form part of the lifestyle scenario Fuller-Love *et al.* (2006) describe which business roles are intertwined with family needs and a desired quality of life.

Although the majority of respondents were not born in Wales (72.3%), results indicate that they have lived in the area for an average of 20 years (13.52 standard deviation), and over half have worked in their creative area for over 20 years (Figure 3). Over half of those involved in the study earn under £10,000 per annum for their creative work (Figure 4). Of

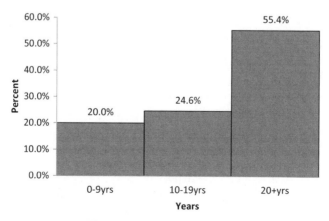

Figure 3. Years in creative work.

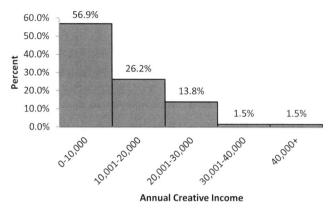

Figure 4. Annual creative income.

the 56.9% who earn under £10,000, over a quarter of these are aged between 55 and 64 years. For a significant number of those involved in the study, their creative income contributes to between 80% and 100% of their average annual income (Figure 5), while just 3% earn over £30,000 for their creative work. This suggests that periphery regions attract, retain and facilitate sustainable craft enterprises.

Collectively, these results indicate craftspeople are more likely to operate sustainable enterprises, but that these firms show little potential for growth; this can be deduced given the low income they receive for their creative work and the length of time they have lived in the area and produced their craft. Craftspeople in Mid and West Wales therefore demonstrate a preference for a quality of life obtainable within rural periphery regions where it is possible to survive on a lower income level; they remain as micro–small businesses through choice. In this respect, the orientation of the craftspeople in Mid Wales is similar to that of the Lifestyler or Idealist identified by Fillis (2006) who have chosen to work in the craft industry because of the lifestyle or engagement with the work involved. This type of modest lifestyle can be described as bohemian by nature.

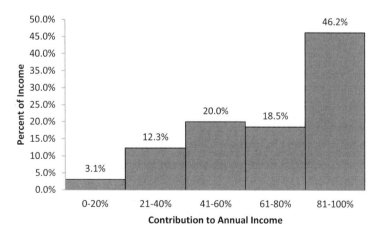

Figure 5. Distribution of contribution creative work makes to overall annual income.

The Bohemian Lifestyle in Relation to Craft Businesses in Mid and West Wales

Ball *et al.* (2010) describe this lifestyle as motivated by the desire to maintain a "personal satisfaction deriving from creativity" (p. 31). This has been highlighted in research by Comunian (2009) and McRobbie (2002) where bohemian attributes are used to identify and explain the importance of self-fulfilment as a motivational factor that can be generated by creative work. The term "creative bohemian" is often used to refer to flexible employment in the creative industries such as open ended contracts, temporary contracts or without any employer. This terminology has been used by Eikhof and Haunschild (2006) to describe the lifestyle of German actors; by Comunian, Faggian and Jewell (2011) in a study of creative graduates and McRobbie (2002) to describe the lifestyle of creative contractors working within core and periphery arts occupations. Wedemeier (2009) also uses this term to describe those working across art forms from audio engineering to design.

The original notion of the Artistic Bohemian relates to a style of living described by Murger (1988) and seen in self-employed artists in the 1950s (Eikhof & Haunschild, 2006). Craftspeople in Mid and West Wales appear to adopt a modest way of life similar to these artists whose lifestyle is based on the desire to create, on a make-do-and-mend attitude and occasional additional employment necessary to supplement creative income. Murger's artists engaged with their work primarily for self-fulfilment, while the production of a saleable product was a secondary concern; their values were therefore bohemian rather than commercially driven. This is true also of those currently involved in creative work, where the experience gained is a strong drive for its continuation. Research by McCauley (1999) involving small creative firms in Scotland found the primary focus was on obtaining the personal satisfaction achieved during the production process; while relaxation, family lifestyle and a sense of accomplishment are listed by the Craft and Hobby Association as reasons to engage in this sector. A recent survey of online craft sellers indicated that people make their craftwork because they like the act of making (Barford, 2012).

The bohemian lifestyle choice is prevalent in periphery regions where it is facilitated by particular external conditions, such as a low cost of living. In a study by Collis *et al.* (2011), a third of visual artists and musicians identified affordability as one of the main reasons for living in a rural area where they could pursue creative work from home-based studios. This is also a consideration for craftspeople in Mid and West Wales; the average craft-related income in Wales is £18,594 (Barford, 2012), yet for the enterprises based in Mid and West Wales the figure is much lower, at an average of £10,000. The rural and low cost location of Mid and West Wales provides an attractive base from which to work. Barriers to industry investment such as limited transport networks, resources and ICT infrastructure described by Fuller-Love *et al.* (2006) may deter other creative industries, particularly those depending on high-level technology, but do not appear to be of particular concern to the craftspeople in this study, the majority of whom have been living and working in the area for significant length of time.

The low cost of living in rural locations may prove attractive to the crafts enterprise; however, the bohemian characteristics of the owner/managers involved in this industry contrast clearly with the qualities of a flexible, dynamic and creative workforce the Innovation Strategy for Wales (Welsh Assembly Government, 2012a) highlights as necessary for business growth. Instead, research into industry in Wales suggests the decision to start or continue micro or small businesses in rural periphery regions is often motivated not by commercial gain but bohemian values such as a desire to live in a preferred area or to earn an income from an activity that they enjoy (Haven-Tang and Jones, 2008). The modest lifestyle that the owner/manager of the craft enterprise follows appears to fit in with this, and their bohemian values lie at the core of the mismatch between rural craft enterprises and government business incentives. Creative organizations in Wales do not generate the regional economic wealth expected from those working within the creative industries because not all those working within this sector equate success with business growth; therefore, the one size fits all approach to policy-making in the creative industries is not suitable for those working within the rural and periphery regions of Mid and West Wales.

Conclusion

The lack of research into, or acknowledgement of, the craft industry in Wales has meant that craft has remained invisible to creative policy-makers who instead focus on the type of creative potential found in urban areas throughout the UK. As demonstrated in this study, the lifestyle practiced by owner/managers of micro and small craft businesses based in Mid and West Wales is not compatible with the attributes of the creative workforce highlighted in the Innovation Strategy for Wales (Welsh Assembly Government, 1012a). This concentration on urban creativity has resulted in an approach to creative economic development in rural areas that attempts to mimic the conditions of cultural hubs despite vastly differing geographic, economic and social realities (Oakley, 2011). The high ratio of ageing workers and lower-than-average income levels identified in this study indicate craft enterprises in this region operate according to a desired quality of life that is not aligned to the commercial profit-driven criteria evident in the 2004 Creative Industries Strategy. Although this Strategy set out to accelerate the growth of creative businesses as seen in ICT and other fast growth creative areas (Hargreaves, 2010), not all small creative firms are commercially orientated, as demonstrated both in this study and in the work of Chaston (2008). This is particularly true for craft enterprises in Mid and West Wales.

Policy-makers may view the creative enterprise as capable of leading economic revival in periphery regions yet those operating in Mid and West Wales do not exhibit this anticipated growth because owner/managers follow a lifestyle that is characteristic of the current occupants within periphery regions. Small craft enterprises in Wales remain small because owners/managers have no desire to expand them. They do not appear to follow a lifestyle aligned to delivering economic wealth through creative innovation. Government strategies attempting to foster local enterprise through such creative innovation are mismatched to creative output in periphery regions because they adopt a generic approach focused on the type of creativity found in urban areas. It is clear that the modest lifestyle of the creative worker in Wales is not compatible with the growth making strategies government is pursuing.

Hargreaves (2010) suggests that without sustained effort and investment in ICT to capitalize on licensing in Wales there is a danger that the creative industries will weaken and this will directly impact on the economic output of the country; yet data from the sector skills council indicate that the creative industries currently account for just 1–1.1% of the total economic output in Wales. Rural areas may appear to harbour a wealth of potential with high self-employment rates and strong potential for small business creation and innovation which governmental initiatives are designed to develop, yet these areas have neither the infrastructure to support the type of urban innovation required for growth, nor the type of workforce necessary to implement it.

In this context, perhaps there is little cause for policy-makers in Wales to include the craft enterprise in its regional strategy, yet this sector does remain significant to the local economy in its ability to sustain rather than grow. Over half the respondents in this study have worked in their creative area, and in their current location, for an average of 20 years; in this context although these enterprises do not exhibit a high level of growth they remain in business. In excluding them the majority of the creative workforce in Wales is under represented and therefore current policies remain misaligned to a large section of the population. Instead, we recommend further investigation into the craft enterprise in Wales to understand why they are attracted to this area, what attributes they bring, and the indirect contribution of the craftsperson to the periphery regions of Wales in terms of the tourism industry. Periphery regions clearly attract and facilitate this type of creative output, it would be wise therefore to acknowledge and develop further understanding of the craft industry in Wales.

Disclosure statement

No potential conflict of interest was reported by the author(s).

References

Ball, L., Pollard, E., Stanley, N. & Oakley, J. (2010) *Creative Career Stories*, Report 477, London: Centre for Learning and Teaching in Art and Design, University of the Arts.
Barford, V. (2012) *BBC News Magazine*, November 8. Available at http://www.bbc.co.uk/news/magazine-19599168 (accessed 8 November 2012).
Bryman, A. (2008) *Social Research Methods*, 3rd ed. (New York: Oxford University Press).
Burns, J., Gibbon, C. & Rosemberg, C. (2012) *Craft in an Age of Change* (London: BOP Consulting).
Chaston, I. (2008) Small creative industry firms: A development dilemma? *Management Decision*, 46(6), pp. 819–831.
Collis, C., Felton, E. & Graham, P. (2010) Beyond the inner city: Real and imagined places in creative place policy and practice, *Information Society: An International Journal*, 26(2), pp. 104–112.
Collis, C., Freebody, S. & Flew, T. (2011) Seeing the outer suburbs: Addressing the urban bias in creative place thinking, *Regional Studies*. doi:10.1080/00343404.2011.630315
Comunian, R. (2009) Questioning creative work as driver of economic development: The case of Newcastle-Gateshead, *Creative Industries Journal*, 2(1), pp. 57–71.
Comunian, R., Faggian, A. & Jewell, S. (2011) Winning and losing in the creative industries: An analysis of creative graduates career opportunities across creative disciplines, *Cultural Trends*, 20(3–4), pp. 291–308.
Creative Business. (2012) Creative Business. Summary of 'The Green Paper'. Available at http://creativebusiness.org/ (accessed 20 March).
Day, G. & Thomas, D. (2007) Rural needs and strategic response: The case of rural wales, *Local Economy*, 6(1), pp. 35–47.
DCMS. (2001) *Creative Industries Mapping Document 2001* (London: Department of Culture, Media and Sport).
Econactive. (2010) *Aberystwyth Arts Centre: The Economic Context* (Cardiff: Econactive Ltd).
Eikhof, D. R. & Haunschild, A. (2006) Lifestyle meets market: Bohemian entrepreneurs in creative industries, *Creativity and Innovation Management*, 15(3), pp. 234–241.
Fillis, I. (2006) Art for art's sake or art for business sake: An exploration of artistic product orientation, *Marketing Review*, 6(1), pp. 29–40.
Fillis, I. (2008) The internationalisation process of the smaller firm: An examination of the craft microenterprise, *The Open Business Journal*, 1(1), pp. 53–61.

Fillis, I. (2009) Profiling the behaviour of people working with crafts, in: L. Valentine & G. Follett (Ed) *Past, Present and Future Craft Practice*, pp. 124–135 (Dundee: University of Dundee).

Florida, R. (2002) *The Rise of the Creative Class* (New York: Basic Books).

Fuller Love, N. Midmore, P., Thomas, D. & Henley, A. (2006) Entrepreneurship and rural economic development: A scenario analysis approach, *International Journal of Entrepreneurial Behaviour & Research*, 12(5), pp. 289–305.

Hargreaves, I. (2010) *The Heart of Digital Wales: A Review of Creative Industries for the Welsh Assembly Government* (Cardiff: Welsh Assembly Government).

Haven-Tang, C. & Jones, E. (2008) Labour market and skills needs of the tourism and related sectors in Wales, *International Journal of Tourism Research*, 10(4), pp. 353–363.

Hull, A. (2010) A winning wales: An integrated strategy for sustainable economic development, *Planning Practice & Research*, 19(3), pp. 329–343.

Jones, R. J. & Sloane, P. J. (2007) Low pay, higher pay and job satisfaction in Wales, *Spatial Economic Analysis*, 2(2), pp. 197–214.

Kent, R. (2007) *Marketing Research: Approaches, Methods and Applications in Europe* (London: Thomson Learning).

Lorenzen, M. & Vaarst Andersen, K. (2011) Different creative cities: Exploring Danish data to adapt the creative class argument to small welfare economies, *Creative Industries Journal*, 4(2), pp. 123–136.

McCauley, A. (1999) Entrepreneurial instant exporters in the Scottish arts and crafts sector, *Journal of International Marketing*, 3(1), pp. 67–82.

McDermott, E., Venus, J., & Vincentelli, M. (2007) *The Role of Flow in the Motivation of Women Potters and Ceramic Artists in Wales*. Unpublished (Aberystwyth: Aberystwyth University).

McRobbie, A. (2002) Clubs to companies: Notes on the decline of political culture in speeded up creative worlds, *Cultural Studies*, 16(4), pp. 516–531.

Morgan, B. (1996) An endogenous approach to regional economic development: An emergence of Wales, *European Planning Studies*, 4(6), pp. 705–716.

Murger, H. (1988) *Scenes de la Vie de Boheme* (Paris: Gallimard).

Oakley, K. (2011) In its own image: New labour and the cultural workforce, *Cultural Trends*, 20(3–4), pp. 281–289.

Office for National Statistics. (2012) *Regional Data: Workforce in Wales* (Cardiff: ONS).

Scott, A. J. (2010) The cultural economy of landscape and prospects for peripheral development in the twenty-first century: The case of the English Lake District, *European Planning Studies*, 18(10), pp. 1567–1589.

Stough, R. R. (2009) Leadership and creativity in regional economic development, *European Planning Studies*, 18(4), pp. 613–627.

Walters, R. & Lawton Smith, H. (2002) Regional development agencies and local economic development: Scale and competitiveness in high-technology Oxfordshire and Cambridgeshire, *European Planning Studies*, 10(5), pp. 634–649.

Wedemeier, J. (2009) The impact of the creative sector on growth in German regions, *European Planning Studies*, 18(4), pp. 506–520.

Welsh Assembly Government (2012a) *A Welsh Government Response to the Call for Evidence on an Innovation Strategy for Wales* (Cardiff: Welsh Assembly Government).

Welsh Assembly Government (2012b) *City Regions Task & Finish group: Definition and Criteria* (Cardiff: Welsh Assembly Government).

Welsh Assembly Government (2012c) *Micro-Business Task and Finish Group Report* (Cardiff: Welsh Assembly Government).

Winther, L. & Hansen, H. (2012) *Report on the Third Research Seminar of the RSA Research Network on Creative Regions* (York: Regional Studies Association).

Towards the Creative and Knowledge Economies: Analysing Diverse Pathways in Spanish Cities

MONTSERRAT PAREJA-EASTAWAY* & MARC PRADEL i MIQUEL**

*Research Group "Creativity, Innovation and Urban Transformation", Department of Economic Theory, University of Barcelona, Barcelona, Spain, **Research Group "Creativity, Innovation and Urban Transformation", Department of Sociology Theory, University of Barcelona, Barcelona, Spain

ABSTRACT Until 2007, many Spanish cities developed ambitious policies and programmes to foster the creative economy in a context of economic expansion mainly driven by the growth of the real estate sector. The goal was common but the means were considerably diverse. Currently, the development of creative sectors and the emergence of new economic activities in Spain have to cope with the deep economic recession affecting the country: given the considerably different specializations and prospects of employment creation, cities' strategies differ from one to the next. In this paper, these differences are explored through the analysis of four Spanish cities: Madrid, Barcelona, Bilbao and Valencia. First, we analyse how different paths of industrialization and modernization paved the way for different forms of transition towards the creative economy. Secondly, we elaborate on how the local context, defined by the set of actors interacting and the existence of economic traditions, frames a specific vision on creative and knowledge industries. Finally, the paper indicates to what extent the development of the creative economy in the four Spanish cities depends on the combination of trajectories and disruptive changes.

Introduction

The transformation of economic activity that globalization entails identifies as key sectors those incorporating high added value from creativity and knowledge (Sassen, 2009). In this context, cities and their metropolitan areas face new competitive parameters that usually require rethinking traditional strategies of survival in the international arena, covering not only the discovery of innovative economic patterns but also new approaches to competitiveness. In recent decades the world's major cities have experienced a significant shift towards such activities, creating or attracting them, seeking to improve regional or metropolitan competitiveness.

Cities have limited resources and are basically defined by three elements; their own economic pathways, the agents involved and the policies that they develop (Musterd & Gritsai, 2013). Despite the importance of traditional and contemporary location theories, the conditions for creating or stimulating creative knowledge regions in the context of a global economy are certainly dependent on urban history and the economic tradition of the territory: different paths of industrialization and modernization pave the way for different forms of economic transition. Path dependence is stressed as a clear determinant of current urban strategies and, definitely, as a variable to be taken into account in defining economic challenges (Mahoney, 2000; Lambooy, 2002; Musterd et al., 2007). The diversity of world cities is huge in terms of dimension, economic specialization and trajectory; they could hardly follow the same strategy to attract economic activity.

During the last three decades, the Spanish economy has experienced major changes marked by modernization and internationalization. These were also decades of remarkable economic growth, with rates consistently higher than those of the Euro-zone countries. However, this growth has not been achieved without major chronic imbalances related to a GDP growth based on real estate expansion and the low rate of productivity achieved since the country entered the EU (Pareja-Eastaway & Turmo, 2013). Spain is one of the countries where the current crisis has seriously hit the economic system and the societal structure. Therefore, the analysis of how the four larger metropolitan cities, that is, Barcelona, Bilbao, Madrid and Valencia, have reacted to this major shock, their similarities and differences, together with their successes and failures, becomes of paramount importance. Despite their different economic specializations, GDP per capita and population size (see Table 1), these four territories are currently coping not only with the economic crisis but with the demands of a new global order where cities become the nodes of competition and innovation.

The main objective of this paper is to discuss the elements that contribute to a better competitive position for four Spanish city regions: Barcelona, Bilbao, Madrid and Valencia. These cities are considered as examples of the alternatives adopted by many Spanish cities, providing arguments to appropriately design policies to strengthen and improve those aspects that are considered as critical in a period of economic crisis and public

Table 1. Main socio-economic characteristics of the four city regions (2012)

	Catalonia (*)/ Barcelona (+)/ Barcelona city (x)	Basque Country (*)/ Bizcaya (+)/ Bilbao (x)	Madrid (*)/ Madrid (+)/ Madrid (x)	Valencia (*)/ Valencia (+)/ Valencia (x)
Population	7,539,618/ 5,552,050/ 1,620,943	2,184,606/ 1,158,439/ 351,629	6,483,680/ 6,498,560/ 3,233,527	5,117,190/ 2,580,792/ 797,028
Surface (sq.) (*)	32,113	7234	8029	23,255
Provinces	4	3	1	3
Municipalities	947	261	179	542
GDP contribution (*)	18.6%	6.2%	17.6%	9.6%

Source: INE (*) Autonomous Community; (+) Province; (x) City.

austerity. In particular, we aim to identify the role of path dependency and "top-down" approaches in the current strategies adopted by each metropolitan region: the different historical endeavours towards the creative and knowledge economy are assessed, together with a special focus on the articulation of governance in the territory and specific actors' involvement in the process.

In order to do this, the results of CREAURBS ("Creativity and Knowledge: pillars for a new urban competitiveness", 2010–2012), a research project funded by the Spanish Ministry of Economy and Competitiveness, are used. This study compares the aforementioned four metropolitan cities and their ability to compete in the international arena. The methodological approach we followed in this project was both quantitative and qualitative. In addition to the exploitation of the existing primary data provided by the INE (National Institute of Statistics), the Spanish Office of Patents and Brands, the Ministry of Economics and Competitiveness and the Spanish Social Security system, we conducted a survey in 2011 (CREAURBS Survey) with 250 creative and knowledge managers and workers, as well as 25 in-depth interviews with representatives of key actors (policy-makers, stakeholders, creative and knowledge companies) in the four metropolitan regions. As the focus of this paper is on political and economic changes, we present here some of the results of the qualitative interviews carried out with policy-makers and key experts or stakeholders.

First, we summarize the most relevant issues to be taken into account when looking at the relevance of path dependency in the context of urban competitiveness. Secondly, we analyse how different paths of industrialization and modernization paved the way for different forms of transition towards the creative economy in Spain and how the local context, defined by the set of actors interacting and the existence of economic traditions, frames a specific vision on what the creative industries are and how to promote them. Finally, the paper indicates to what extent the pathways of their economic development and governance models provide better tools to promote their competitiveness.

Path Dependency, Urban Competitiveness, and Creative and Knowledge Sectors

Historically, urban economic development has been nourished from the traditional theories of company location based on the existence of agglomeration economies and synergies between actors (Beccatini, 1979; Amin & Thrift, 1992; Porter, 1998). Later, other arguments have been developed based on the belief that the city environment and its quality of life, in short, the availability of "soft" factors, might be decisive in the location of talented people. The cities' ability to attract and retain talent and creativity has been considered one of the most determinant variables for improved positioning within the urban competition scene (Landry, 2000; Florida, 2002).

Although the location of economic activity usually follows some incentives, such as benefiting from the externalities created between companies and the synergies between different productive processes, the impact across the territory strongly depends on the available technology, the structure of the market and previous patterns of industrialization. The benefits of the effects of attracting certain economic activities to the city essentially depend on how the territory is involved and connected with the existence of these effects (Scott, 2006). In particular, the economic links established between companies go hand-in-hand with the proliferation of a diverse range of social interactions that, although based in the economic fabric, go further in the establishment of personal and professional mutual understandings, favouring the transmission of spillovers from this complex network to the real world (Jacobs, 1972). This is particularly true in the creative and knowledge sectors that consider human capital, talent, as a decisive input in making the most of the opportunities associated with the new economy.

Economic histories and cultural and political processes created and developed in regions highlight their historical record; their temporal belonging to the market economy, industrial development, geo-political characterization and the impact of public policies (Kovács et al., 2007). Two spheres of great magnitude are relevant in studying the competitive city of today: the economic and the social. Beyond thoughts around economic indicators and their magnitude, the scope of the social and organizational structure of the territory indicates a uniqueness explained by the role of certain factors for promoting the city's attractiveness, such as the diverse composition of its society, its political traditions, and the whole set of politicians, stakeholders and policies promoting and stimulating creativity and innovation at a regional level (Storper & Scott, 2009; Ponzini & Rossi, 2010).

The governance mechanisms, rooted by definition in the city's social and institutional substrate, might enhance different strategies by public and private bodies seeking to stimulate creativity and knowledge. They can differ considerably according to some specific items, being capable of changing the result of the measures taken: the timeframe of initiatives, more or less involvement by relevant stakeholders, and the consensus reached are some matters to be considered in analysing the contribution of governance to the success of adopted measures (Pareja-Eastaway & Pradel i Miquel, 2010). Evidence shows that cities reinvent themselves successively in order to adapt to the requirements of the times, particularly in the knowledge economy, making an extensive use of public policies (Crossa et al., 2010). Nevertheless, success or failure in adopting specific measures goes beyond the setup or the efficiency of action: the historical legacy and specificities of the territory where the policy is implemented play a relevant role. In that sense, the following questions gain remarkable significance in understanding the urban response to the new economic landscape:

- What has been the role played by the existing path dependency of cities in adapting to this changing environment?
- To what extent has the flexibility provided by the articulation of a certain governance model in a particular context also influenced this adaptation?
- What could be the combination between benefitting from trajectories and creating a completely brand new context in a top-down approach?

Divergence in Economic, Cultural and Institutional Pathways in Spanish Cities

To understand local variations on policies and economic activities among cities in the creative field, we must pay attention to the diverging historical development paths of the territories, and their constitution as territories as such. Here, territories are understood as social constructions emerging from stable social relations in a geographical area, including economic relations, political organization and reciprocity practices (Keating, 1998, 2001). In fact, looking at the history of the industrialization of cities and the pathways they have followed, we can understand not only current needs and priorities, but also the compound of the constellation of local actors and a set of norms and values on economic relations that frames political decisions (Scott, 2006; Musterd & Murie, 2010; Musterd & Gritsai, 2013). Although it is too far from our aim to present an exhaustive analysis of the four cities' development paths, in this section we take a look at the configuration of pathways in Barcelona, Bilbao, Madrid and Valencia which may be taken into account as four different models freely adopted by many other cities in Spain. Three different elements are stressed: (1) the configuration of their economic profile since early industrialization, (2) the emergence of different cultural traditions and (3) their wide diversity in urban governance models.

Configuration of the Economic Profile since Early Industrialization

Spanish cities have different paths of industrialization and modernization in their economic structures, linked to the general pattern of reshaping traditional economic specialization in Spain. We have focused the analysis on four cities that represent divergence in economic, cultural and institutional pathways under three different elements that, to our understanding, shape the diversity in the current morphology of Spanish cities: time of industrialization, urban development and public–private involvement.

In contrast to other countries, Spain suffered a weak and uneven process of industrialization during the nineteenth century, because of the capacity of the Ancient Regime structures to resist modernization and to remain in control of political power. A common project for the bourgeoisie was difficult to reach as the interests of actors of the different cities were not always the same (Solé-Tura, 1974). The four cities show different strategies to control political and economic power: the bourgeoisie in Barcelona and Bilbao developed nationalist political projects to defend their interests, whereas the elites in Madrid and Valencia remained attached to the centralist state model. These differences can be explained through the different paths of industrialization.

Barcelona and Bilbao were the two earliest industrial cities in the country, together with small municipalities in their regions. Both cities experienced slightly different processes but, by the end of the century, they were strongly industrialized with a deep transformation in their urban morphology. These two cities were receiving incoming population from the countryside, especially Barcelona, which became the second most populated city of Spain at the end of the nineteenth century with around half a million inhabitants, very similar to Madrid, which was the first. Madrid's complete industrialization did not take place until the second half of the twentieth century. During the nineteenth century, its position as capital of the country allowed for the development of services and cultural institutions, as well as the development of a relevant financial sector. Finally, Valencia maintained agriculture as its main economic activity, but modernized production through industrial processes, mechanization and innovation, allowing for the emergence of industries outside the city, with several industrial districts serving the needs of agricultural economic activity and later expanding to the rest of the country.

During the post-war period, centralist policies brought increasing relevance to Madrid in terms of industrial GDP during the second half of the century, and decreasing relevance to the smallest provinces of Valencia and Biscay (see Table 2).

Due to their industrial expansion, from 1854 Barcelona spread beyond its city limits and soon absorbed nearby municipalities, whereas Bilbao expanded along the Ria (the estuary of Bilbao), the natural waterway that allowed for iron trading. In fact, by the second half of

Table 2. Contribution of the four provinces to the national industrial GDP (1955–1985)

	1955	1967	1975	1985
Barcelona	24.9	24.3	22.9	19.5
Madrid	8.9	13	13.2	12.2
Valencia	6.3	5.2	5.8	6
Biscay	7.3	6.8	7.3	5

Source: García Delgado (1990).

the nineteenth century, Spanish cities faced major transformations with the demolition of walls, urban expansion, urban renewal and the improvement of urban services. This transformation contributed to the capital accumulation of the bourgeoisie (Capel, 1975). Madrid, strongly favoured by the modernization of the state, underwent this process in the context of a non-heavily industrialized city. The modernization project of the national government was based on a centralized communication infrastructures network with the aim of transforming Madrid into a large metropolis, similar to London or Paris. Madrid accumulated administrative, political and cultural institutions, including the Royal Court, the parliament, national galleries and museums, and other institutions. Its relevance as a capital brought about the emergence of services-oriented companies, including from the hotel industry, education services, trade, transport, and financial and real estate sector companies, among others. There were also certain forms of industrialization linked to the administration and the state apparatus, including railway reparation companies, the National Coinage and Stamp Factory and the telecommunications company.

Madrid's urban expansion reflected this dualism between strong services sectors and incipient industries, with the former tending to locate in the north and the latter concentrating near the railway stations in the southern part of the city (Méndez *et al.*, 2006). Finally, Valencia was an atypical case of urban and economic development as its main activity remains agriculture and the city remains linked to farming land. Its economic expansion was linked to the modernization of agricultural production based mainly on wine and orange production. This modernization allowed for the emergence of chemical, metallurgy and wood industries in order to provide materials for food production. Food industries became themselves a relevant sector. Because of this specific model of industrialization, industrial location was based on communication networks preserving part of the land for agricultural purposes and creating industrial districts from different sectors outside the city.

The economic and political development of cities in Spain suffered a dramatic shift with the Spanish Civil war and the victory of Francoist troops in 1939. Local actors in economic development were dependant now on the centralized decisions of the dictator, and local traditional economic elites had to share power with leaders of the victorious gang. In this framework, the regime promoted a fascist model of industrialization based on the so-called National Industrial Institute (INI) copying the Italian fascist model. Through the INI, the state promoted the creation of national companies, the reconstruction of infrastructures and the creation of large industrial complexes. Thus, the industrialization of Madrid and the reinforcement and modernization of industries in Bilbao and Barcelona were clear results of a process with uneven success. Industrial sectors in Valencia, for their part, took advantage of the protected national market, consolidating industrial districts in certain sectors such as furniture or toy making.

These different patterns of industrialization brought about different economic actors ruling the city, as well as different forms of organization of the working class, and the canalization of social conflict. Moreover, how the local bourgeoisie of each city tried to influence nationally based decisions also differed. All of these strategies consolidated diverse local pathways that have continued through time. With such different processes of industrialization, the strategies to face de-industrialization and the crisis in the 1970s were also different, particularly after the Spanish transition to democracy (1976–1981), when there was a shift towards decentralization with the creation of regions and the capacity of cities to develop their own policies (Brugué et al., 2001; Pradel, 2012).

The Emergence of Different Cultural Traditions

The political configuration of the local bourgeoisie also has an influence on the development of cultural traditions and, therefore, on how the emergence of cultural industries is accommodated, paving the way for the generation of new dynamics with de-industrialization (Keating, 2001). Madrid and Barcelona were the main centres of development of cultural and leisure industries since their modernization: the emergence of new lifestyles, the diversity of companies and activities, and the consolidation of the bourgeoisie brought about the materialization of economic activities that nowadays can be considered as "creative sectors" (for instance, advertising, radio, cinema, theatre, performing arts or publishing). In Madrid, the creation of state cultural institutions, such as the National Library (1836), national museums and theatres, paved the way for the emergence of private cultural initiatives as well as economic activity dependant on these public institutions. Besides, the concentration of political power in Madrid brought about the emergence of media industries, especially newspaper agencies and publishing houses.

Nevertheless, until the end of the Civil War, the development of cultural industries in Madrid was shadowed by the strength of Barcelona, which became the cultural capital of Spain (Rodríguez Morató, 2008). As has been stated, since the end of the nineteenth century the Barcelonese bourgeoisie supported a political project around Catalan nationalism, which meant the promotion of Catalan culture; private actors and cultural associations fostered institutions and cultural resources to spread this. At the same time, cultural sectors such as publishing or leisure industries increased their relative weight due to population growth, the improvement of literacy amongst the bourgeoisie and the apparition of leisure time. Due to its innovative industrial environment, Barcelona was also the scene of the rise of pioneering industries such as the first Radio station in Spain, EAJ1 Radio Barcelona and the first film studios.

Workers also promoted their own cultural institutions and associations, mainly based on the promotion of anarchist and republican ideas through culture that contributed to bringing dynamism to Barcelona and Madrid. By contrast, there was no sensible development of cultural industries in Bilbao and Valencia. Due to the unwillingness of its local bourgeoisie, Bilbao did not develop large cultural institutions, there were no significant clusters of cultural industries, and the Basque culture remained mainly rural without a role in the development of such industries. In Valencia, which shared cultural elements with Barcelona, there was a certain cultural emergence following the Catalan trend with the emergence of Catalan–Valencian culture and the creation of cultural institutions, but there was no clear link between the support for these institutions and a political nationalist project because of the embeddedness of the Valencian bourgeoisie among the elites of the capital city.

After the Civil War (1936–1939), cultural industries suffered a contraction as cultural sectors were heavily controlled by the regime. Centralist policies also concentrated cultural industries in Madrid. The creation of the National Radio (1938) and Television (1956) companies in Madrid meant the concentration of filming activity in that city, as well as radio and part of the music industries. Besides, the position of Madrid as the capital of Spain reinforced the role of its cultural institutions. Barcelona, the former capital of cultural industries, saw the emergence of a countercultural movement around Catalan culture that had an impact on music and publishing. Moreover, Barcelona had a long concentration of publishing companies that continued during the Francoist period and also participated in the Catalan recovery since the 1970s. The return to democracy would again change the hegemonic actors ruling the cities and the framework for cultural industries.

Shaping Diverse Governance Frameworks

The Spanish transition and the return of democracy (1976–1981) brought a new governance framework to the country in which decentralization was a key element. For the first time, the constitution foresaw the existence of a regional level or Autonomous Communities (A.C.) and devolved competencies for the municipalities. In practice, the development of A.C. meant a concentration of power and funds in regional administrations, whereas the local level received new possibilities for policies in different fields, but scarce resources to develop them (García-Milà, 2003). The central government tended to increasingly decentralize policies such as healthcare, employment and education, but without developing a comparable decentralization of funds. Besides, after 40 years of forced centralization, both regional and local administrations were reluctant to integrate their policies vertically with other levels of government, or to collaborate with other administrations at the same level.

This new democratic framework was developed under a severe industrial crisis, an effect of the excessive protection of the national market during Francoism and the delayed effects of the oil crisis. By the end of the 1970s, Spanish cities had to face a double challenge: modernising the economy in a context of industrial crisis and providing citizens with services and resources lacking since the fifties. Like many others, the four cities faced these challenges from different departing points: Madrid, as the capital of the country, had a relevant financial sector and a strong presence of the services sector in its economy. Besides, it had developed an industrial sector with innovation capacity (García Delgado, 1990). Barcelona had a diversified industry with the incipient emergence of tourism, even though there had been a movement from traditional industrial activities such as textile, towards more lucrative sectors such as the real estate sector. Tourism was also growing in Valencia, which became the holiday destination of the Madrid population. The availability of land due to the agricultural basis of the city allowed a rapid reconversion of the economy towards tourism, with the construction of hotels and apartments and the growth of the real estate sector. Finally, Bilbao, like many other cities already specialized in heavy industries, suffered from its excessive specialization in the metallurgic sector. After two decades of intense growth, Bilbao's Fordist industries declined significantly (Eizaguirre, 2012, p. 105) despite a relevant financial sector and a favourable tax regime.

As we will see later, the 1980s were the period of large revitalization projects and new urban policies within the framework of democracy in which local governments adapted the existing legal framework and created new governance tools for decision-making, like partnerships and other forms of public–private collaboration. These efforts to overcome the crisis were taken at the same time that regional governments were established and started to assume competencies and develop legislation. Thus, the governance framework of each city was increasingly diverse, depending to a great extent on the political action and the legislation of the regional government. In the four cases we find patterns of low levels of integration between local and regional governments regardless of the political parties ruling them, and new governance arrangements based on public–private partnerships to promote urban regeneration and the transformation of the economy.

In Barcelona and its metropolitan region, leftist parties became hegemonic and promoted social-democratic forms of economic development based on social dialogue and the involvement of the citizenship in decision-making processes (Blackeley, 2005). The Catalan government, ruled by conservative nationalists, by contrast, promoted less interventionist policies with the centralization of decision-making in the regional government, and liberal approaches that framed the possibilities at a local level. Moreover, the regional government limited the possibility of a metropolitan authority. Facing this situation, Barcelona tended to promote voluntary partnerships with other city councils, as well as societal and private actors.

In Madrid, the regional government could play a role as the *de facto* metropolitan authority, but conflict soon emerged with the central city regarding the development of policies. Until 1995, the Autonomous Community was ruled by the Socialist party, but that year there was a shift towards the conservative Partido Popular, which also brought a shift in the orientation of policies and the legislative framework towards a neoliberal, non-interventionist approach. Valencia followed a similar pattern, as in the 1990s the same conservative party took power both in the city council and the regional government. Economic actors in Valencia followed the previous path of linking their economic activities to the capital and orientated their efforts towards the real estate sector and leisure tourism, with part of the customers coming from the capital.

In Bilbao, an integrated approach between administrations took place from the 1980s with the collaboration of local, provincial, regional and national levels to develop the physical transformation of the city, which was considered key to economic renewal, even though this approach lacked a metropolitan vision and a strong economic basis (Eizaguirre, 2012, p. 108). These large transformations took place in parallel with the efforts of private actors, promoting industrial innovation, and the important role of civil society actors.

Summarising, strategies developed in the 1980s and the 1990s must be framed in a context of increasing decentralization of decision-making that brought about different scenarios. In this context, the promotion of creativity and innovation takes different orientations. In Madrid and Valencia, liberal approaches promote the central role of private actors in urban renewal and economic development, whereas in Barcelona, the city council plays a more central role developing cultural and economic promotion policies through public–private partnerships in which the city council takes the lead. In Bilbao, the significant activity of public administrations in urban renewal is completed by strong private actors playing a role in industrial innovation and civil society, being able to obtain resources for different purposes, including actions against social exclusion, and for culture, creativity and innovation initiatives.

Approaching Creative and Knowledge Sectors from Urban Diversity in Spain

Now that we have depicted the historical trajectories and multi-level governance frameworks of the four cities, we are in a position to better understand how creative and knowledge industries have been accommodated in each case study since the 1990s. Due to methodological problems (lack of available data for city regions), data used in this section refer to the Autonomous Communities (A.C.), our four case studies being their capitals. Each city has developed different approaches to the fostering of creativity and knowledge: we explore, on the one hand, the economic capacity to accommodate the new sectors and, on the other, the use of culture throughout the celebration of events or the building of flagship museums or monuments.

The Economic Capacity to Accommodate Creative and Knowledge Sectors

According to the data provided by the Spanish National Institute of Statistics (INE), the contribution of creative and knowledge sectors to employment differs between city regions: while in the A.C. of Madrid they represent nearly 30%, Valencia and the Basque Country exhibit the lowest percentage (around 20%), and we find the A.C. of Catalonia with around 25%. However, the composition of employment between creative and knowledge sectors varies between all territories during the period 2009–2011. Creative and knowledge sectors participate in total employment in considerably different ways: creative sectors contribute around 4–6% of the total employment and knowledge sectors' contribution oscillates between 12% and 22%. A common characteristic of the four regions is that knowledge activities perform better than creative sectors, exhibiting unemployment rates below the average and almost no employment destruction (Pareja-Eastaway & Turmo, 2013).

The presence and recognition of each territory's economic trajectory award the area with uniqueness and places its growth on a basis determined by the dynamics of each region without diminishing the importance of "top-down" urban policy strategies for supporting the sectors considered necessary and fully emerging in the local context. In Madrid, for example, a combination of non-interventionism and a strong top-down approach has been the case. On the one hand, the market and the city's previous specialization have shaped a certain development of creative and knowledge activities:

> We can consider different approaches. One of them is to be more interventionist, in other cases less. The case of Madrid, I would say that's pretty extreme in the field of non-interventionism. In fact, an element that I think may serve to illustrate this issue is the following: the Community of Madrid, which in the 90s developed a series of regional research and development plans, for the past three years there is no regional plan for research and development. (Head of Research, Foundation Madrid+i, 2012)

On the other hand, Madrid has certainly opted for a top-down approach to stimulate knowledge sectors but on a larger scale:

> There is a de facto priority (in Madrid): Right now there are about a dozen clusters formed in the Community of Madrid. The fact that these clusters are created under the auspices of the Community of Madrid itself through the Department of Economy and an institution that helps

coordinate them called Madrid Network. This is an element of prioritisation and policy development. (Head of Research, Foundation Madrid+i, 2012)

This is also the case, for instance, of the 22@Barcelona, this city's innovation district. The positive economic performance of the area has probably determined the spread of this type of strategy to the rest of the city. As one informant states:

> In fact, when the current mayor Trias assumes his mandate, the first thing he says is: we are going to work on the "@isation" of the city. In this sense I would say that there is consistency, because in these 10 years of history, the 22@ project not only agglutinated all political parties but also has been recognised. There has been consistency with a different change on the focus over time. (Head of Barcelona Growth Office, 2012)

Catalonia and the Basque Country reflect a clear specialization in most manufacturing activities, some of which are knowledge intensive. The manufacturing specialization is lower in Valencia, with an impact on labour-intensive activities, and null in the A.C. of Madrid. However, Madrid has strong expertise in an important part of service activities, particularly quaternary and quinary sectors and, among them, those closely related to productive entrepreneurial activity. Clearly, the weight of these sectors in the Madrid region exceeds the needs of the region itself, which means that it is clearly oriented towards export, both to domestic and international markets (González-Lopez, 2009).

The Basque country shows clear specialization in knowledge sectors and a reduced participation in employment in creative industries. However, as we will see in depth later, this has an effect on the dynamism and the role of civil society, and, consequently, on the possibilities for creativity and innovation:

> I think that you have here (Bilbao) ... a very specific creativity, very specific, very different. Bilbao does not have the cosmopolitanism that Barcelona may have, or the proximity to economic sources that Madrid may have, Bilbao has dynamism, a much richer civil society. (President, Creativity Zentrum, 2012)

The A.C. of Valencia's participation in employment creation in these sectors is more focused on creative sectors (around 5%) than on knowledge (between 10% and 14%, for the whole period). Catalonia and the A.C. of Madrid are leaders in knowledge and also in creative sectors. In this regard, when analysing creative sectors and their evolution we see that in the Basque Country employment in creative sectors is significantly less relevant than in the rest of the city, due to the long tradition in heavy industries and the historical role of the lack of cultural industries in the area. At different points in time, Madrid, Barcelona and Valencia have developed these cultural sectors, linking them to: being a State Capital (Madrid); the push of an autonomous bourgeoisie using culture as a means of self-representation (Barcelona) or the more recent commitment to promoting national and international tourism (Valencia).

Patterns of industrialization and historically dominant sectors explain some differences in the development of creative and knowledge industries. Although Barcelona took the lead in the process of industrialization from the very beginning, the growth of Madrid after the Spanish Civil War turned the two cities into industrial cities with a great diversity of economic activities. Within this diversity, cultural industries and other activities could emerge and consolidate. By contrast, Bilbao, even though it was a pioneering city in industrialization, rapidly specialized in heavy industries, which required at that time vertical integration and strong financial capital. In this environment of strong concentration of economic activity in certain sectors such as metallurgy, the absence of consistent development of cultural industries became a clear consequence. According to an informant, this has clearly marked out the future areas of specialization of the city of Bilbao:

> Industry has to be a key sector forever in Bilbao, because if we are surviving in the Basque Country it is because industry represents 33% of our economy, which does not occur in other territories. (Contact at Lan Ekinza, Employment Promotion Office, 2012)

This process of development clearly influences the fact that attempts to promote new sectors and the tertiarization of the economy in the case of Bilbao simultaneously encounter constraints and opportunities: for instance, when we compare employment in knowledge sectors in the A.C. of Valencia and the Basque Country, the Basque Country shows a stronger position. In fact, the push for the knowledge economy is understood in the Basque Country as the modernization of existing industrial activities and the attraction of new sectors that can be easily attached to the existing environment.

In spite of that, the redevelopment of the Ria in Bilbao and the creation of the Guggenheim can be understood as attempts to foster the tertiarization of the city through the attraction of new sectors and the internationalization of the image of the city. In this regard, this large urban renewal process has elements in common with Barcelona's redevelopment of the Poblenou Area, in which new infrastructure for knowledge is being developed. These initiatives depart from considering former industrial areas as empty spaces and key areas for the urban development of the city: in both cases, public authorities have assumed a leading role promoting policies to foster the agglomeration and clustering of relevant targeted sectors in these areas. Clustering policies in Barcelona were based on concentrating public or semi-public knowledge-based companies in the area to create the critical mass for attracting other private companies promoting collaboration and exchange between them. These approaches have been strongly controversial, as shown by different authors, in their capacity to attract new creative and knowledge economic activity (Rodríguez *et al.*, 2001; González, 2006; Casellas & Pallares-Barbera, 2009; Martí-Costa & Pradel, 2012).

In Valencia, the organization of industry in small clusters outside the city and the modernization of food industries paved the way for transformation into a tourist centre since the 1970s, transforming the city towards the service economy with a noticeable role for the real estate sector as the leader of economic activity. This development is closely linked with the creation of economic networks with Madrid, as the city became one of the most important tourist destinations for the population of the capital: the growth of tourism was linked with a shift in the strategy of economic and political actors in Valencia who were traditionally tied to Catalonia.

The Use of Culture (International Events, Flagship Projects, etc.) to Reinvent the City

From the return of democracy, city councils started ambitious processes of urban redevelopment where culture was central. In these processes, real estate actors had a prominent role as developers and were also involved in decision-making. In fact, urban regeneration projects were largely funded on increasing land value, expecting future returns after the development. Besides, these projects were accompanied by policies aimed at fostering human capital, incentivising the creation of new companies and attracting talent, even though we find different patterns in the four cities.

In Barcelona, the nomination for the Olympic Games of 1992 was the starting point of a physical and economic transformation of the city towards a service economy, with a strong role for tourism and culture. As the head of research at the Barcelona Municipality confirms:

> BCN was not a typical tourist city, seen from outside the city was rather industrial and business oriented (...) BCN is now one of the leading cities in terms of urban tourism attraction in Europe. This is mainly a result of the transformation of the city that took place because of the Olympic Games in 1992 (Head of Research, Economic Promotion Area, Municipality of Barcelona, 2012)

The nomination for the Games allowed for strong collaboration between local, Catalan and Spanish governments, creating possibilities for a massive transformation of the city, including the creation of new transport infrastructures, the creation of cultural institutions in the city centre (MACBA, CCCB) and the reurbanization of part of the industrial district of the city. As stated previously, at the beginning of the 1990s, the city council proposed to finish the urban transformation of the city through rebuilding its former industrial neighbourhood: Poblenou. Between 1996 and 2000 the city council defined the project 22@ as an urban regeneration project to foster the new economy and started urban regeneration in the neighbourhood, such as the extension of the Diagonal Avenue to the sea. In the first proposals, the project was promoted as fostering the communication economy or the information economy. Later, explicit claims for the knowledge economy were launched and finally, in 2006, some references to creativity were included. It should be stressed that in Barcelona, despite culture having definitely contributed to creating the city brand (Pareja-Eastaway *et al.*, 2013), support for creative, and particularly knowledge, sectors has been reinforced since 2011. As an informant assesses:

> We cannot live under the illusion that we have the brand and that we have the product. Barcelona is a very attractive brand, a brand that appeals to people, but this fact cannot hide (...) that, or we increase the amount of creative companies in this discussion or Barcelona will end up as a space for tourism. (Head of Creative Industries Institute, Municipality of Barcelona, 2012)

In Madrid, the strategy was based on promoting the services sector and the cultural industries through urban regeneration directed at improving and taking advantage of the existing cultural institutions in the city. In 1992 Madrid was declared European Capital of Culture, which brought about a growing strategy on culture as a motor for economic growth. The physical regeneration of the city centre and the promotion of new creative neighbourhoods were part of this strategy. The creation of new cultural facilities such as Medialab or "Caixaforum Madrid" in the city centre reinforced the role of the Barrio de las Letras, a central neighbourhood that includes the main cultural institutions of the city (Museo del Prado, Museo Reina Sofía, Museo Thyssen, etc.). Moreover, the attraction of foreign investment and the promotion of knowledge industries in the south of the metropolitan region were also salient. The development of large transport infrastructures by the central government, such as the High Speed Train and the expansion of the airport, reinforced the role of Madrid as the capital of the state, and the concentration of financial capital. In this regard, Madrid continued its historical development path as the capital of the state with strong reliance on service sectors. According to one informant:

> There is one aspect that clearly makes Madrid different, which is its capital status. This fact meant that, especially after the post-war, Madrid concentrated a lot of research resources. Madrid represented approximately 50% of the country's resources in research. (Head of Research, Madrid+i, 2012)

Thus, according to this framework, Madrid's strategy for promoting the creative economy relies on the strong role of cultural resources, and the concentration of film, TV and music industries in the area.

Bilbao and Valencia underwent processes of regeneration during the 1990s with different objectives. In the case of Bilbao, there was a double strategy based on continuing with the modernization of the remaining industry in the metropolitan area and the redevelopment of Bilbao Ria into a new service-oriented area promoted by the Guggenheim museum. The approach to the promotion of creativity and knowledge in Valencia was strongly linked to the growth of the tourism and real estate sectors that had been taking place since the 1990s. Several developments in the 1990s were directed at fostering tourism and leisure industries. The most ambitious development, nonetheless, was the creation of the complex "Ciutat de les arts i les Ciències" (City of Arts and Sciences). The complex is nowadays the main tourist attraction of the city, and has also served for the general promotion of the real estate sector. In the same vein, the city council has pushed for the organization of large sport events such as the F1 and the Sailing America's Cup. As one informant states:

> I think that in the city of Valencia there is very traditional thinking about which are the engines of innovation and urban growth. I think that tourism is in the mind of public authorities (conferences, but also cruises, or seasonal, or related to low-cost companies). Another bet is logistics. I think that the port of Valencia is the clearest flagship of what the authorities think is the future of the city. (Professor, University of Valencia, 2012)

Thus, even using the rhetoric of culture and creativity, we find different strategies and different policy approaches to the development of these sectors. These strategies depend to a great extent on previous development and specific political cultures in economic development.

Concluding Remarks: Identifying Elements of Economic Success in the Transformation of Urban Regions in Spain

As we have seen, path dependency frames policy decision-making and strategic conceptions on how to develop creative and knowledge sectors. Urban trajectories paved the way for different strategies and views on the development of the creative and knowledge economy, and for different degrees of development of these sectors.

This paper aimed at identifying the elements that contribute to a better economic position for four Spanish cities regarding (a) the role played by historical trajectories in the adaptation to a changing global environment and, particularly, the ability of cities to accommodate creative and knowledge industries, (b) the role of governance in the provision of flexibility to make adaptation easier and (c) the successful combination of top-down approaches with local trajectories.

Table 3 summarizes most of these elements. The industrialization path, governance arrangements, the use of culture for the promotion of the city and the role of tourism might be key variables for understanding their current position in the Spanish urban hierarchy. Moreover, the role of each city in the Spanish multi-level governance framework also explains political decisions and the forms of engagement between the public administration, private actors and civil society.

As we have seen, the different positions of the creative and knowledge sectors in each city depends to a great extent on the historical development path, but also on the policies that local actors have promoted. In this regard, the economic trajectories of the four city regions differ and the relevance of creative and knowledge sectors is uneven. Territorial traditions referring to the "way of doing", as well as political coalitions, are relevant to understand the situation of each city region. Economic trajectories are relevant in the four city regions but top-down approaches, mainly at the local level and promoting the clustering of companies, have also played a key role, particularly in knowledge sectors.

The use of culture has been common in the four cities as a means for promoting the city through an image based on cultural matters. However, their cultural path dependency differs in terms of both the typology of cultural agents established and their top-down approach to culture through the construction of cultural resources and facilities. In terms of the built environment, Bilbao, Barcelona, and to a lesser extent Madrid, have faced large urban renewal processes to transform their industrial areas into services economy neighbourhoods, with urban infrastructures oriented towards tourism, knowledge-intensive activities and creative industries. Nevertheless, in these processes of urban transformation, real estate interests have also played an important role, contributing to the definition of the renewal projects. In Valencia, on the other hand, the reconversion of agricultural land into urban land has been a response to increasing tourism and real estate sectors, without a clear need for the redevelopment of industrial spaces, which were mainly outside of the city. Both Barcelona and Bilbao are looking to rebuild their industrial economic centres as new industrial districts of the creative and knowledge economy. Madrid promotes the deployment of creative industries in the shadow of a powerful cultural policy based on building up cultural facilities. In Valencia, the creative industries are heavily rooted in the territory, with an eminently local vocation.

Barcelona exhibits a long-lasting tradition of promoting its internationalization through culture while Valencia, for instance, indicates a two-sided approach: on one side, it is highly attached to the citizenship (musical societies or "Fallas" associations) and, on the other, the organization of large events and the construction of cultural facilities (Ciudad de las Ciencias y de las Artes) as a means for internationalization, following, to a certain extent, the successful model of Barcelona.

Madrid certainly follows a top-down approach to culture, enhancing the value of the historical heritage of cultural resources and territories where culture and artists or intellectuals played a key role. In addition, the capital status is remarkable in attracting the headquarters of media companies.

Tourism is relevant as a powerful economic sector in Spain; these four areas have specialized throughout time in different types of tourism despite the traditional Spanish

Table 3. Synthesis of path dependency variables per city region

	Industrial development	Economic specialization	Governance structures	Historical competitive advantage	Uses of culture	Tourism
Barcelona	Pioneer	Specialized in diversity	Dismantling power during CW, regional and local battle for income resources	Powerful trade centre/harbor Current design advantage based on textile and architecture path dependency	Event-related • International Exhibition (s) • Olympic Games • Forum of Cultures Strong key cultural sectors • Architecture • Publishing	Strongly related to culture, business and events
Bilbao	Pioneer	Heavy manufacturing	Fiscal autonomy at the AC level which benefits the city Institutional and associative life strongly attached to the productive activity	Transforming heavy manufacturing sectors into knowledge High labour quality	Flagship project-related • Guggenheim • Euskalduna congress-Hall	Not dominant, but increasing since the installation of Guggenheim
Madrid	Late	Bureaucratic services structures (public services and companies) High degree of internationalization	Capital effect, but strong competitiveness between regional and city council of Madrid	Benefits for central geo-political situation (i.e. infrastructures) Strong financial sector	Facilities-related • Paseo del arte • Barrio de las Letras Event-related • ARCO (Contemporary Art Festival)	Business and leisure
Valencia	Late	Economic specialization based in agricultural modernisation	Weak articulation of governance, leadership of the Valencia municipality	Land availability and agricultural tradition	Facilities-related • Ciutat de les Arts i les Ciències Attached to citizenship	Strongly related to leisure

Source: Own elaboration.

approach based on leisure and good weather. It is of outstanding importance in cities such as Barcelona and Valencia, with less relative weight in Madrid when compared to other economic sectors, and shows late development in Bilbao.

Although there are common characteristics in the four cities, governance articulation differs from one city to the next, with better or weaker integration depending on the ability of actors to promote themselves and the interests they seek. In this regard, we find weak coordination between regional and local levels which brings, on the one hand, increasing competitiveness of projects promoted at a local level and, on the other, new forms of governance for coordination between levels and scales of government. We find, for instance, increasing competitiveness between cities within the same metropolitan region to attract creative and knowledge industries, and new mechanisms of governance between them to avoid these trends, promoted often by the regional government.

Policies and approaches in the creative and knowledge economies are developed clearly from the second half of the 1990s and are distinctly influenced by the historical development of each city, helping to shape the already existing trends and policies being developed since the 1980s. Aligning our arguments with those provided by Musterd and Kóvacs (2013), path dependency and the historical context should be taken into account in the articulation of policies aiming for better urban competitiveness on the basis of creativity and knowledge, even when the city faces disruptive transformations. The unique characteristics of the four cities we have analysed exhibit their own strength upon which their future challenges should be achieved. Even though the financial crisis constrains possibilities for public policies, still surviving economic actors show prevalence in decision-making; attempts can be found in the four cities to maintain and adapt their strategies to the new context shaped by a new global order, but also a diminishing role for public authorities.

The creation of new contexts for the creative and knowledge industries does not necessarily mean forgetting the previous trajectories of the city: top-down approaches for economic development can be based on a new reading of the past, focusing on the elements that brought about economic agglomeration. For instance, creating a narrative of the historical development of craftsmanship or creating new platforms for firms that are at the same time based on historical institutions. Thus, rather than merely translating experiences or recipes from one local context to another, cities can profit from knowledge and policy transferability, but simultaneously learn from their past and promote new forms of innovation, formulating their own version of policies to foster the creative and knowledge economies.

Acknowledgements

The authors are extremely grateful to the members of the CREAURBS research team.

Disclosure statement

No potential conflict of interest was reported by the authors.

Funding

This work was supported by the Spanish Ministry of Economy and Competitiveness [CSO2012-39373-C04-01].

References

Amin, A. & Thrift, N. J. (1992) Neo-Marshallian nodes in global networks, *International Journal of Urban and Regional Research*, 16(4), pp. 571–587.

Beccatini, G. (1979) Dal "settore" industriale al "distretto" industriale: Alcune considerazioni sull'unità di indagine dell'economia industriale, *Rivista di Economia e Politica Industriale*, 1, pp. 7–21.

Blackeley, G. (2005) Local governance and local democracy: The Barcelona model, *Local Government Studies*, 31(2), pp. 149–165.

Brugué, Q., Gomà Cardona, R., & Subirats, J. (2001) Multilevel governance and Europeanization: The case of Catalonia, in: K. Featherstone & G. Kazamias (Eds) *Europeanization and the Southern Periphery*, pp. 95–117 (London: Frank Cass).

Capel, H. (1975) *Capitalismo y morfología urbana en España* (Barcelona: Los Libros de la Frontera), 142 pp. (4th ed. 1983).

Casellas, A. & Pallares-Barbera, M. (2009) Public-sector intervention in embodying the new economy in inner urban areas: The Barcelona experience, *Urban Studies*, 46(5–6), pp. 1137–1155.

Crossa, V., Pareja-Eastaway, M., & Barber, A. (2010) Reinventing the city: Barcelona, Birmingham and Dublin, in: S. Musterd & A. Murie (Eds) *Making Competitive Cities*, pp. 67–92 (London: Blackwell-Wiley).

Eizaguirre, S. (2012) Innovació social i governança urbana: entitats socialment creatives a Barcelona i Bilbao, PhD Thesis, Universitat de Barcelona, 2012.

Florida, R. (2002) *The Rise of the Creative Class and it's Transforming Work, Leisure, Community and Everyday Life* (New York: Basic Books).

García Delgado, J. L. (1990) La economía de Madrid en el marco de la industrialización española, in: J. Nadal & A. Carreras (Eds) *Pautas regionales de la industrialización española (siglos XIX y XX)*, pp. 219–256 (Barcelona: Ariel).

García-Milà, T. (2003) Fiscal federalism and regional integration: lessons from Spain. Available at http://www.crei.cat/people/gmila/book1_july03.pdf

González, S. (2006) Scalar narratives in Bilbao: A cultural politics of scales approach to the study of urban policy, *International Journal of Urban and Regional Research*, 30(4), pp. 836–857.

González-López, M. (2009) Euro Commentary: Regional differences in the growth patterns of knowledge-intensive business services: An approach based on the Spanish case, *European Urban and Regional Studies*, 16, pp. 101–106.

INE (National Institute of Statistics) (several years) INEbase. Available at: http://www.ine.es/en/inebmenu/indice_en.htm

Jacobs, J. (1972) *The Economy of Cities* (London: Cape).

Keating, M. (1998) *The New Regionalism in Western Europe* (Cheltenham: Edward Elgar Publishing).

Keating, M. (2001) Governing cities and regions: Territorial restructuring in a global age, in: A. J. Scott (Ed) *Global City-regions: Trends, Thoery, Policy*, pp. 371–390 (Oxford: Blackwell).

Kovács, Z., Murie, A., Musterd, S., Gritsai, O., & Pethe, H. (2007) *Comparing Paths of Creative Knowledge Regions* ACRE Report 3, Amsterdam: AMIDSt, University of Amsterdam.

Lambooy, J. (2002) Knowledge and urban economic development: An evolutionary perspective, *Urban Studies*, 39(5–6), pp. 1019–1035.

Landry, C. (2000) *The Creative City: A Toolkit for Urban Innovators* (London: Earthscan).

Mahoney, J. (2000) Path dependence in historical sociology, *Theory and Society*, 29(4), pp. 507–548.

Martí-Costa, M. & Pradel i Miquel, M. (2012) The knowledge city against urban creativity? Artists' workshops and urban regeneration in Barcelona, *European Urban and Regional Studies*, 19(1), pp. 92–108.

Méndez, R., Michelini, J. J., Sánchez, S., & Tébar, J. (2006) *Informe anual 2006. Observatorio industrial de Madrid* Ayuntamiento de Madrid, 146 pp.

Musterd, S. & Gritsai, O. (2013) The creative knowledge city in Europe: Structural conditions and urban policy strategies for competitive cities, *European Urban and Regional Studies*, 20(4), pp. 343–359.

Musterd, S. & Kóvacs, Z. (Eds) (2013) Place-Making and Policies for Competitive Cities (London: Wiley-Blackwell).

Musterd, S. & Murie, A. (Eds) (2010) Making Competitive Cities (Chichester: Wiley-Blackwell).

Musterd, S., Bontje, M., Chapain, C., Kóvacs, Z., & Murie, A. (2007) *Accommodating creative knowledge. A literature review from a European perspective* ACRE Report 1, AMIDSt, University of Amsterdam.

Pareja-Eastaway, M. & Pradel i Miquel, M. (2010) New economy, new governance approaches? Fostering creativity and knowledge in the Barcelona Metropolitan Region, *Creative Industries Journal*, 3(1+2), pp. 29–46.

Pareja-Eastaway, M. & Turmo, J. (2013) La necesaria transformación del modelo productivo en España: el papel del territorio. *Documents d'Anàlisi Geogràfica*.

Pareja-Eastaway, M., Chapain, C., & Mugnano, S. (2013) Success and failures I city-branding policies, in: S. Musterd & Z. Kóvaks (Eds) *Place-making and Policies for Competitive Cities*, pp. 149–171 (London: Wiley-Blackwell).

Ponzini, D. & Rossi, H. (2010) Becoming a creative city: The entrepreneurial mayor, network politics and the promise of an urban renaissance, *Urban Studies*, 47(5), pp. 1037–1057.

Porter, M. (1998) Clusters and the new economies of competition, *Harvard Business Review*, 76(6), pp. 77–91.

Pradel, M. (2012) *Governança, innovació econòmica i social en dos territoris subnacionals europeus: el Vallès Occidental (Catalunya) i el Black Country (West Midlands)* (Universitat de Barcelona).

Rodríguez, A., Martinez, E., & Guenaga, G. (2001) Uneven redevelopment: New urban policies and socio-spatial fragmentation in Metropolitan Bilbao, *European Urban and Regional Studies*, 8(2), pp. 161–178. doi:10.1177/096977640100800206

Rodríguez Morató, A. (2008) La emergencia de una capital cultural Europea, in: M. Degen & M. García (Eds) *La Metaciudad: Barcelona, transformación de una metrópolis*, pp. 45–64 (Barcelona: Antrhopos).

Sassen, S. (2009) Cities Today: A New Frontier for Major Developments. ANNALS AAPSS, 626, November 2009.

Scott, A. J. (2006) Creative cities: Conceptual issues and policy questions, *Journal of Urban Affairs*, 28(1), pp. 1–17.

Solé-Tura, J. (1974) *Catalanismo y revolución burguesa. La pell de brau* (Madrid: cuadernos para el diálogo).

Storper, M. & Scott, A. J. (2009) Rethinking human capital, creativity and urban growth, *Journal of Economic Geography*, 9(2009), pp. 147–167.

Creative Regions on a European Cross-Border Scale: Policy Issues and Development Perspectives

THOMAS PERRIN

Faculty of Geography and Planning, University Lille 1, Research Centre TVES, Villeneuve d'Ascq, France

ABSTRACT *This article discusses the creative and cultural policies that are developed on a European cross-border scale. It provides a comparative case study of the Pyrenees-Mediterranean Euroregion, located on the French–Spanish eastern border and the Greater Region between Luxembourg, Germany, Belgium and France. The analysis is based on the concept of cultural development, which is related to Euroregions to emphasize the uses of culture, identity and creative resources in strategies of territorial attractiveness and institutional capacity-building. The analysis then shows how the dynamics of cultural development concretely impact Euroregional policies: implications, or even strengthening, of arts and creativity in cross-cutting policies—tourism and sustainable development, promotion of cultural diversity and the human dimension of development. Furthermore, these dynamics underline the contribution of cultural policy to the construction of territoriality, and subsequently the contribution of Euroregions to the territorial and cultural construction of Europe.*

1. Introduction

Encouraged by the Council of Europe action in favour of cross-border cooperation[1] and supported by funding from the European Union (EU) regional policy, the European territorial authorities have developed numerous networks and projects of cooperation. Accordingly, over a hundred "Euroregions" have been created. Although the term refers to different types of cooperation and clusters, it is a generic description to designate more or less structured organizations on both sides of a European border, sub-state territorial authorities joined together in the pursuit of objectives and joint projects, based on shared interests and within project areas (Durà *et al.*, 2010).

Among the various actions developed in the Euroregions, culture appears as an area of frequent cooperation, giving rise to a particular form of cultural policy, which we can refer to as "Euroregional cultural policy". The phrase encompasses the cultural projects and schemes involving actors from different territories of a Euroregion, the implementation of which is supported by the regional authorities, when they are not the initiators, but can also involve the participation of other institutions or bodies, the most important of which is the EU. The concept of culture—polysemic and elusive—is understood here in terms of "cultural policy", that is, culture as an object of public policy, as defined and announced through the actions of the official authorities (Mulcahy, 2006).

Like in any other type of cultural policy, the thematic of "cultural development" is gaining increasing importance in the cross-border context. This approach developed within the normative paradigm of the knowledge and smart economy, largely based on cognitive and intangible resources and on the notion of sustainable development, in which creative and cultural activities are considered fundamental resources. In this context, culture and creativity have progressively appeared to be concrete assets for the development and the attractiveness of territories, and factors of social cohesion (Scott, 2007; Bernié-Boissard et al., 2010). The EU authorities illustrated this trend by adopting in June 2011 the Council's conclusions on the contribution of culture to the implementation of the Europe 2020 strategy "for a smart, sustainable and inclusive growth" (réf. 2011/C 175/01). However, this trend is not without controversy as to its impact on the purpose and nature of cultural policies and actions.

This article discusses the current challenges facing cultural development by transposing them on a European cross-border scale. The main hypothesis is that the general evolution of cultural policies impacts the conducting of Euroregional cultural action but, at the same time, due to their particular cross-border and transnational context, Euroregional policies can renew and enrich the thinking and the practices of cultural development.

The analysis is based on a comparative study of several cases of Euroregional cultural policy: mainly the Pyrenees-Mediterranean and the Greater Region Euroregions, supplemented by other examples in which culture is mobilized as a separate and salient sector of Euroregional cooperation. This mainly qualitative analysis uses documentary and bibliographic sources as well as the data that were collected during fieldwork with the institutions, artists and cultural operators, in the context of a Ph.D. research (Perrin, 2013).

The Pyrenees-Mediterranean Euroregion was established in October 2004. It combines the French regions of Languedoc-Roussillon and the Midi-Pyrénées with the Spanish autonomous communities of Catalonia, Aragon and the Balearic Islands (Figure 1).[2]

Cultural policy is one of the strategic axes of the cooperation and is part of the stated aims of the Euroregion, which were defined in 2004. Support schemes have been implemented: creation of a cultural portal on the Internet, a genuine "cultural showcase" aspiring to become both a resource centre and platform for the networking of operators; launching calls for specific projects to fund Euroregional cultural and artistic initiatives, one of the only areas where such calls have been launched, cross-border mobility grants for cultural actors and annual organization of forums for cultural stakeholders. Culture is one of the areas of intervention that has been integrated and strengthened within the common structure created in 2010 to pilot the Euroregion: the Pyrenees-Mediterranean European Grouping for Territorial Cooperation (EGTC).[3]

The Greater Region, meanwhile, includes the German "Länder" states of Saarland and Rhineland-Palatinate, the French region of Lorraine, the Grand Duchy of Luxembourg and

Figure 1. Euroregion Pyrenees-Mediterranean.
Source: http://www.euroregio.eu.

three Belgian federated entities: Wallonia and the French and German-speaking communities of Belgium (Figure 2).

The formation of this Euroregion in the 1990s finds its origin in a process initiated from 1960 to 1970 in the "Sar-Lor-Lux" space (Dörrenbächer, 2006). In 2007, the Luxembourg authorities wished for the full involvement of all members of the Greater Region as European Capital of Culture of Luxembourg. This cross-border dynamic cultural cooperation was then perpetuated by the establishment in 2008 of the cultural association of the Greater Region: "Espace culturel Grande Région/Kulturraum Großregion" (Figure 3).

After presenting the notion of cultural development, the Euroregions cross-border context is analysed with conceptual patterns that emphasize the uses of culture, identity and creative resources in territorial strategies of attractiveness and capacity-building (van Houtum & Lagendijk, 2001; Leresche & Saez, 2002; Saez, 2009). Following this theoretical approach, the analysis then shows how the dynamics of cultural development concretely impacts Euroregional policies: implication or even strengthening of arts and creativity in cross-cutting policies—tourism and sustainable development, promotion of cultural diversity and the human dimension of development. Furthermore, these dynamics

Figure 2. Greater Region.
Source: https://www.123go-networking.org.

underline the contribution of cultural policy to the construction of territoriality, and subsequently the contribution of Euroregions to the territorial and cultural construction of Europe.

2. Culture, Creativity and Cross-Border Development

2.1. A Polymorphic Notion, from Cultural Development to Creative Economy

As Saez (2009) shows in his analysis of the current issues of territorial cultural policies, the notion of cultural development refers to the balance between both regimes of cultural policy, on the one hand cultural democratization and widespread access to a conventional offer, and on the other hand cultural democracy aimed at expanding content and the consideration of expressions and artistic and cultural requests in all their diversity, with no hierarchizing approach. Accordingly, cross-cutting and interculturality become the main characteristics of cultural development. One of the most representative expressions of this approach is the adoption of Agenda 21 for Culture by almost 225 cities, associating cultural policy with the wider issues of sustainable development, such as environmental, citizenship, land or cultural diversity issues.[4]

In addition, cultural development issues and their advocacy by the public authorities are related to wider socio-economic evolutions (Bernié-Boissard *et al.*, 2010). Cultural development was gradually associated with the development of the cultural economy or development "by" the cultural economy, which appears to be the "new dynamic front of contemporary capitalism" (Daviet & Leriche, 2008, p. 4). In 2005, a report by the

Organization for Economic Cooperation and Development (OECD) has shown how culture can be a lever for the organization of territory and local development, particularly through the promotion of cultural tourism, the formation of cultural districts or cultural sectors. This economic paradigm shift is reflected at an EU level[5] in the so-called Lisbon and Gothenburg and Europe 2020[6] development strategies, positioning creative activities as drivers of innovation and economic and territorial development. 2009 was labelled "European Year of Creativity and Innovation" and in June 2011 the European Council adopted conclusions on the contribution of culture to the implementation of the Europe 2020 strategy "for smart, sustainable and inclusive growth".[7]

In the relationship between culture, creativity, development and territories, a social dimension accompanies the economic dimension, where cultural development should contribute to developing human capital, promoting cultural and linguistic diversity (Bonet & Négrier, 2008). In this approach, culture is mobilized to foster social and territorial cohesion, to fight against exclusion. Cultural diversity is considered to be a social asset that must be valued. The defence of cultural diversity appears as a feature of the European model of cultural economy (Daviet & Leriche, 2008, pp. 9–10) and the EU has labelled

Figure 3. Luxplus 2007 and the Espace culturel Grande Région: continuity in branding.
Source: http://www.espaceculturelgr.eu.

2008 "European Year of Intercultural Dialogue". At a global level, the Convention for the Protection and Promotion of the Diversity of Cultural Expressions, adopted within the framework of UNESCO came into force in 2007 and the United Nations decided to make 2010 "International Year for the Rapprochement of Cultures".

2.2. *The Euroregions as Territories of Development*

If the dynamics of cultural development mainly concerns urban and metropolitan areas, areas "of creativity and cultural invention" par excellence (Saez, 2009, p. 12),[8] in the economic reality of globalization, the activity often spreads beyond city centres and metropolitan territory, on a larger regional scale that has some relevance for Euroregional organizations.

> The extension of an urban center and the localization strategies (of activities) may well acquire a cross border dimension (...) the projection of clusters and specific externalities may be carried out on a cross border basis, and in fact it is often the case. (Letamendía, 2010, p. 81)

This Euroregions dimension is also linked to the specificities of the European urban network, which positions metropolitan areas, alongside "global cities", as major players in the world-system (Daviet & Leriche, 2008, p. 8). Urban networks form the backbone of Euroregions and these two dynamics are subject to similar strategies of cooperation, fostered by institutional support devices, whether intercity or interregional cooperation. The Greater Region is committed to building a cross-border polycentric metropolitan area. The development of the Pyrenees-Mediterranean space is based largely on the strength of its cities, Barcelona, Toulouse, Montpellier, and the challenge is to find the balance between urban hypertrophy and weak rural areas.

In the Euroregions analysed, the current cultural development issues in economic, social and geopolitical terms are reflected in the cultural policy discourses. This is both a means of reconciliation between people and territories on both sides of the border and an asset for external projection outside the territory, its attractiveness and competitiveness: promoting a whole economic sector and its potential benefits in terms of creativity and innovation, tourism industry support and more broadly, contribution of cultural marketing to the inclusion of territory within the EU framework, or in the global socio-economic networks.

The Greater Region as European Capital of Culture for a period of one year aimed to position this territory on the European or even global map, the founding declaration of the Pyrenees-Mediterranean Euroregion aims to make "the Euroregion become a reference place within international artistic and creative circuits".[9] The same external projection determination can be found in the cultural agenda of the Alps-Mediterranean Euroregion, located on the Franco-Italian border[10]: its member regions wish to establish a "common portfolio" of Euroregion cultural projects to set up a joint promotion in foreign markets such as North America, Australia, Japan, China and India.

Consequently cultural policy occupies a unique place in the distinction strategies of many Euroregional groupings, which includes the patterns of consumption of cultural products as elements of social distinction and assertiveness that Pierre Bourdieu highlighted and which was not without effect on the growth of the cultural economy (Leriche & Scott, 2005, p. 209). However, this "territorial distinction" goal can give way to different strategies and issues, which are present in Euroregional policies.

3. Euroregional Cultural Development: Dynamics and Issues

3.1. *"Creative City" vs. "Participative Town": Which Euroregion Model?*

In the analysed Euroregions we find the two trends of cultural development as identified by Saez (2009, p. 14): the creative City on the one hand, "positioning strategy specific to geo-cultural marketing" and the participative Town on the other hand, which "seeks to promote the different areas of the town including the most deprived and the numerous 'communities' intersecting".

In the Pyrenees-Mediterranean Euroregion, the majority of projects selected and supported in the framework of calls for cultural projects since 2006 leaves a large share to contemporary forms, innovative productions and emerging or "techno-creative" disciplines: street and circus arts—staunchly labelled as networks of excellence in the Midi-Pyrénées and as might be called in Catalonia, an "exceptional sector", where the main structures offering a renewed approach to the circus tradition in Spain can be found; interdisciplinary between dance and digital arts; design, photography and contemporary art (Perrin, 2013). The 2008 Euroregional cultural encounters, held at the Museum of Contemporary Art in Palma de Mallorca, had as a main theme the links between innovation, research and culture. The Euroregion established a "Technological and Cultural Laboratory" funded by the EU programme for cooperation in the transnational area of South-West Europe.

Consequently, the cultural identity promoted in the Pyrenees-Mediterranean Euroregion seems to be the object of a renewed approach, less confined to the strict limits of a cross-border area of mythologized cultural homogeneity, more open to contemporary issues such as the creative identity of a territory as a factor of attractiveness and economic development. However, the orientation of the "Euroregional cultural corpus" towards creativity could ultimately only be the response of a (Euro)regional "realpolitik" to repository evolution of EU programmes according to the priorities of the Lisbon-Gothenburg and Europe 2020 agendas, as part of a financial attraction strategy. Therefore, such a "creative drift" consisting of "manufacturing devices", certainly consistent with the times, involves the risk of "going over the existing to place an order".[11] The majority of cultural players encountered in different fields[12] agree with this fact: when the authorities implement a new system of cultural cooperation, too often this is carried out without identification, without taking into account and without capitalizing on actions and experiences already carried out in the field. This also corresponds with the idea of a "neo-elitist illusion of widespread creativity" that must be overstepped (Bonet & Négrier, 2008, p. 210). In addition, the emphasis on the innovative dimension or technology use may risk founding creativity on techniques and means, on a creative device rather than on the meaning of the works produced.

In the Greater Region and the rest of the 2007 cross-border cultural capital year, the cultural policy reflects a more participative approach to cultural development, with the emphasis not only on creativity and innovation, but also, and in particular, cultural diversity as a means of living together—40% of the inhabitants of the Grand Duchy of Luxembourg are foreigners and 162 nationalities are represented. The research and mobilization of a new public with youth and immigrant communities was one of the objectives for the year 2007 and is part of the specifications of the "Espace culturel Grande Région". However, such an agenda requires sound financial footing, available so far certainly, but which an economic crisis may weaken. This reminds us of another territory and the organization of "Bethune regional cultural capital of Nord-Pas-de-Calais". Originally planned for 2009, the event had to be postponed to 2011 for financial reasons mainly.[13]

3.2. *Functional Identity vs. Cultural Identity of Territories*

The examples discussed also illustrate the development patterns of polycentric urban regions as they have been defined in the case of the Ruhr in Germany and the Basque country in Spain (van Houtum & Lagendijk, 2001). These patterns conceptualise the identity of metropolitan regions in three dimensions: strategic, functional and cultural identity. The strategic identity aims to enhance competitiveness and attractiveness by synergy, cooperation and networking between territories. Cultural identity refers to the collective representation of the territory, a dynamic and evolving process, where positioning the territory, toponymy, mapping and heritage come into play. The notion of functional identity refers to the—economic, political, social—elements that embody and thereby legitimize the development of one or another territorial form.

While the functional identity of the Ruhr is not doubted, notably based on specific economic history, the authorities are setting up a strategy to "remodel" and "mobilize" a common cultural identity that, on the contrary, seems to be lacking. Essen has also placed its title of European Capital of Culture 2010 under the label "Ruhr 2010". The situation in this metropolitan area appears quite similar to that of the Greater Region. Conversely, in the Basque Country, it is the strong cultural identity that supports the construction of a functional and geo-strategic image of the territory—"the Basque Country competitive in Europe"—even though the functionality of this space seems far from being accomplished. It is closer to the Pyrenees-Mediterranean space, which has a cultural identity affirmed and structured around an "Occitan-Catalan" axis. There are also discrepancies and interactions between functional, cultural and geo-strategic identities in the Euroregional Franco-Belgian space, highly integrated yet not free from cultural differences, shaped by the Franco-Flemish linguistic policy split which partly contributed to the failure of the institutionalization of the Euroregion between Kent, the Nord-Pas-de-Calais and the three Belgian regions, between 1991 and 2004.

Therefore, these Euroregions illustrate different types of cross-border cultural mobilization of territories in a context of international competition: either cultural or identity resources can be put at the service of economic competition, or cross-border territories can be converted into cultural and identity resources to resist this competition (Leresche & Saez, 2002, p. 93). While the Pyrenees-Mediterranean Euroregion does not, strictly speaking constitute an integrated economic cluster, despite countless potential synergies and a certain cooperation experience in this area, culture is mobilized above partnership. The strengthening of a Euroregional cultural capital, especially as these territories have a fairly typical cultural identity, is seen as a catalyst for integration in other fields, and as a factor to achieve sustainable development "based on innovation as well as social and territorial inclusion", the main objective of the Euroregional partnership (Morata, 2007, p. 5). It is almost a reverse situation in the Greater Region: the cultural agenda appears to be a viable means of strengthening—and so doing of legitimizing—a high functional identity, embodied in the history of the Sar-Lor-Lux "mining triangle" and today in the daily cross-border flow of workers within the Euroregion.

From an operational point of view, the discourses and strategies of cultural development have a concrete impact on Euroregional cultural policies and on the institutional development of Euroregions.

4. Culture, Creativity and Construction of Territoriality in the Euroregions

4.1. *The Cross-cutting Approach to Cultural Policies*

Cultural development strategies—particularly at the level of territorial authorities—often lead to inclusion of cultural policy into cross-cutting policies, the most common cross-cutting approach being the contribution of cultural policy to fostering creativity, innovation and attractiveness.

Another trend of this cross-cutting approach is the interaction between cultural and tourism policies. The Euroregional Pyrenees-Mediterranean fifth cultural days in June 2010, focused on the "New Tourism" theme. One of the stated objectives was the merger between culture and tourism to promote lesser-known destinations, the development of routes around recently valued heritage elements—industrial heritage—or highlighting mountain or rural tourism. Such projects can also be based on a pooling of institutional networks such as, for example tourism promotion centres of the Government of Catalonia, Languedoc-Roussillon offices abroad called Les Maisons du Languedoc-Roussillon, or the "Para-Euroregional" tourism partnership between Catalonia and Midi-Pyrénées, which was launched in 2009 and which in 2010–2011, was inserted into the larger programme "Catalonia year in France", a series of activities and events organized in Lyon, Montpellier, Nantes and Toulouse.[14] The interpenetration between cultural policies and tourism is seen as a development issue for the Alps-Mediterranean Euroregion too, where the tourism industry is one of the major sources of income. Indeed, according to a prospective work on European polycentrism (Baudelle *et al.*, 2002), we can see that these two Euroregions are at the junction of the "golden belts" of the EU space, and at the heart of a "Fun Belt (...) incorporating trendy seaside resorts in the Balearics, the Riviera and the Basque Country", which feature as the "Mediterranean golden banana", or even" as a "European California" (Baudelle *et al.*, 2002, p. 130).[15] And the development of such spaces implies a process of "gentrification of non-technopolitan regions in the vicinity of the (European) metropolis, by valuing their natural, cultural and heritage amenities for a settlement of definite residences, double residences or temporary residences for well-off populations, whether active or retired" (Baudelle *et al.*, 2002, p. 129). This gives cultural policy a special place in the development strategies and attraction of these areas (Figure 4).

Moreover, if the "marriage" between culture and tourism can be an added value for the sustainable development of the Pyrenees-Mediterranean Euroregion, it is not only because of the weight of the tourism sector in the economies of member regions (Morata, 2007, p. 35). Valuing cultural tourism can take on a dimension that is not only economic, but also ecological or educational, having the effects of new repercussions for the sector while renewing the relationship with the environment. In 2011, the Pyrenees-Mediterranean EGTC launched a call for project "Euroregional tourism and climate change", in order to sensitise the tourism sector to the impact of this activity on climate change and consequently promote a new "tourism culture" in the Euroregion. In 2012, a call was made for projects contributing "to the efficient use of resources (water and energy), through communication, information, research and demonstration and training activities". Members of the Alps-Mediterranean Euroregion, in their contribution to the public consultation on the Green Paper of the European Commission on Territorial Cohesion,[16] insist on the preservation of natural environments and the links between the environment and sustainable tourism.

CREATIVE REGIONS IN EUROPE

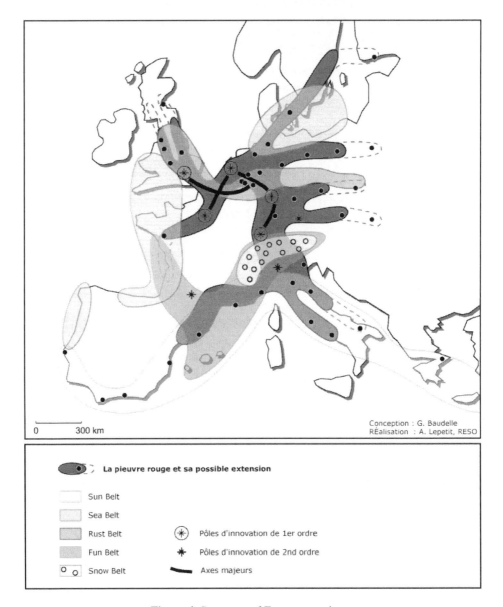

Figure 4. Structures of European territory.
Source: Baudelle *et al.* (2002).

On such subjects, artists can allow an interesting and relevant "dialogue with the territory" (Saule-Sorbé, 2000). For example, on the issue of artificial soil related to the metropolization of spaces, that had consequences on the Mediterranean coast, the Catalan artist Joan Rabascall made a series of photographs "Paisatges Costa Brava" (1982). David Goldblatt carried out a work between 1999 and 2002 on luxurious "neo-Tuscan"-inspired residential complexes built in the South African countryside, the photographs of which are in the collections of the Museum of Contemporary Art in Barcelona. More broadly, we can cite the work of André Mérian on "landscape and its territory, its transformation and evolution", on the relationship between urbanization and the natural environment, particularly in the Mediterranean region.[17] The Pyrenees-Mediterranean Euroregion funded the project "Pyrenees: Art and Ecology in the 21st century", developed from 2010 to 2012 and combining contemporary art and ecology, with the aim to broadcast scientific knowledge on the threats of global warming through artistic language.[18]

Accordingly, artists and cultural professionals can be important actors to nourish the meta-geographic perceptions of territory and identity: "artistic work is strong enough not only to renew the perspectives of landscape perception but also imbue it with a strong capacity for political influence" (Amilhat Szary, 2012, p. 222). In this way, the junction between a territorial project and the visions and productions of artists and designers could contribute to the emergence, in the Euroregions context, of a cross-border "geopoetic".[19]

4.2. The Challenge of Cultural Diversity: From Euroregions to European Construction

Cultural diversity is the other major issue of cultural development. It appears to be a spearhead of cultural cooperation in the Greater Region, in connection with a particular context of multilingualism and multiculturalism, especially involving two trilingual states, two linguistic communities in Belgium and over 160 nationalities in Luxembourg. In the Pyrenees-Mediterranean Euroregion, the constitutive declaration states that cultural diversity is a "creative force" and emphasizes the importance of sharing, within the Euroregion, "experiences of multiculturalism". In Catalonia, the defence of cultural diversity is also a means of legitimizing its own cultural autonomy and therefore its own identity of "Stateless Nation". During preparation of a new External Action Plan presented in 2010, the Catalan Government made cultural diplomacy one of its priorities in the strategies of "nation branding".[20]

These issues also highlight the potentialities of the Euroregional context as a layout of different dynamics, aspirations and demands of cultural diversity, between pluralism and nationalism, cultural globalization and particularities. For example, this context may allow overcoming of "stereotyped and stratified" regional identities that leave little room for expressions of diversity and non-regional cultures (Syssner, 2009).

A Euroregional head of cultural affairs of the Catalan Government hypothesized that "cross border experience will one day produce a cross border narrative, a fantasy novel or multiple identity".[21] The philosopher and artist Fischer (2011) argues for "peripherism" that he defines as the search for harmony between unity and fragmentation of contemporary societies, a search that embodies by numerous aspects the construction of cross-border territoriality such as Euroregions, and through them European construction.

Consequently, Euroregional devices and EU devices in many ways appear as two sides of the same coin. A Euroregional cultural project is often regarded as a first step towards EU programmes. Euroregional projects themselves are rarely developed without mobilizing funding from the EU. Moreover culture, through its potential visibility and its high symbolic charge, is a privileged field of action to bring meaning to Euroregional capacity building, and the institutional strengthening of Euroregions may bring about a meta-geographical change in the perception of the European territory (Durà *et al.*, 2010, p. 33). The geographer Baudelle (2005) notes that some representations of the European space, such as the "European Sun Belt" or the "European California", which are particularly important for some Euroregions analysed, could be an "avant-garde scene" a "prototopos (...) foreshadowing the future Europe".

5. Conclusion: The "In-between" Perspective

By its very nature, the Euroregional scale lies in a territorial, geopolitical and institutional in-between. Indeed Euroregional cultural policies also falls within an "in-between dialectic", to find the right balance and articulation between "creative" or "participatory" models, between representation and experience/living of the territory, or between diversity and intercultural dialogue, where cultural policy "faces its new intercultural destiny" (Bonet & Négrier, 2008, p. 210). In the absence of dialogue and contact between cultures, multiculturalism and cultural diversity may lead to cultural communitarianism of societies, of different but fixed identities, making diversity more of a constraint than a wealth. "Understanding is accepting not to understand everything. What matters is that which is 'between', the relationship to others. (...). Intercultural dialogue is found on the edge, on the boundary, which implies a constant struggle" (de Bernard, 2008, p. 17). The cultural and artistic environment is cosmopolitan by essence, traditionally internationalized and has a globalized logic of action. Hence, is it not one of the most adapted to project across borders ... to be better able to reinvest? As a cultural actor recalled "we are different on either side of the border, we do not think the same way, we do not understand each other and that is what is interesting".[22] While the parties and political dialogue with xenophobic trends are making a comeback and, among others, Samuel Huntington's well-known thesis on the "clash of civilizations" is experiencing some growth in Europe, the German Chancellor Angela Merkel noted a total failure of the model of a multicultural Germany, where different cultures harmoniously live side-by-side,[23] which re-launches the debate on the middle path that should be found between inclusion and cultural communitarianism, on the passage from multicultural to intercultural. Thus, if the Euroregional experience can be considered an antechamber of the cultural and territorial construction of Europe, it not only reflects the progress, but also the obstacles and dead ends of such a construction.

The observation of Euroregional cultural policies underlines the issues and challenges of cultural globalization. Indeed, the Euroregional dynamics emphasizes quite at the same time the identity dimension of cultural policies, the interactions between culture, identity and territory, and the increasing place of culture and cultural matters as major issues of the international relations. Furthermore, the development of Euroregions illustrates, on the one hand, a "return to territory" movement despite the crossing of the borders, and on the other hand a dialectic between distinction/differentiation and dilution/integration – on identity, territorial and cultural levels –, which characterizes the processes of globalization.

> Today we are living with discourses of globalization and hybridity which have paradoxically created both an illusion of a "borderless world" and a world in which borders have multiplied [...] They are even folded into the identities of individual subjects. (Schimanski & Wolfe, 2010, p. 40)

CREATIVE REGIONS IN EUROPE

In this way, one of the main challenges facing the "creative euroregions" is to advocate European construction and cultural diversity, while preserving regional identities and sub-state prerogatives.

Acknowledgements

Translation carried out with the support of UMR PACTE CNRS and Pierre-Mendès University France – Grenoble II.

Disclosure statement

No potential conflict of interest was reported by the author.

Notes

1. Notably through the European Outline Convention on Transfrontier Cooperation between Territorial Communities or Authorities of 1981, known as the Madrid Convention.
2. Since 2006, Aragon has suspended its participation to the Euroregion.
3. This legal status was created in 2006 by EU law to facilitate and promote cross-border cooperation. Regulation EC n° 1082/2006 of the European Parliament and of the Council, of 5 July 2006.
4. Initially, Agenda 21, or Action 21, is an action plan for the twenty-first century founded on sustainable development and adopted in the framework of the United Nations organization by 173 governments during the earth summit held in Rio in 1992. It calls on local authorities to take steps to implement the plan locally—local Agenda 21—in particular through participatory mechanisms. The representative interregional organization "United Cities and Local Governments" (UCLG), which unites cities worldwide, is at the origin of the Agenda 21 project for culture, adopted in 2004 at the 2004 Universal Forum of Cultures in Barcelona, which is also the headquarters of the UCLG.
5. "Community" is used here in "relation to the European Union", excluding of course a context or remarks indicating another use of the term.
6. In Lisbon in March 2000, Heads of State and Government of the EU fixed a strategy for 2010, aiming to make Europe "the most competitive and the most dynamic knowledge-based economy in the world". The Gothenburg European Council in June 2001 expanded this strategy to protect the environment and create a sustainable development model. Although, this agenda has been a failure in achieving its objectives, in late 2010 the EU adopted a new "Europe 2020" strategy for "smart, sustainable and inclusive growth".
7. (Ref. 2011/C 175/01).
8. Cf. also La ville créative: concept marketing ou utopie mobilisatrice? Special dossier, "L'Observatoire. La revue des politiques culturelles", n°36 hiver 2009–2010: http://www.observatoire-culture.net
9. Available at http://www.euroregio.eu (accessed 27 January 11).
10. Between the French regions of the Rhône-Alpes and Provence-Alpes-Côte d'Azur, and Ligurie, Piémont and the Aoste Valley in Italy.
11. Interview with an expert on European cultural policies, July 2009.
12. In the two main fields, but also in the Alps-Mediterranean Euroregion in the Franco-Italian border and the Eurometropole Franco-Belgian Lille-Kortrijk-Tournai.
13. "La Voix du Nord" of 25 October 2008.
14. Catalan village with vacation ideas for all, representation of castellers (human towers), medieval folk shows and parade of traditional Catalan characters and figures, gastronomic tasting and sale of local products, etc.
15. By analogy with the "Blue Banana" of Europe, the concept of "golden banana" refers to the coastal strip between the Spanish Levant and the Eastern Alps, from Valence to Genoa.
16. The consultation took place from October 2008 to February 2009. Contributions, almost 400 are available on http://ec.europa.eu/regional_policy (accessed 03 March 12).
17. http://www.documentsdartistes.org/artistes/merian/repro.html (accessed 03 March 12). André Mérian also worked on the transformation of the Toulouse suburbs after the explosion of the AZF factory.

18. Project developed by the cultural operators Caza d'Oro (Midi-Pyrénées), Casa d'Art i Natura (Catalonia) and Les Isards (Languedoc-Roussillon).
19. To resume the denomination of the intellectual movement initiated by the writer and poet Kenneth White. In reference to this movement, Saule-Sorbé (2000, p. 90) coined the term "geo-poetic" to designate the geographical dimension of the creative process
20. Cf. seminar on "La diplomàcia cultural. Reflexions i propostes des de Catalunya". Barcelona, 2–4 December 2009.
21. Participation of Estanislau Vidal-Folch during the Luxembourg meeting of the European Association of Towns and Regions of greater Europe for culture, 12 and 13 October 2007.
22. "Dimensions et perspectives culturelles des eurorégions". Roundtable conference organized by the Culture Department of the Rhône-Alpes region. Avignon, 12 July 2009.
23. During a speech in front of the youth wing of her own political party in October 2010: "Angela Merkel: German multiculturalism has 'utterly failed'", *The Guardian*, Sunday, October 17, http://www.guardian.co.uk (accessed 3 December 2012).

References

Amilhat Szary, A-L. (2012) Walls and border art: The politics of art display, *Journal of Borderlands Studies*, 27(2), pp. 213–228.

Baudelle, G. (2005) *Figures d'Europe: une question d'image(s)*, Norois. Environnement, aménagement, sociéte, no. 194, 2005/1. Available at: http://norois.revues.org (accessed 3 December 2012).

Baudelle, G., Guy, C., & Ollivro, J. (2002) Les scénarios de l'espace européen, in: G. Baudelle & B. Castagnède (Eds) *Le Polycentrisme en Europe. Une vision de l'aménagement du territoire européen*, pp. 107–154 (La Tour d'Aigues/Paris: Aube/DATAR edition).

de Bernard, François. (2008) Towards new paradigms? Europe, globalization and the perception of new opportunities, in: A-M. Autissier (Ed) *Intercultural Dialogue(s) in Europe*, pp. 17–19 (Paris: Culture Europe International).

Bernié-Boissard, C., Chastegner, C., Crozat, D., & Fournier, L-S. (Eds) (2010) *Développement culturel et territoires* (Paris: L'Harmattan).

Bonet, L-L. & Négrier, E. (Eds) (2008) *La fin des cultures nationales? Les politiques culturelles à l'épreuve de la diversité* (Paris: La Découverte).

Daviet, S., & Leriche, F. (2008) "Nouvelle" économie culturelle : existe-t-il un modèle français?, Conference Arts, territoires et nouvelle économie culturelle, May 6–7, Québec. Available at: http://chairefernanddumont.ucs.inrs.ca/Mai2008/Arts.html (accessed 3 December 2012).

Dörrenbächer, H. Peter, (2006) *From the "mining triangle" to the "Greater Region". The institutionalization of the "SaarLorLux" Euroregion*. Working papers online n°12. Available online at: http://www.iuee.eu (accessed 3 December 2012).

Durà, A., Oliveras, X., & Perkmann, M. (2010) Las regiones transfronterizas: balance de la regionalización de la cooperación transfronteriza en Europa (1958–2007), *Documents d'Anàlisi Geogràfica*, 56(1), pp. 21–40.

Fischer, H. (2011) Mitoanàlisi de la frontera, in: O. Jané & E. Forcada (Eds) *L'Afrontera. De la dominació a l'art de transgredir*, pp. 45–58 (Catarroja: Editorial Afers).

van Houtum, H. & Lagendijk, A. (2001) Contextualising regional identity and imagination in the construction of polycentric urban regions: The cases of the Ruhr area and the Basque country, *Urban Studies*, 38(4), pp. 747–767.

Leresche, J-P. & Saez, G. (2002) Political frontier regime: Towards cross border governance?, in: M. Perkmann & N-L. Sum (Eds) *Globalization, Regionalization and Cross Border Regions*, pp. 77–99 (Basingstoke: Palgrave Macmillan).

Leriche, F. & Scott, A-J. (2005) Les ressorts géographiques de l'économie culturelle: du local au mondial, *L'Espace géographique*, 34(3), pp. 207–222.

Letamendía, F. (2010) Cooperación europea transfronteriza: regulación, historia y trabajo, *Documents d'Anàlisi Geogràfica*, 56(1), pp. 71–88.

Mulcahy, Kevin V. (2006) Cultural policy: Definitions and theoretical approaches, *Journal of Arts Management, Law, and Society*, 35(4), pp. 319–331.

Morata, F. (Ed) (2007) *A Sustainable Development Strategy for the Pyrenees-Mediterranean Euroregion: Basic Guidelines* (Barcelona: CADS/Catalunya government). Available at http://www.iuee.eu (accessed 3 December 2012).

Perrin, T. (2013) *Culture et eurorégion. La coopération culturelle entre régions européennes* (Brussels: Éditions de l'Université de Bruxelles).
Saez, G. (2009) *Les collectivités territoriales et la culture* Cahiers Français 348, pp. 8–14, Paris: La Documentation française.
Saule-Sorbé, H. (2000) Du sentiment géographique en art: quelques exemples du dialogue entre artistes et territoires, en Sud-Ouest, *Sud-Ouest Européen*, n°8, pp. 83–90.
Schimanski, J. & Wolfe, S. (2010) Cultural production and negotiation of borders: Introduction to the Dossier, *Journal of Borderlands Studies*, 25(1), pp. 38–49.
Scott, A-J. (2007) Capitalism and urbanization in a new key? The cognitive-cultural dimension, *Social Forces. International Journal of Social Research*, 85(4), pp. 1465–1482.
Syssner, J. (2009) Conceptualizations of culture and identity in regional policy, *Regional and Federal Studies*, 19(3), pp. 437–458.

Factors Explaining the Spatial Agglomeration of the Creative Class: Empirical Evidence for German Artists

CHRISTOPH ALFKEN, TOM BROEKEL & ROLF STERNBERG

Institute of Economic and Cultural Geography, Leibniz University of Hanover, Hannover, Germany

ABSTRACT *The paper contributes to the on-going debate about the relative importance of economic and amenity-related location factors for attracting talent or members of the creative class. While Florida highlights the role of amenities, openness and tolerance, others instead emphasize the role of regional productions systems, local labour markets and externalities. The paper sheds light on this issue by analysing the changes in the spatial distribution of four groups of artists over time: visual artists, performing artists, musicians and writers. Little evidence is found for amenity-related factors influencing the growth rates of regional artist populations. Moreover, artists are shown to be a heterogeneous group inasmuch as the relative importance of regional factors significantly differs between artistic branches.*

1. Introduction

There is an on-going debate about the creative class, creative industries and creative regions. These notions are indivisibly connected to Richard Florida's work. Florida (and followers) highlight amenities, openness and tolerance as the key factors behind the geographic mobility and regional agglomeration of creative people (Florida, 2002a, 2002b; Florida *et al.*, 2008; Florida & Mellander, 2010). The notion "amenities" is ambiguously used in the literature and comprises the climatic, cultural, recreational as well as aesthetic aspects of a regional environment (Storper & Manville, 2006). Their role is of particular interest to us because recently they have been used to explain increasing urban economic and population growth (Glaeser *et al.*, 2001; Clark *et al.*, 2002). This stimulated investments in amenities, which then became a fashionable policy tool that attracted talented and creative people.

Florida's concept of the creative class is frequently criticized, however (Glaeser, 2005; Peck, 2005; Markusen, 2006; Storper & Scott, 2008; Scott, 2010), and the very broad, one may even say "fuzzy", definition of the creative class in particular has provoked criticism.

While there is considerable empirical evidence backing Florida's hypotheses, it primarily relates to US metropolitan areas (Florida, 2002a; Florida et al., 2008; Florida & Mellander, 2010). Some empirical studies focus on regions outside the US. For instance, Fritsch and Stuetzer (2009), Krätke (2010), Mossig (2011), Möller and Tubadji (2004) and Wedemeier (2010) investigated these issues for Germany.

In order to test Florida's hypotheses, most existing studies closely follow his approach in empirical assessment. However, this implies that the broadness of Florida's theory frequently blurs empirical findings as well (Marrocu & Paci, 2012). In addition, in empirical investigations many studies apply static approaches and ignore the inherently dynamic nature of spatial agglomeration processes.

The present study aims at overcoming some of these shortcomings. Firstly, in contrast to most existing studies we focus on one subgroup of the creative class, namely artists. In addition, we further disaggregate artists into four groups: visual artists, performing artists, musicians and writers. This allows for sounder theoretical discussions and empirical investigations of the spatial distribution and the spatial dynamics of creative people, avoiding the fuzzy definition of the creative class.

Secondly, besides the factors put forward by Florida (e.g. amenities, openness and tolerance), we consider a broad array of economic factors that are known to influence the mobility and growth of human capital. In this sense, Florida's hypotheses are confronted with concepts emphasizing regional productions systems, local labour markets and externalities (see Storper & Manville, 2006; Storper & Scott, 2008).[1]

The paper focuses on the following four questions:

(1) How are artists distributed across German regions?
(2) How does their distribution change over time?
(3) Which location factors are associated with the regional growth rates of freelance artists?
(4) To what extent can sub-groups of artists explain why their distribution, growth rates and other factors differ?

We seek to answer these questions using quantile regressions and a unique data set covering 412 German regions for the years 2007–2010.

The results show that population growth, the presence of universities, variations in crime rates and externalities explain the agglomeration of artists in regions. More precisely, population growth and localization externalities are identified as being two central determinants which influence the growth of regional artistic populations. It is also shown that some branches of artists (e.g. visual artists and writers) experience negative growth effects if they are over-proportionally present in a region. Moreover, our study identifies considerable heterogeneity within the group of artists when it comes to factors explaining their regional agglomeration over time.

The paper is structured as follows. The next section lays out the theoretical background on the agglomeration of the creative class in space. Section 3 introduces the data and the empirical approach. Then Section 4 introduces the empirical model, the results are presented and discussed in Section 5. Section 6 concludes the study.

2. Theoretical Considerations

The debate about the creative class has received considerable attention in the Economic Geography literature. Florida (2002a, 2005a, 2005b, 2008) prominently argues that the agglomeration of members of the creative class in particular regions can stimulate its economic development and prosperity. He puts forward the concept of the "3 Ts" to describe the relationship between tolerance, talents and technology. The starting point of the chain of arguments is an open and tolerant climate in urban and amenity-rich places. This climate then attracts members of the creative class who are highly mobile and react to this stimulus by migrating. Subsequently, the resulting geographical agglomeration of members of the creative class draws high-tech-companies seeking human capital to the region, which in turn leads to higher start-up rates of technology-based companies. Members of the creative class might even begin the latter themselves. As a result, a cumulative process of knowledge and technology-based growth is induced (Florida, 2002a).

Consequently, researchers try to understand the reasons behind variations in the agglomeration of members of the creative class across regions. Studies dealing with this issue can broadly be attributed to two different streams of literature. On the one hand, there are the studies building on the ideas of Richard Florida, and these particularly emphasize the role of certain amenity-related factors. In contrast, there is a more traditional view which sees the economic factors relating to the structure of regions' economies and population as the primary driving forces of the agglomeration of the creative class (Storper & Manville, 2006; Storper & Scott, 2008; Asheim & Hansen, 2009). We first present Florida's arguments in more detail before coming back to this literature. Some of the arguments relate to the creative class in general, while others are related to artists—which are subject to our empirical analyses—in particular.

2.1. Amenity-Related and Tolerance Factors

Florida argues that members of the creative class prefer to live in regions showing a number of characteristics, which means these regions are more likely to observe an agglomeration of creative people over time. In particular, this includes an open and tolerant climate and amenities. In Florida's view, tolerance reflects "low barriers to entry for human capital" (Florida, 2002b, p. 750). A tolerant environment is open to new ideas and entrepreneurs, and this means that it attracts human capital in general, but especially creative people who need such an environment to constantly develop new and unconventional ideas. In addition, Florida claims that creative people are eccentric and they may have faced discrimination themselves. They seek communities with people who share their values, or who are at least open-minded. The values include self-expression, sexual norms, gender roles and ecological awareness, which are all characteristics of tolerant societies (Florida, 2002a). He argues that tolerance helps to attract human capital, accelerates spill-overs and human capital externalities and reflects an environment that is risk-oriented and associated with self-expression (Florida et al., 2008).

Other dimensions are the tolerance towards foreigners and social capital. Florida (2002a) reports a positive correlation between the concentrations of foreign-born population members and creative class members, but negative correlations with respect to the share of the non-white population. However, research by Putnam (2007) highlights that ethnic diversity does not necessarily indicate tolerance. In the short run, ethnic diversity even seems to foster intolerance and lowers trust, altruism and community cooperation. Societies benefit from social integration only in the long run. Navarro *et al.* (2012) confirms this by identifying a negative effect of the share of foreigners on the concentration of the creative class in Spanish municipals.

This ambiguity suggests the existence of different types of social capital. For instance, Putnam (2000) differentiates between "bridging" and "bonding" social capital. Bonding social capital describes closed social groups, associations or networks. Individuals sharing similar characteristics form these groups. Such characteristics include gender, religion, sexual orientation, socioeconomic status, etc. In contrast, bridging social capital characterizes groups, associations or networks that link individuals that vary in these characteristics. Thus, the former scrutinizes the idea that social capital is always positive and facilitates externalities and spill-overs (Coffe & Geys, 2007; Geys & Murdoch, 2010).

Both types of social capital can be of particular importance for artists and conducive to a creative milieu. Artists heavily rely on (local) social interaction and trust to exploit their creativity economically (Banks *et al.*, 2000; Eikhof & Haunschild, 2006; Currid, 2010), making social capital an attractive regional characteristic.

Amenities matter in a similar fashion. "'Amenity' can mean many things, including good weather, a shore-line, ethnic diversity (or its absence), options for dining and entertainment, cultural offerings and aesthetically beautiful architecture" (Storper & Manville, 2006, p. 1252). Florida argues that these amenities have a crucial influence on the location decision of creative people. They desire self-fulfilment economically, but at the same time appreciate leisure (Florida, 2002a).

2.2. *Economic Factors*

Contrasting these amenity-related factors are economic location factors that influence the spatial distribution of the creative class and its dynamics. For some time these have been highlighted in concepts of regional productions systems, local labour markets, and externalities (see Storper & Manville, 2006; Storper & Scott, 2008).

The first, and somewhat, trivial reason for variations in the distribution of the creative class is the non-uniform distribution of the population. Naturally, highly populated cities are, all things being equal, home to more members of the creative class in absolute terms than smaller cities. What is more important is that the relationship between the population size and the presence of the creative class can induce different types of localization externalities. This may cause the spatial distribution of the creative class to differ from that of the general population.

The most important effects in this respect are related to localization/Marshal externalities (see Beaudry & Schiffauerova, 2009). These externalities may be subject to a critical mass effect, although if the absolute number of the creative class exceeds a certain threshold, positive localization externalities may unfold. One may think of potential knowledge spill-over, shared institutions, shared supplier and customer pools, and the benefits of local competition in this respect.

Related but not identical to this are localization externalities induced by the relative number of members of the creative class, meaning the relationship between the absolute number and a region's population matters.[2] Diametrical effects are possible in this case. On the one hand, a high relative agglomeration can foster knowledge spill-over effects, the awareness of creative communities and their political power (Currid, 2010). On the other hand, competition and rivalry for customers, suppliers and resources (e.g. public funding of arts) may rise as a consequence of an increasing relative agglomeration (Hauge & Hracs, 2010). Since some members of the creative class (e.g. artists) tend to be less prosperous in terms of resources they may be highly sensitive to increasing factor prices—e.g. affordable spaces for galleries—as a consequence of high relative agglomeration (Peck, 2005).

In addition to localization, the creative class may also be subject to urbanization & Jacobs externalities (Jacobs, 1969). For instance, a larger absolute number of the creative class may go hand in hand with higher diversity. This in turn increases the creative potential of knowledge spill-over.

Another relevant demographic characteristic is the age structure of a region's population. For instance, Bader and Scharenberg (2010) highlight the view that younger populations are generally more open to new ideas and are potentially more interested in cultural and artistic activities. For this reason, a young population may offer a more attractive consumer structure for artists.

Another characteristic of the regional economic structure is the relevance of tourism. Tourism is associated with artists, who in general are known to attract tourists from outside the region (Currid, 2009). Many artists provide products and services which are consumed by tourists. These products and services can relate to high culture like opera, museums and ballet or to popular culture like musicals, festivals and street culture. Accordingly, the higher demand for artists' products by tourists makes regions more attractive for some artists. The same applies to the general economic situation in a region, as regional income may determine the demand for the products and services of artists. However, artists seem to attach less importance to material aspects as they are more spatially mobile (Menger, 1999; Florida, 2002a; Markusen, 2006).

2.3. Research Gaps

Both literature streams provide good arguments for the influence of certain regional characteristics on the spatial distribution of the creative class. We therefore simultaneously consider the factors put forward in both streams. Given the existing empirical evidence on Florida's amenity-related factors, we expect these to be generally more relevant than the economic factors. This motivates the first hypothesis.

> H1: Amenity-related location factors have a stronger relative importance for the spatial agglomeration of artists than traditional factors.

Section 2.2 highlights the idea that, from a theoretical point of view, localization externalities are either related to the absolute number of the creative class living in a region or to their relative agglomeration. Most existing studies model these externalities as being related to the agglomeration of general economic activities—e.g. population density—in a region however (cf. Lorenzen & Andersen, 2009; Clifton et al., 2013).[3] Accordingly, there is still little empirical evidence on the source of localization externalities in this context, though we suspect it to be the most important factor among the economic factors. H2 takes up this issue:

H2: Localization externalities are the most important economic factor explaining the agglomeration of artists. These externalities emerge from the agglomeration of artists and not from the agglomeration of economic activity in a region.

When empirically testing the hypotheses, we also seek to overcome a number of weaknesses limiting many existing studies. The most important one relates to the definition of the creative class. Florida puts forward the notion that members of the creative class "... engage in complex problem solving that involves a great deal of independent judgment and requires high levels of education of human capital" (Florida, 2002a, p. 8). In contrast to common approaches in human capital literature, his definition is not based on individuals' educational attainment, and instead he refers to the individuals' occupation. Therefore the definition is based on what people do instead of what they know. Moreover, Florida divides the creative class into two groups. Members of the "Super-Creative Core" belong to professions like scientists, engineers, university professors, artists, designer, etc. They are "... producing new forms or designs that are readily transferable and widely useful ..." (Florida, 2002a, p. 69). The second group consists of workers in knowledge-intensive industries, financial services, legal services, health care and business management. This group is called "creative professionals". Their creativity shows in their ability to solve specific problems in everyday business (Florida, 2002a).

This straightforward conception is especially appealing to practitioners from economic or urban development agencies. However, it is subject to severe criticism within the scientific community. These critics in particular refer to the "fuzzy" definition of who belongs to the creative class.

For instance, Markusen (2006) argues that Florida conflates creativity with high levels of education. In addition, Glaeser (2005), using simple regression models, shows that a variable for education attainment outperforms the creative core variable in explaining regional economic growth.

Florida's definition of the creative class is also problematic from an occupational point of view. It includes occupational subgroups that are arguably creative like dental hygienists, but it does not consider marine engineers. Moreover, the creative class is very heterogeneous, making common spatial behaviours or similar economic effects unlikely. Due to this heterogeneity, Markusen (2006) even refuses to call it "class" according to the sociological or political conception. "Corporate lawyers are conservative while trial lawyers are liberal; engineers tend to be moderate to conservative, and artists more liberal" (Markusen, 2006). Using Florida's definition of "creative class" consequently makes it difficult to "... disentangle which effects on local performances are due to their creativeness and which to their education" (Marrocu & Paci, 2012, p. 371).

In the empirical investigation we therefore focus on just one particular subgroup of the creative class, namely artists. Artists are undoubtedly creative and members of Florida's creative class: "... the presence of a significant bohemian concentration signals a regional environment or milieu that reflects an underlying openness to innovation and creativity. This milieu is both open to and attractive to other talented and creative individuals" (Florida, 2002b, p. 56).

One may even say that artists pioneer the preferences of the whole (however being defined) creative class (Lorenzen & Andersen, 2009).

Despite being a subgroup of the creative class, artists are still heterogeneous from an occupational point of view. They are subject to a variety of production and consumption schemes. For instance, visual artists and writers can easily transport their work over distances, whereas for musicians and performing artists—at least partly—co-location to their consumer (i.e. their audience) is a necessity. Writers and visual artists frequently work on their own. In contrast, performing artists and musicians usually need to cooperate and build teams in order to become successful (Markusen, 2006). Such differences in production and consumption schemes are likely to have severe implications for artists' spatial behaviour. For instance, it seems reasonable that visual artists and writers are most free in their location decisions, while musicians and performing artists are more likely to prefer to be close to other artists.

In summary, we follow Florida in that the creative class has a specific economic value that is primarily related to what they actually do and less related to its members' formal education, however, at least in the empirical analyses, it is essential to consider the specifics of the production and consumption schemes to which artists are subject. This is because these schemes define incentives and boundaries to individuals' spatial behaviour. Artists are no exception in this respect. This motivates the third hypothesis of the paper.

H3: Specifics of production and consumption schemes shape the spatial agglomeration processes of artists. In the case of artists, these schemes particularly alter the influence of localization externalities.

3. Empirical Approach and Data

3.1. *Dependent Variables*

Missing longitudinal data frequently constrains researchers to cross-sectional investigations, and these dominate the existing empirical research on the spatial agglomeration of the creative class (see, e.g. Hansen, 2007; Clifton, 2008; Florida *et al.*, 2008; Boschma & Fritsch, 2009; Fritsch & Stuetzer, 2009). However, agglomeration processes are dynamic in their very nature, so cross-sectional analysis delivers only limited insights into these processes. Thanks to the availability of panel data, we follow the few existing studies that apply a dynamic approach (cf. Wenting, 2008; Wedemeier, 2010).

Econometrically, we seek to identify regional factors correlating to the growth of regional artist populations. We first estimate the growth rate of an artist population in region "r" on the basis of its relative annual (*t*) growth for each year between "2007" and "2010":

$$\Delta \text{Artists}_{t,r} = \frac{\text{Artists}_{t,r} - \text{Artists}_{t-1,r}}{\text{Artists}_{t-1,r}}.$$

In order to reduce the effect of stochastic noise in the growth rates, we focus on the (normalized) mean growth rate from 2007 to 2010.

$$\Delta \text{Artists}_r = \frac{\sum_{p=1}^{P} (\Delta \text{Artists}_{p,r} - \Delta \text{Artists}_p)}{P}$$

with *p* indicating the period (2007–2008, 2009–2009, 2009–2010), *P* the number of periods, and $\Delta \text{Artists}_p$ as average growth of artists in Germany.

Information on the annual growth of artists is derived from data of the Social Security Insurance for Artists and Writers ("Künstlersozialkasse"). This organization was introduced in West Germany in 1983 and the new federal states in 1992. Its purpose is to integrate freelance artists and writers into the social insurance system by contributing to the members' premium for compulsory statutory pension, health and long-term nursing care insurance. Members are visual and performing artists, musicians, journalists and people teaching in these fields. Their activities have to be profit-oriented and they have to be recognized as an artist/writer in their professional community (Künstlersozialkasse, 2011).

Freelance artists are a minority in the creative class in Germany. According to Fritsch and Stuetzer (2012) creative occupations only amount to 14.3% on the whole work force in 2007. Creative professionals account for 11.8%, the creative core for 2.2%, and employed bohemians, 0.2%. The share of freelance artists is even lower, with barely 0.2% (Fritsch & Stuetzer, 2012, pp. 8–9).

Following Fritsch and Stuetzer (2009), we use German districts (Kreise) as units of observation. These regions represent the smallest spatial units for which such data are available. There are 412 of these administrative units in Germany in the year 2010.

For these 412 districts, we know the numbers of residing artists for each year between 2007 and 2010. The numbers can be disaggregated into four branches: visual arts, performing arts, musicians and writers. Our data cover only a subsample of all German artists and writers, as we observe only self-employed artists, leaving all artists in dependent employment unobserved. By looking at those freelancers, we capture the (potentially) most mobile group of artists because their geographic mobility is not constrained by job-availability. Or, in the words of Markusen (2006, p. 1926): "High levels of self-employment make plausible some of the claims made for creative class members—that they are more footloose and apt to choose a place to live before committing to employment or marketing efforts." Moreover, if these artists expand their businesses they are likely to hire other artists as dependent employees, and this makes them a pull-factor for the mobility of other artists. Nevertheless, caution is needed when generalizing our findings to artists working in dependent employment.

3.2. Independent Variables

3.2.1. Economic factors explaining migration.

For the 412 regions, we seek to identify the characteristics that explain growth or decline in regional artist populations. In the following section a number of regional characteristics are presented that are most likely to play a role in this context.

The first block of regional characteristics represents economic factors or variables which are central in traditional theories on spatial human capital accumulation and concentration.

The first and probably most important factor in this respect is "the absolute agglomeration of artists" (ART07) in the year 2007. It is an indicator of a critical mass of artists present in a region. As discussed in Section 2, such a critical mass is needed to unfold localization externalities which can stimulate the regional growth of the number of artists.

Contrasting these are localization externalities related to the "relative number of artists per inhabitant" (ARTPC07), or artists' spatial agglomeration. These effects are not related to the absolute number of artists of regions, but are instead related to their relative importance in the local economy. The two factors approximating localization externalities are constructed from the same data as the dependent variable.

Factor UNI encompasses the "number of graduates from artistic" and those from "cultural disciplines" (per inhabitants), "the number of students" (per 1000 inhabitants) and the "share of inhabitants between 18 and 30". Therefore we capture artists that are endogenously "created" within a region. The share of young population and students indicates, at least in innovation-driven economies, a tolerant and vibrant environment which is open to new ideas and interested in cultural and artistic activities, and therefore might be particularly important for artists (Bader & Scharenberg, 2010).

Information about the numbers of university graduates for the two disciplines was obtained from the Federal Statistics Office of Germany. Statistics about the number of students and the share of young population was obtained from the INKAR data set.

The factor TOUR is foremost related to the "number of beds per tourist enterprise" and "the number of overnight stays per tourist enterprise" in 2007. It controls for touristic activities in a region. Natural amenities like the forest area, water area and recreation area per inhabitant are associated with this factor as well.

We further consider the factor EAST. Due to the different social, economical and political developments of West Germany and the former GDR after World War II there are still significant structural differences between the two parts of Germany. These differences manifest in a high regional "unemployment rate" and financial support by the state or related organizations in East German regions ("support of urban development, KfW support of infrastructure development, GRW support of infrastructure development (€ per inhab)").

Two additional factors are population growth (ΔPOP) and GDP per capita growth (ΔGDP). They are primarily used as control variables. The first, population growth, is particularly important, because given a stable share of artists in a population, the population growth will also induce an increase in the number of artists in a region.

Information on the variables used to construct the regional factors (TOUR, UNI, EAST, ΔPOP, ΔGDP) is taken from the INKAR ("Indikatoren und Karten zur Raum- und Stadtentwicklung") data set which is published by the Federal Institute for Research on Building, Urban Affairs and Spatial Development (BBSR, 2012) or from the Federal Statistics Office of Germany.

3.2.2. *Amenity and tolerance factors.* The second block summarizes the factors that are particularly emphasized by Florida to make regions attractive for the creative class, i.e. artists.

The German Weather Service (Deutscher Wetterdienst, DWD) provides data for the first factor in this set ("30 yearly mean of temperature", "number of sunshine hours" and "precipitation"). The variable "mean temperature per year over 30 years" for a region shows the highest loadings and serves as a proxy for natural amnesties. Research from Glaeser *et al.* (2001) provides evidence for the effect of the climate on the distribution of human capital. Moreover, Florida (2002a) claims that the creative class are more attracted by amenities than overall human capital in general.

We consider crime as a disamenity impacting regions' attractiveness for movers. There exists considerable evidence that crime or the change of crime levels influences the population growth of cities and neighbourhoods (Cullen & Levitt, 1999; Ellen & O'Regan, 2009). However, we argue that artists are particularly sensitive to high crime rates.

Lloyd (2002) shows with a case study of Wicker Park in Chicago, and Pratt (2009) on Hoxton in London, that artists occupy run-down neighbourhoods and help to transform them. Accordingly, the factor CRIME is likely to influence the spatial distribution of artists. The variables "street crime offences per inhabitant" and the "robberies per inhabitant" are most associated with this factor. Information on these two variables is taken from the so-called "Deutscher Lernatlas 2011" (German learning atlas 2011), which is published by the Bertelsmann foundation (Bertelsmann Stiftung, 2011).

Lorenzen and Andersen (2009) empirically investigate the rank size rule of the creative class compared to that of the rest of the population. They show that the slope for the creative class is steeper. Their explanation is that members of the creative class are attracted to central places because of specialized consumer preferences (e.g. restaurants, cafés, entertainment, museums) and specialized job preferences (employees who work in high-technology industries) (Lorenzen & Andersen, 2009). According to Florida (2002a), this especially applies to artists, who will therefore be overrepresented in urban areas. We take this argument into consideration with the factor URBAN. It is mainly loaded to the variables "population density" and "price of construction land (€ per m^2)". Information for these variables is again taken from the INKAR database. In addition, the factor URBAN comprises the variables "share of foreigners" and "share of unemployed foreigners". These two variables relate to the importance of openness and tolerance in attracting creative class members (Florida, 2002a). They not only account for tolerance, but also capture the quality of foreigner integration into the regional society or regional labour market, respectively. Both are obtained from the "Lernatlas" as well.

One might argue that urbanity and tolerance towards foreigners might play different roles in attracting creative-class members, but they cannot be statistically disintegrated in our analysis.

Social capital is also considered because it is an important pull-factor for artists. The factor SOCIAL is strongly correlated with the "share of inhabitants committed to churches and religion", "committed to youth" and *committed to elderly*. The *Lernatlas* serves as a data source here.

Lastly, the factor CUL_AMENITY can be identified. The variables "visitors of museums (per 100 inhab.)" and "visitors of theatres and concerts (per household)" load high on this factor, whereas, "the number of cinema screens (per 100,000 inhab.)" are only weakly associated with this factor. Therefore CUL_AMENITY mainly represents the consumption of high culture in a region. The variables are derived from the INKAR data set.

3.2.3. *Reducing the dimensionality.* For the construction of the variables, we generally use the average of their annual values over the four years 2007–2010. However, this is not possible for all variables because the time series is not available or is unreliable due to reforms in the district delineations. In these instances we use the corresponding values of 2008 or 2009 (see Table A1 in the appendix).

The previously presented regional characteristics are empirically strongly correlated, and many of them are likely to approximate the same (underlying) regional factor. We take this into account and reduce the dimensionality by means of a factor analysis. The factor analysis groups variables were based on their common statistical variance in order to extract a smaller number of factors. The number of factors is determined using the Kaiser criterion. It suggests extracting as many factors as there are eigenvalues larger than one in the variables' correlation matrix (see Figure A1 in the appendix). According to this criterion, we extract eight factors from the 33 regional characteristics. The eight factors are then interpreted according to the rotated factor matrix providing information on the variables' loading (see Table A1 in the appendix).

However, not all regional characteristics enter the factor analysis. We excluded those variables that are of a different kind and those that are of special interest from a theoretical point of view. The factor analysis condenses only level variables. In light of their dynamic nature, population growth and GDP per capita growth are not included, but instead remain independent control variables. The relative and absolute numbers of artists per region play an outstanding role (see theoretical discussion in Section 2) and therefore these factors are also kept independent.

The extracted factors and the four independent variables are summarized in Table A1 in the appendix.

4. Model

Figure 1 visualizes the non-normal distribution of the mean annual (trend-corrected) growth rates. We rely on quantile regressions (also known as least-absolute deviation regression), because they are less impacted by outliers and more appropriate when the dependent variable is not Gaussian (see for a discussion Koenker & Hallock, 2001; Coad & Rao, 2006). To further increase the reliability of the results, we employ bootstrapped standard errors allowing for robust and reliable statistical inference (Elfron, 1979).

In addition, our statistical analysis shows that the growth rates are not spatially auto-correlated (Moran's $I = 0.04$, sig. $= 0.08$) and the residuals of the quantile regression analysis (Moran's $I = 0.04$, sig. $= 0.10$). As a result we do not need to account for geographic dependencies in the estimations.

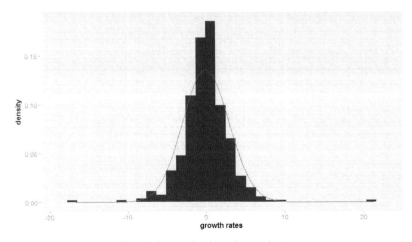

Figure 1. Distribution of growth rates.
Source: KSK, own calculation.

5. Empirical Results

5.1. *Spatial Distribution of Freelance Artists in Germany*

Before presenting the results of our analyses, we provide some brief impressions on artists' spatial distribution and its change over time. The map in Figure 2 illustrates artists' relative and absolute spatial distribution in Germany in the year 2010. The mean is about 422 artists per district (SD = 1819.2).[4] Not surprisingly, the largest number of artists is

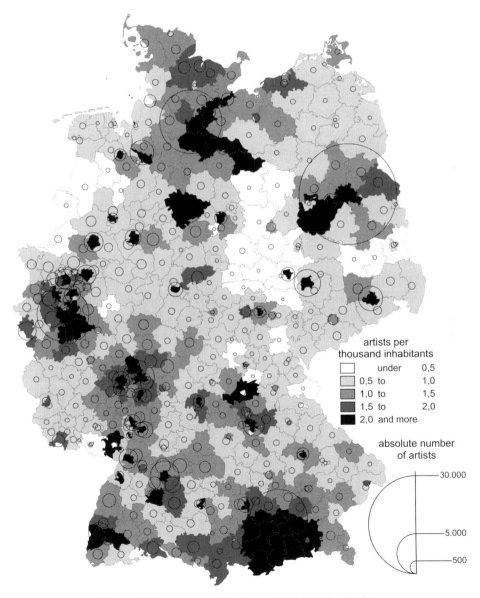

Figure 2. Distribution of freelance artists 2010 by districts.
Source: KSK, own calculation.

found in Berlin (31,525). Next is Hamburg with 12,642 artists, which is followed by Munich (10,646), Cologne (8665), and Düsseldorf (3220). A correlation test confirms that the absolute number of artists and the size of the regional population strongly correlate ($r = 0.9^{***}$).[5]

Interesting insights are also obtained by looking at the distribution of the relative artist numbers. The mean of all regions is 1.36 artists per inhabitant (SD = 1.16). While Berlin still ranks first with 9.1 artists per 1000 inhabitants, Cologne (8.6) now ranks second, and Munich third (7.9). The two cities are followed by Hamburg (7.1) and Freiburg im Breisgau (6.7). These patterns suggest that artists do indeed prefer living in urban regions, which is further substantiated by the correlation of $r = 0.6^{***}$ between the share of artists and population density.

Figure 2 reveals some surprising agglomerations of artists. For instance, significant agglomerations of artists are observed in regions on the coast of the Baltic Sea, in the Alpine foreland, and in a number of other rather remote regions. Since these regions are known as very touristic places, it may hint at this factor being relevant.

Some further interesting insights are gained when disaggregating the numbers of artists into different branches. Figure 3 depicts the share of artists from four different branches in 2010. The largest branch is visual artists, next are musicians, writers and performing artists.

The spatial distribution of the four branches somewhat diverges from that of the aggregated one (see Table 1). While the absolute rankings are still dominated by large cities (Berlin, Hamburg, etc.), some comparatively smaller cities such as Hanover and Stuttgart appear to be important locations for artists of particular branches.

The importance of smaller cities becomes even more evident when the numbers of artists are set into a relationship with the regional population size. For instance, relative to its population, Düsseldorf has the second highest agglomeration of visual artists. Freiburg im Breisgau is (in relative terms) an important region for performing artists, and even more important for musicians. Musicians in particular turn out to be less concentrated in big cities—Weimar and Freiburg im Breisgau ranking first and second—as compared to

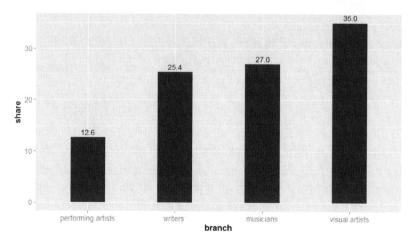

Figure 3. Share of branches 2010.
Source: KSK, own calculation.

Table 1. Ranking of the distribution of freelance artists per branch

	All artists		Visual artists		Performing artists		Musicians		Writers	
Rank	Absolute	Per inhabitants	Absolute	Per inhabitants	Absolute	Per inhabitants	Absolute	Per inhabitants	Absolute	Per inhabitants
1	Berlin	Berlin	Berlin	Berlin	Berlin	Berlin	Berlin	Weimar	Berlin	Cologne
2	Hamburg	Cologne	Hamburg	Düsseldorf	Hamburg	Cologne	Hamburg	Freiburg i. B.	Hamburg	Munich
3	Munich	Munich	Munich	Munich	Cologne	Munich	Munich	Berlin	Munich	Berlin
4	Cologne	Hamburg	Cologne	Hamburg	Munich	Freiburg i. B.	Cologne	Cologne	Cologne	Hamburg
5	Düsseldorf	Freiburg i. B.	Düsseldorf	Cologne	Stuttgart	Hamburg	Hanover	Karlsruhe	Frankfurt a. M.	Starnberg
6	Frankfurt a. M.	Weimar	Frankfurt a. M.	Starnberg	Frankfurt a. M.	Potsdam	Frankfurt a. M.	Hamburg	Düsseldorf	Bonn
7	Stuttgart	Starnberg	Stuttgart	Darmstadt	Düsseldorf	Weimar	Stuttgart	Würzburg	Leipzig	Freiburg i. B.
8	Hanover	Düsseldorf	Hanover	Weimar	Hanover	Stuttgart	Leipzig	Munich	Stuttgart	Frankfurt a. M.
9	Leipzig	Frankfurt a. M.	Leipzig	Freiburg i. B.	Leipzig	Düsseldorf	Dresden	Starnberg	Hanover	Heidelberg
10	Dresden	Potsdam	Dresden	Stuttgart	Dresden	Starnberg	Bremen	Leipzig	Bonn	Düsseldorf
11	Bremen	Stuttgart	Bremen	Landsberg a. L.	Bremen	Frankfurt a. M.	Freiburg i. B.	Dresden	Bremen	Landsberg a. L.
12	Freiburg i. B.	Darmstadt	Nuremberg	Frankfurt a. M.	Freiburg i. B.	Leipzig	Düsseldorf	Heidelberg	Rhein-Sieg-Kreis	Potsdam
13	Nuremberg	Landsberg a. L.	Münster	Münster	Nuremberg	Münster	Karlsruhe	Stuttgart	Freiburg i. B.	Leipzig
14	Bonn	Leipzig	Karlsruhe	Potsdam	Essen	Darmstadt	Nuremberg	Regensburg	Munich, Land	Mainz
15	Essen	Münster	Freiburg i. B.	Karlsruhe	Bonn	Baden-Baden	Essen	Mainz	Dresden	Munich, Land

Source: KSK, own calculation.

the other branches. The ranking for writers suggests that these have a preference for an urban environment, because cities like Cologne, Munich, Berlin and Hamburg are ranked high, however an attractive landscape (Starnberg[6]) seems to be a valid substitute.

To get a better understanding of the extent to which artists are spatially concentrated we estimate the coefficient of variation (CV).[7] Accordingly, performing artists are most concentrated (CV = 5.85), followed by writers (CV = 4.95), visual artists (CV = 4.23), and musicians (CV = 3.16). Compared to the overall population (CV = 1.16), the spatial concentration of artists proves to be very high. We also find a very skewed distribution of the share of artists in certain branches per region (Figure 4). The share of musicians varies most strongly, with values between 0.0% and 100.0% (SD = 8.8).

This implies that there are regions without any registered self-employed musicians and there are other regions that exclusively host this type of artist. The share of the other branches varies much less (SD: 6.3–7.8). In general, most regions show a mix of artistic branches.

5.2. Change of the Distribution over Time

The number of artists in German regions increased by 7.5% from 161,958 in the year 2007 to 174,086 artists in 2010 (Figure 5).

Regional growth rates between 2007 and 2010 range from 38.5% to 80.0%. The mean growth is 5.6%, with the standard deviation being 9.1%. Accordingly, we find considerable variation in regional growth. This is visualized in Figure 2, showing the growth of artists per region between 2007 and 2010. Interestingly, we observe a quite ambiguous pattern: regions with fast growing artist populations are large core regions like Hamburg, Berlin and Dresden and remote regions with low population counts such as Weimar, some regions on the Baltic Coast and some regions near the Alpine Foreland. A similar picture is obtained for negative growth rates that characterize regions with substantial agglomerations (share of artists in total population) of artists (e.g. Freiburg im Breisgau) and regions with low artist agglomerations (e.g. Bamberg). However, Table 2 reveals that the most extreme growth between 2007 and 2010 is observed for regions

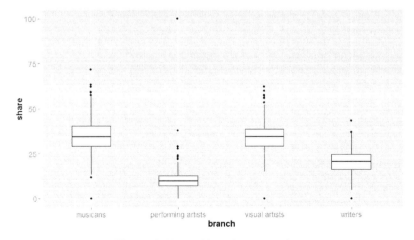

Figure 4. Share of branches per region.
Source: KSK, own calculation.

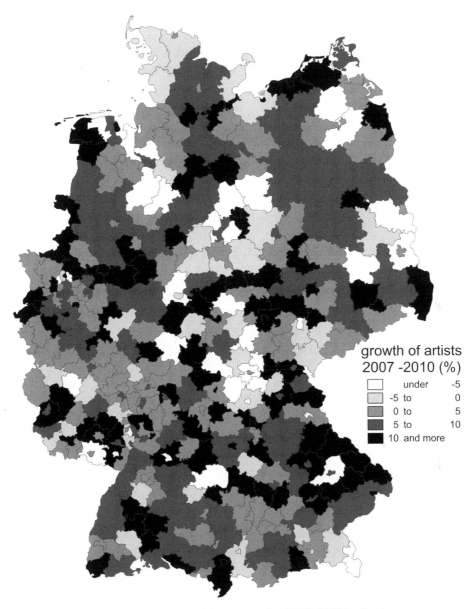

Figure 5. Growth rates of freelance artists 2007–2010 by districts.
Source: KSK, own calculation.

with low absolute numbers of artists. However, it is not a size effect that explains the magnitude of growth, as the correlation between growth and the number of artists in a region is insignificant (Figure 6; see also Figure 7).

The growth patterns of the four branches differ considerably: The number of performing artists grew fastest, by 11.8% from 2007 to 2010. They are followed by musicians with 10.0%, writers with 6.6%, and visual artists with a 4.8% growth (Figure 8).

Table 2. Ranking of growth rates 2007–2010

Rank	Name	Absolute	Percentage
1	Burgenlandkreis	10	80.0
2	Kroch	11	34.9
3	Tirschenreuth	8	31.4
4	Nordvorpommern	21	28.6
5	Remscheid	18	27.9
⋮			
44	Berlin	4203	15.4
⋮			
121	Hamburg	1015	8.7
⋮			
181	Cologne	568	7.0
⋮			
211	Munich	490	4.8
⋮			
267	Düsseldorf	61	1.9
⋮			
408	Peine	−14	−16.2
409	Cochem-Zell	−10	−17.1
410	Straubing-Bogen	−14	−17.6
411	Suhl	−11	−25.9
412	Altmarkkreis Salzwedel	−21	−38.5

Source: KSK, own calculation.

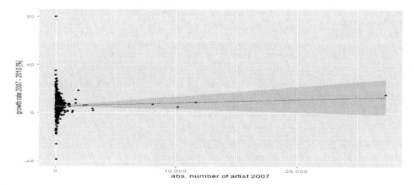

Figure 6. Correlation of growth rates and number of freelance artists.
Source: KSK, own calculation.

5.3. *Factors Explaining the Variation in Regional Growth Rates of Freelance Artists*

5.3.1. Determinants of freelance artists' total population growth. The previous section highlighted the existence of significant variations in the growth of regional artist populations. In the following section we explore to what extent these relate to regions' endowments with Florida's amenity-related theory and with other economic factors.

The results of the quantile regressions are shown in Table 3. The first model (All) is estimated with respect to the growth in artists' total regional populations, i.e. no

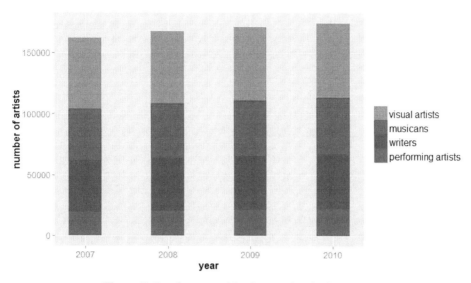

Figure 7. Development of freelance artists in Germany.
Source: KSK, own calculation.

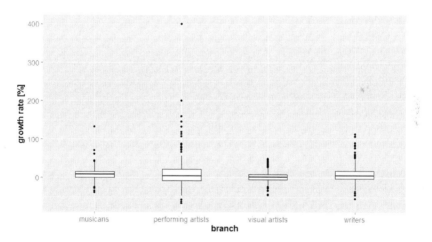

Figure 8. Regional growth rates of branches.
Source: KSK, own calculation.

differentiations are made between branches of artists. The other models represent the results for the four branches (musicians, writers, visual and performing artists).

The model for the growth of artists' total populations (All) reveals that population growth (ΔPOP) and urbanization (URBAN) are the best predictors for growth of regional artist populations. There might be two reasons for population growth to become significant. Firstly, increasing populations may "automatically" imply increasing numbers of artists if they represent a more or less fixed share of the population. In addition, population

Table 3. Quantile regressions

Variables	All	Musicians	Writers	Visual	Performing
ART07	0				
ARTPC07	−0.208				
ΔPOP	0.462**	0.420	0.402	0.470**	0.242
ΔGDP	−0.016	0.015	−0.058	−0.018	−0.120
EAST	0.322	−0.665	0.548	0.700**	0.559
URBAN	−0.404**	−0.082	0.155	−0.308	−0.705
UNI	−0.065	0.007	0.264	−0.187	1.547***
TOUR	0.047	0.239	0.085	−0.088	0.196
CRIME	0.129	0.009	−0.093	0.607**	0.152
SOCIAL	0.071	−0.297	0.042	0.082	0.170
TEMP	−0.153	−0.087	0.130	−0.135	0.560
CUL_AMENITIES	−0.205	−0.374	−0.291	0.073	−0.202
MUSIC07		0.001			
MUSICPC07		−1.033			
PERF07					0.007
PERFPC07					−11.888
VIS07				0.001	
VISPC07				−1.010*	
WRIT07			0.002		
WRITPC07			−5.426**		
(Intercept)	0.703	0.874	0.851	0.841*	0.074

Source: KSK, own calculation.
Signif. codes, ***0.01; **0.05; *0.1.

growth makes regions more attractive for artists as it implies an increasing demand for artistic products and services.

In contrast to Florida's argumentation, we do not find artist populations growing stronger in urban regions. On the contrary, the factor URBAN is negatively related to growth rates. This factor is strongly associated with an urban environment (higher population density and prices of construction land), and with the presence of foreigners and their participation in the labour market (see factor loadings in Table A1 in the appendix). Higher cost of living in cities can explain the negative effects. Artists are less prosperous in economic terms than the rest of the creative class, therefore they are more sensible to increasing factor prices—e.g. affordable spaces for galleries—as a consequence of high relative agglomeration (Peck, 2005).

Putnam (2007) delivers insight about the negative effects of the presence of foreigners. His research reveals that in the short run ethnic diversity fosters intolerance and lowers trust, altruism and community cooperation, and only in the long run can societies benefit from social integration.

Another explanation is that in the observed period there is tendency of convergence of the concentration of regional artists'. Urban regions with a relatively high level of artists' concentration did not grow as fast as urban regions with a comparatively low level of artists' concentration.

No other factors show significance in the model, and therefore we can evaluate our first two hypotheses with respect to the factors driving the growth of artists' populations in regions. According to hypotheses H1, Florida's amenity-related factors are expected to be more relevant than the economic factors. We clearly reject this hypothesis with respect to natural or cultural amenities. None of these factors are significantly related to artists' growth rates. Nevertheless, urbanity and tolerance—two other factors put forward by Florida—seem to have effects on artists, but are diametrical to his argumentation. Moreover, we have to reject hypothesis H2. There is no statistical evidence that agglomeration effects related to the size of regional artists populations impact the latters' growth.

5.3.2. *Differences between the branches.* The models for the four artist branches reveal the existence of significant differences between the branches. Population growth positively relates to the growth of regional communities of visual artists. A similar effect is not observable for the other three branches. This finding might hint at the relevance of variations of production and consumption schemes among the branches. Visual artists are more strongly dependent on local demand and cannot advertise their products and services as easily as artists of other branches. In particular, for writers it seems very reasonable to assume that they are able to transmit their products (i.e. written text) easily across large geographical distances. Similarly, the products and services offered by performing artists and musicians are relatively unaffected by geographical distance as these artists frequently go on tours outside their home region.

We observe positive and significant coefficients for CRIME and EAST in the model of visual artists' population growth, though the results are somewhat counter-intuitive. Why would visual artists in particular be attracted to regions showing above-average crime rates? The same applies to EAST, which suggests that these artists' populations grow more in regions belonging to the former GDR. A potential explanation for both coefficients might be that visual artists seek regions offering abundant and cheap space to set up art galleries and studios. This is particularly the case for regions in the former GDR, with low property prices and available space in abandoned industrial properties. The radical break with the past not only freed space literally, but also figuratively by providing opportunities to transform cultural and social norms by artistic means. However, this explanation remains speculative at the moment and calls for more research on the individual level.

Visual artists are the only artists benefiting from population growth. This might be due to the fact that especially performing artists and musicians present their performances to wider audiences by touring. In contrast, visual artists seem to be more dependent on their home base. Their art is likely more strongly related to the local context and refers to symbolic, historical and localized knowledge, which is particularly meaningful for local communities.

In contrast to the overall model, localization externalities matter in explaining the growth of visual artists and writer populations. According to our results, the two branches are subject to negative localization effects that come into effect when these artists are overrepresented in the regional population (negative coefficient of VISPC07 and WRITPC07). Visual artists are particularly dependent on the public support of cultural infrastructure such as museums and galleries, and as a result negative externalities may arise when public expenditures for this infrastructure, which constitute supply and demand, do not rise proportionally to their numbers. In contrast to visual artists, we lack a persuasive explanation in the case of writers. As argued above, the local surroundings of writers impact their supply and demand conditions only to a limited extent. We also expected that these individuals particularly benefit from intensive interaction and exchange with other writers. Accordingly, this finding clearly contradicts our expectations and deserves more research in the future.

Performing artists' populations increase more in regions characterized by a student milieu (positive coefficient UNI). There are three probable explanations. Firstly, performing artists are comparatively immobile, and therefore they frequently remain in the region where they obtain their university degree. Secondly, university students represent an important demand group for their products and services. Thirdly, university regions are usually characterized by the presence of highly educated individuals, i.e. people who work in the high-tech industries which also strongly demand the performances of these artists.

The results for the models on the disaggregated artists' growth rates clearly suggest that hypothesis H3 has to be confirmed. Specific production and consumption schemes of artist branches alter the effect of regional factors on the agglomeration of artists. In this sense, artists are a heterogeneous group, implying that we can confirm hypothesis H2 exclusively for visual artists and writers. We do not find an effect of localization externalities for the branches of musicians and performing artists. This heterogeneity among artists is confirmed by Faggian et al. (2012). These authors also find pronounced differences within the group of bohemian graduates regarding their spatial behaviour and careers (location choice, starting a job, full vs. part time work, income and self-employment).

However, we do not find convincing evidence for the relevance of amenity-related factors emphasized by Florida and followers. With the exception of universities, no empirical evidence is found for the factors highlighted in this literature stream such as amenities, openness and, urbanity. Accordingly, we have to reject hypothesis H1 for models on the basis of the disaggregated artist growth rates as well.

6. Conclusion

The paper contributes to the on-going debate on what regional factors make regions attractive for the creative class. In order to avoid the problematic definition of the creative class, we focused on the spatial distribution of artists and its temporal change. Using quantile regression and panel data on 412 German districts, it was shown that the amenity-related factors put forward by Florida and followers fail to explain the agglomeration processes of artists. In contrast, the results clearly confirm the relevance of economic factors which are central in the literature on regional productions systems, local labour markets and externalities. Next to population growth, urbanity, crime and localization externalities in particular play significant roles. Such externalities are related to negative effects which come into existence when the number of regional artists becomes too large in comparison to the population.

The paper delivers two more advancements to the existing literature. Firstly, by disaggregating the group of artists into four branches, the paper identifies branch-specific production and consumption schemes altering the importance of regional factors. Accordingly, even this comparatively small group of artists is significantly heterogeneous when it comes to the factors explaining their regional agglomeration.

Secondly, the study advances existing empirical approaches on this topic. This particularly concerns its focus on artists' population growth instead of the more common empirical analysis of the absolute artist population size. In addition, it clearly concentrates on a subgroup of well-identifiable members of the creative class and models branch-specific localization externalities as a function of the number of artists in a region.

Nevertheless, there are a number of shortcomings that need to be pointed out. First and most importantly, the data do not allow for differentiating between endogenous growth and migration. The change in the number of artists in a region, i.e. migration, depends only to a certain extent on regionally exogenous factors. Despite the above-average spatial mobility of artists postulated (but not empirically backed up) by Florida, the change in the number of artists in any given region should depend more on the behaviour of the endogenous artists than on migration to and from that region. In terms of the stock (the endogenous stock of artists in a region), the question arises of whether it is growing or declining (independently of migration). In general, the characteristics of the region itself are likely to be more important as factors in the changes in the number of endogenous artists than those of other regions. When investigating the importance of particular regional factors, many studies—including the present study—just look at the net change in the number of members of the creative class in that region. However, this number is subject to inter-regional migration of members and changes in the endogenous stock of members. Regional factors of the kind investigated in the present study may play completely different roles in the two processes. For instance, universities provide degrees of artistic or cultural disciplines and thereby "transform" inhabitants into artists. They also attract young people interested in a career in a creative job or sector from outside the region. When they graduate, those students stay in their university's region and enlarge its population of the creative class (Florida et al., 2008). These two different roles remain unobserved when investigating the net change in the number of regional creative class. Accordingly, future studies need to disaggregate the net change into the net result of migration and the net change due to regional endogenous processes. Regional characteristics then need to be evaluated to see whether they have an impact on migration decisions or if they stimulate a region's endogenous potential of the creative class.

The second shortcoming of the present study is the potential underestimation of the role of amenities, because our indicators predominantly focus on cultural and natural amenities. Other amenities might be relevant as well. For instance, we did not test for the "coolness" of German regions, which Florida claims to matter in this respect (Florida, 2002a).

It is generally difficult to empirically approximate intangible location characteristics like amenity-related factors. Accordingly, the larger explanatory power of economic factors in our models might be due to the fact that the available statistical data capture their inter-regional variance more precisely than in the case of amenity-related factors

Thirdly, our analyses made use of regionally aggregated data. Accordingly, we missed processes at the micro (individual) level (e.g. gender, age, income, etc.), which might be unrelated to regional characteristics. Future research therefore needs to employ data at the individual level, including information on artists' spatial mobility.

Despite these shortcomings, our findings have crucial implications for policy-makers in general, and particularly for those who are potentially inspired by Florida's ideas to support the regional agglomeration of the creative class. Firstly, this concerns the questionable importance of amenities, because we did not find them to be associated with any empirical effect on the agglomeration of artists. Secondly, support programmes need to seriously consider the significant differences among the groups of artists. Given the severe heterogeneity within this relatively small sub-group of the creative class, it may be doubtful whether suitable policies can be designed for the creative class as a whole (for a detailed discussion, see Sternberg, 2012).

Acknowledgements

This work was prepared in the context of the research project "Creative Lower Saxony: regional distribution, spatial mobility, start-up potentials and economic relevance of creative people". Our thanks go to the participants of the third research seminar "Creative Regions in Europe: Challenges and Opportunities" of the Regional Studies Association Research Network in Copenhagen for their helpful comments on an earlier version of this article. Moreover, we would like to thank Jürgen Schneider from the Social Security Insurance for Artists and Writers providing regional data on artists and the anonymous referees for their useful suggestions.

Funding

The project was funded by the Ministry for Science and Culture of Lower Saxony [grant number 76202-17-5/10] in the period from 2011 to 2015.

Notes

1. We distinguish between economic and amenity-related location factors. One can find the distinction between soft and hard location factors in the literature, too.
2. Following Brenner (2004), we call the relative number of members of the creative class in relation to the overall population "relative agglomeration".
3. A potential reason for this might be the lack of longitudinal data, which is a requirement for such analyses.
4. SD = standard deviation.
5. *, ** and *** indicate significance at the levels of .1, .05 and .001, respectively.
6. Starnberg is located between Munich and the Alps with the beautiful landscape of Lake Starnberg.
7. The variation coefficient is the ratio of a variable's standard deviation and mean.

References

Asheim, B. & Hansen, H. K. (2009) Knowledge bases, talents, and contexts: On the usefulness of the creative class approach in Sweden, *Economic Geography*, 85(4), pp. 425–442.
Bader, I. & Scharenberg, A. (2010) The sound of berlin: Subculture and the global music industry, *International Journal of Urban and Regional Research*, 34(1), pp. 76–91.
Banks, M., Lovatt, A., O'Connor, J., & Raffo, C. (2000) Risk and trust in the cultural industries, *Geoforum*, 31(3), pp. 453–464.
BBSR. (2012) *Indikatoren und Karten zur Raum- und Stadtentwicklung in Deutschland und in Europa* [Indicators and Maps of Urban and Regional Development in Germany and Europe]. CD-ROM. Bonn.
Beaudry, C. & Schiffauerova, A. (2009) Who's right, Marshall or Jacobs? The localization versus urbanization debate, *Research Policy*, 38(2), pp. 318–337.
Bertelsmann Stiftung. (2011). *Deutscher Lernatlas 2011* [German Learning Atlas 2011]. Available at http://www.deutscher-lernatlas.de (accessed 25 February 2012).
Boschma, R. A. & Fritsch, M. (2009) Creative class and regional growth: Empirical evidence from seven European countries, *Economic Geography*, 85(4), pp. 391–423.
Brenner, T. (2004) *Local Industrial Clusters: Existence, Emergence and Evolution*. (London: Routledge).
Clark, T. N., Lloyd, R., Wong, K. K. & Jain, P. (2002) Amenities drive urban growth, *Journal of Urban Affairs*, 24(5), pp. 493–515.
Clifton, N. (2008) The "creative class" in the UK: An initial analysis, *Geografiska Annaler: Series B, Human Geography*, 90(1), pp. 63–82.
Clifton, N., Cooke, P. & Hansen, H. K. (2013) Towards a reconciliation of the "context-less" with the "space-less"? The creative class across varieties of capitalism: New evidence from Sweden and the UK, *Regional Studies*, 47(2), pp. 201–215.
Coad, A. & Rao, R. (2006) Innovation and market value: A quantile regression analysis, *Economic Bulletin*, 15(13), pp. 1–10.

Coffe, H. & Geys, B. (2007) Toward an empirical characterization of bridging and bonding social capital, *Nonprofit and Voluntary Sector Quarterly*, 36(1), pp. 121–139.

Cullen, J. B. & Levitt, D. S. (1999) Crime, urban flight, and the consequences for cities, *The Review of Economics and Statistics*, 81(2), pp. 159–169.

Currid, E. (2009) Bohemia as subculture; "Bohemia" as industry: Art, culture, and economic development, *Journal of Planning Literature*, 23(4), pp. 368–382.

Currid, E. (2010) How art and culture happen in New York. Implications for urban economic development, *Journal of the American Planning Association*, 73(4), pp. 37–41.

Eikhof, D. R., & Haunschild, A. (2006) Lifestyle meets market: Bohemian entrepreneurs in creative industries, *Creativity and Innovation Management*, 15(3), pp. 234–241.

Elfron, B. (1979) Bootstrap methods: Another look at the Jackknife, *Annals of Statstics*, 7(1), pp. 1–26.

Ellen, I. G. & O'Regan, K. (2009) Crime and U.S. cities: Recent patterns and implications, *The Annals of the American Academy of Political and Social Science of the American Academy of Political and Social Science*, 626(1), pp. 22–38.

Faggian, A., Comunian, R., Jewell, S., & Kelly, U. (2012) Bohemian graduates in the UK: Disciplines and location determinants of creative careers, *Regional Studies*, 47(2), pp. 183–200.

Florida, R. (2002a) *The Rise of the Creative Class*. (New York: Basic Books).

Florida, R. (2002b) Bohemia and economic geography, *Journal of Economic Geography*, 2(1), pp. 55–71.

Florida, R. (2005a) *The Flight of the Creative Class: The New Global Competition for Talent*. (New York: HarperBusiness).

Florida, R. (2005b) *Cities and the Creative Class*. (London: Routledge).

Florida, R. (2008) *Who's Your City?: How the Creative Economy Is Making Where to You Live the Most Important Decision of Your Life*. (New York, NY: Basic Books).

Florida, R. & Mellander, C. (2010) There goes the metro: How and why Bohemians, artists and gays affect regional housing value, *Journal of Economic Geography*, 10(2), pp. 167–188.

Florida, R., Mellander, C. & Stolarick, K. (2008) Inside the black box of regional development—human capital, the creative class and tolerance, *Journal of Economic Geography*, 8(5), pp. 615–649.

Fritsch, M. & Stuetzer, M. (2009) The geography of creative people in Germany, *Journal of Foresight and Innovation Policy*, 5(1), pp. 7–23.

Fritsch, M. & Stuetzer, M. (2012) The geography of creative people in Germany revisited, in: C. Mellander, R. Florida, B. Asheim & M. Gertler (Eds.) *The Creative Class Goes Global*, pp. 210–226 (Abbingdon: Routledge).

Geys, B. & Murdoch, Z. (2010) Measuring the "bridging" versus "bonding" nature of social networks: A proposal for integrating existing measures, *Sociology*, 44(3), pp. 523–540.

Glaeser, E. L. (2005) Review of Richard Florida's "The rise of the creative class", *Regional Science and Urban Economics*, 35(5), pp. 593–596.

Glaeser, E. L., Kolko, J. & Saiz, a. (2001) Consumer city, *Journal of Economic Geography*, 1(1), pp. 27–50.

Hansen, H. K. (2007) Technology, talent and tolerance—the geography of the creative class in Sweden, *Economic Geography*, 85(4), pp. 425–442.

Hauge, A. & Hracs, B. J. (2010) See the sound, hear the style: Collaborative linkages between indie musicians and fashion designers in local scenes, *Industry & Innovation*, 17(1), pp. 113–129.

Jacobs, J. (1969) *The Economy of Cities*. (New York: Random House).

Koenker, R. & Hallock, K. F. (2001) Quantile regression, *Journal of Economic Perspectives*, 15(4), pp. 143–156.

Krätke, S. (2010) "Creative cities" and the rise of the dealer class: A critique of Richard Florida's approach to urban theory, *International Journal of Urban and Regional Research*, 34(4), pp. 835–853.

Künstlersozialkasse. (2011). *Künstlersozialversicherung: Soziale Sicherung für Künstler und Publizisten* [Social Security Insurance for Artists and Writers]. Wilhelmshaven.

Lloyd, R. (2002) Neo-bohemia: Art and neighborhood redevelopment in Chicago, *Journal of Urban Affairs*, 24(5), pp. 517–532.

Lorenzen, M. & Andersen, K. V. (2009) Centrality and creativity: Does Richard Florida's creative class offer new insights into urban hierarchy? *Economic Geography*, 85(4), pp. 363–390.

Markusen, A. (2006) Urban development and the politics of a creative class: Evidence from a study of artists, *Environment and Planning A*, 38(10), pp. 1921–1940.

Marrocu, E. & Paci, R. (2012) Education or creativity: What matters most for economic performance? *Economic Geography*, 88(4), pp. 369–401.

Menger, P. (1999) Artistic labor markets and careers, *Annual Review of Sociology*, 25, pp. 541–574.

Möller, J. & Tubadji, A. (2004) *The Creative Class, Bohemians and Local Labor Market Performance—A Micro-Data Panel Study for Germany 1975–2004*, ZEW Discussion Paper 08–135, pp. 1–32.

Mossig, I. (2011) Regional employment growth in the cultural and creative industries in Germany 2003–2008, *European Planning Studies*, 19(6), pp. 967–990.

Navarro, C. J., Mateos, C. & Rodriguez, M. J. (2012) Cultural scenes, the creative class and development in Spanish municipalities, *European Urban and Regional Studies*. doi:10.1177/0969776412448188

Peck, J. (2005) Struggling with the creative class, *International Journal of Urban and Regional Research*, 29(4), pp. 740–770.

Pratt, A. C. (2009) Urban regeneration: From the arts "feel good" factor to the cultural economy: A case study of Hoxton, London, *Urban Studies*, 46(5–6), pp. 1041–1061.

Putnam, R. D. (2000) *Bowling Alone?: The Collapse and Revival of American Community*. (New York: Simon & Schuster).

Putnam, R. D. (2007) E Pluribus Unum: Diversity and community in the twenty-first century. The 2006 Johan Skytte Prize lecture, *Scandinavian Political Studies*, 30(2), pp. 137–174.

Scott, A. J. (2010) Jobs or amenities? Destination choices of migrant engineers in The USA, *Papers in Regional Science*, 89(1), pp. 43–63.

Sternberg, R. (2012) Learning from the Past? Why "creative industries" can hardly be created by local/regional government policies, *Die Erde* 143(4), pp. 293–317.

Storper, M. & Manville, M. (2006) Behaviour, preferences and cities: Urban theory and urban resurgence, *Urban Studies*, 43(8), pp. 1247–1274.

Storper, M. & Scott, A. J. (2008) Rethinking human capital, creativity and urban growthj, *Journal of Economic Geography*, 9(2), pp. 147–167.

Wedemeier, J. (2010) The impact of the creative sector on growth in German regions, European Planning Studies, 18(4), pp. 505–520.

Wenting, R. (2008) Spinoff dynamics and the spatial formation of the fashion design industry, 1858–2005, *Journal of Economic Geography*, 8(5), pp. 593–614.

Appendix

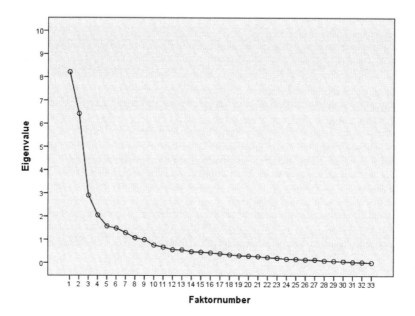

Figure A1. Screeplot.

Table A1. Rotated factor matrix

Variables	EAST	URABN	UNI	TOUR	CRIME	SOCIAL	TEMP	CUL_AMENITIES
GDP per capita 2007	−0.248	0.568	0.329	−0.054	0.306	0.137	−0.071	0.007
Share of employees in manufacturing 2007	−0.070	−0.398	−0.325	−0.07	−0.267	0.183	−0.452	−0.301
Unemployment rate 2007	0.851	−0.038	0.115	−0.043	0.273	−0.220	0.16	0.004
Share of unemployed foreigners 2007	−0.460	0.800	0.049	−0.149	0.077	0.037	0.053	0.013
Share of foreigners 2007	−0.396	0.818	0.139	−0.104	0.146	0.011	0.043	0.008
Population density 2007	−0.163	0.741	0.350	−0.214	0.288	−0.123	0.028	0.203
Price of construction land (€ per m²)	−0.336	0.767	0.185	0.030	−0.017	0.005	0.085	0.277
Support of urban development (€ per inhab.) 2000−2009	0.808	−0.212	0.171	−0.116	0.198	−0.057	−0.181	0.235
KfW support of infrastructure development (€ per inhab.) 2000−2009	0.806	−0.286	0.089	0.137	0.085	−0.091	−0.094	0.180
GRW support of infrastructure development (€ per inhab.) 2000−2009	0.692	−0.201	0.103	0.074	0.186	−0.058	−0.055	0.226
Beds per tourist enterprise 2007	0.031	−0.095	−0.065	0.943	0.021	0.012	−0.106	0.086
Overnight stays per tourist enterprise 2007	0.030	−0.070	−0.029	0.939	0.046	0.009	−0.087	0.109
Street crime offences (per inhab.) 2009	0.268	0.317	0.362	−0.055	0.658	−0.145	0.340	−0.027
Criminal property damage (per inhab.) 2009	0.279	−0.017	0.076	−0.006	0.670	−0.051	0.175	−0.014
Visitors of museums (per 100 inhab.) 2009	0.173	−0.010	0.127	0.305	0.030	0.060	−0.179	0.494
Visitors of theatres and concerts (per household) 2009	0.071	0.095	−0.043	−0.143	−0.085	−0.058	0.213	0.435
Number of cinema screens (per 100.000 inhab.) 2009	−0.011	0.202	0.214	0.132	0.550	0.164	−0.167	−0.015
Net migration (per 1000 inhab.) 2007	−0.646	0.237	0.243	0.032	0.156	0.003	0.146	0.322
Mean size of households 2007	−0.358	−0.371	−0.428	0.058	−0.437	0.171	−0.086	−0.110
Share of inhab. between 25 and 30 years old 2007	0.018	0.276	0.867	−0.097	0.243	0.020	−0.021	0.189
Share of inhab. between 18 and 25 years old 2007	0.286	−0.175	0.731	−0.067	0.232	0.064	−0.085	0.112
Graduates of artistic disciplines (per inhab.) 2007	−0.024	0.502	0.548	0.036	−0.099	−0.077	0.205	−0.039
Graduates of cultural disciplines (per inhab.) 2007	−0.055	0.396	0.752	0.042	−0.104	−0.061	0.185	−0.119
Students (per 1000 inhab.)	−0.040	0.175	0.804	−0.066	0.275	−0.018	0.055	0.038
30 years mean of temperature (year)	−0.094	0.241	0.092	−0.262	0.152	−0.168	0.575	−0.068
30 years mean of number of sunshine hours (year)	0.058	0.094	0.047	0.149	0.038	0.120	−0.052	0.403
30 years mean of precipitation (year)	−0.441	0.196	−0.151	0.257	−0.104	0.024	−0.436	−0.057
Recreation area (m² per inhab.) 2009	0.566	−0.227	−0.081	0.220	−0.059	0.029	0.314	−0.076
Forest area (m² per inhab.) 2009	0.282	−0.349	−0.176	0.337	−0.380	0.135	−0.166	−0.185
Water area (m² per inhab.) 2009	0.417	−0.169	−0.108	0.305	−0.105	0.020	0.143	0.064
Share of inhab. committed to churches and religion	−0.502	0.077	−0.005	−0.007	−0.062	0.592	−0.186	−0.171
Share of inhab. committed to youth	−0.303	0.115	−0.071	0.007	−0.022	0.828	−0.018	0.109
Share of inhab. committed to elderly	0.104	−0.139	0.022	0.042	0.022	0.720	−0.061	0.085

Creative Professionals, Local Amenities and Externalities: Do Regional Concentrations of Creative Professionals Reinforce Themselves Over Time?

JAN WEDEMEIER

Hamburg Institute of International Economics (HWWI), Bremen, Germany

ABSTRACT *This research analyses the impact of the creative sector on total employment and on the creative sector's employment growth in Western Germany's regions from 1977 to 2004. For the analysis, the definitions of the creative sector follow a technologically and culturally oriented definition and, alternatively, Florida's creative class (2002). These approaches are contrasted with a skill-based approach. Using a fixed-effects panel model with time lags, the results support the view that the creative sector fosters the regional growth rate of total employment. The results suggest, moreover, that an initially large share of regional creative professionals pushes the regional concentration of those professions in agglomerated regions further. The driving force behind the concentration of creative professionals is local amenities—measured by bohemians—and it is assumed that knowledge spillovers—possibly accelerated by diversity and close proximity—contribute to this polarization. These results are also confirmed for highly skilled agents.*

Introduction

Explanations for the dynamics of regions are manifold. Important contributions have been made by many economists. Glaeser *et al.* (1992) show that close proximity helps to stimulate the transfer of knowledge and interaction between economics agents. Other explanations are transportation costs (Krugman, 1991), labour market pooling (Marshall, 1890; Krugman, 1991) or the Rosen–Roback framework considering wages, housing costs and amenities (Rosen, 1979; Roback, 1982). A central point for the competitiveness of regions is, however, the ability to attract agents with specific abilities and skills. A sophisticated and excellent regional skill structure is regarded as a major condition for regional employment growth. In particular, creative professionals—who are economic agents working in the fields of education, engineering, science and arts—are supposed to be attracted to the places that are most beneficial to creating employment growth (Florida, 2002; Wojan *et al.*, 2007). Today, the most successful regions seem to be particularly concentrated in idea-producing industries (Glaeser, 2008). The distribution of such places is unequal in space, which is one explanation for regional productivity and economic imbalances.

According to Lucas (1988), the external effects of human capital—generated by formal and informal interaction between people—are a possible explanation for persisting economic differences between regions, i.e. the average skill level of a group of agents might affect the individual level—the productivity level—of agents. Regions with high external effects of human capital probably perform more successfully than other regions. Lucas argues that especially economic agents working in the fields of "arts and sciences—the creative professions" exchange ideas, i.e. the effect of external human capital is common to creative professions (1988, p. 38). The exchange of ideas contributes to the increase in knowledge and productivity. Moreover, he points out that cities facilitate the accumulation of knowledge through the exchange of knowledge and attraction of skilled workers, and much of the economics in cities is "creative" and idea-producing.

Those arguments support Florida's (2002) assumption regarding the importance of agents working in the creative professions. Florida (2002) argues that the economic success and competitive advantages of both cities and regions are based on these creative professionals. They can foster creative and productive processes, resulting in innovation and regional employment growth. He introduces a human capital concept based on occupations, which captures creative abilities ending in economic growth. He further suggests that the regional abundance of creative professionals affects the employment growth of the creative sector, i.e. a self-reinforcing spatial concentration of employment.

Many empirical studies investigate this effect of highly skilled agents, but there is no study that tests this effect for creative professionals. Suedekum (2006, 2008), for example, finds a positive effect of the share of employees with higher education on low- and medium-skilled employment growth, but not on the employment growth of the highly skilled. Because of the latter result, he concludes that skill complementarities are more important for productivity and economic growth than knowledge spillovers. Vice versa, Moretti (2004) finds both spillovers and skill complementarities important for productivity and, consequently, for employment growth.

The primary motivation for this paper comes from Florida's (2002) assumption that the creative professions play a crucial role in employment growth. The work addresses the point that the creative sector fosters total employment growth and the further regional accumulation of creative professionals. (For a general overview of the creative class literature, cf. for instance Clifton, 2008). There is no empirical work so far in the economic literature that tests this primary motivation of the role of creative sector polarization. Furthermore, there are almost no empirical attempts to test the creative sector hypothesis with panel data methods, although exceptions are made by Möller and Tubadji (2009). They investigate the question of whether the regional concentration of the creative class leads to employment and wage growth. They further examine the difference in economic performance of the share of the creative class, bohemians and highly skilled workers. The authors conduct their analysis for 323 NUTS 3 regions and find a positive relationship between the creative class and the regional economic performance as measured by employment and wage growth. Moreover, the creative class indicator outperforms the highly skilled workers indicator.

However, a further improvement to the existing economic literature on the creative sector is that for this research, data over an extraordinarily long time period (1975–2004) are used.

The rest of the paper is organized as follows. The second section brings up the theoretical arguments and some stylized facts relevant to total and sector-specific employment growth. The third section presents the variables for the econometric model, while the model and its specification are presented in the fourth section. In the fifth section, the econometric results are interpreted and discussed. The conclusion is made in the final section.

Employment Growth in the Creative Sector

The theoretical argument relies mainly on a human capital model by Suedekum (2006, 2008). Suedekum investigates with his model the impact of high shares of initial human capital (high-skilled agents) on highly skilled employment growth. As a result of a higher average level of human capital, the average wages of all employment are higher. The skilled agents affect the productivity level of less-skilled agents by human capital externalities; this effect results in higher average wages. However, whether regions with high shares of high-skilled agents further accumulate high-skilled agents also depends on the strength of human capital externalities, which will result in higher skilled wages. These human capital externalities can be generated by formal and informal interaction between agents. One argument is that the exchange of knowledge may affect the wage level of less-skilled agents (Lucas, 1988; Acemoglu, 1996; Suedekum, 2008; Schlitte, 2012). Another explanation is that there is a complementary relation between high-skilled and low-skilled agents (Moretti, 2004; Suedekum, 2008). Moreover, it is assumed that there is a long-run relationship between wage and employment growth. Though human capital externalities are supposed to affect the productivity level and not employment directly, it can be argued that changes in productivity levels have an impact on employment growth for different skill groups. The clustering of more highly skilled agents could positively affect the productivity of low-skilled workers. This effect can be explained by knowledge transfers (for further discussion, cf. Schlitte, 2012). However, empirical results show different effects of productivity depending on the sectoral structure (Appelbaum & Schettkat, 1995; Möller, 2001). Knowledge-intensive sectors are more positively affected by productivity growth, resulting in employment growth, than less knowledge-intensive sectors (Borcherding *et al.*, 2012), and creative professionals are regarded as knowledge-intensive workers (Hansen, 2007).

Suedekum (2006, 2008), however, delivers empirical evidence for his model. As a result, the author finds that German cities with a high endowment of highly skilled agents initially grow faster in employment than unskilled cities. Moreover, cities with initially high shares of highly skilled agents subsequently face lower growth rates in such highly skilled employment. The first effect overwhelms the decline. Hence, he does not observe a self-reinforcing spatial concentration. Suedekum finally concludes that the strength of human capital externalities is not strong enough to affect the average employment wage. In contrast, Moretti (2004) obtains the empirical result for the US that the regional supply of college graduates raises the wages of less-educated groups. Rauch (1993) also shows that the regional concentration of high-skilled agents has a significant influence on the average wages. A further contribution comes, for instance, from Shapiro (2006). Autor *et al.* (2008), furthermore, find empirical evidence for the polarization of earnings growth. Hitherto, the trend has been towards rising wage inequalities by education, age and experience, but also by occupation group. The local skill concentration by education is regarded, moreover, as a major cause for regional growth disparities in Germany (Schlitte, 2012). In contrast, Acemoglu and Angrist (2000) find that the impact of regional human capital on regional growth is weak.

Suedekum (2006, 2008)—but also, for example, Moretti (2004) and Shapiro (2006)—stresses in his model the importance of local amenities. Highly skilled agents are assumed to value local amenities, and these amenities affect their location. Following Suedekum's model, if local amenities are unequally distributed in space, high-skilled agents are disproportionately distributed between cities. Since the characteristic of local amenities can be relatively time-invariant, in the empirics it is suggested that unobserved characteristics across regions be controlled by using region-specific fixed effects. This is especially true for geographical conditions, such as weather or access to the sea.

Local amenities could also include cultural characteristics, such as the share of bohemians—agents working, for example, as artists, publishers or audio engineers—or the diversity of economic agents. Both bohemians and the diversity of economic agents are regarded as factors for the attraction of creative professionals (Florida, 2002; Shapiro, 2006; Boschma & Fritsch, 2009; Wojan *et al.*, 2007). Several other studies research the link between the "quality of place" and the location of the creative class (Andersen & Lorenzen, 2005; Hansen, 2007; Fritsch & Stützer, 2008; Clifton & Cooke, 2009). The general result is that the creative class tends to locate (jobs–fellow–people argument) where the quality of place is high. However, these findings are in contrast to those of Möller and Tubadji (2009), who find that creative professionals prefer to live in strong economic regions and contribute to employment and wage growth. Nevertheless, Möller and Tubadji do not find empirical evidence for Germany that bohemians matter for the attraction of creative agents.

As an alternative approach to the standard literature on human capital, it is suggested than an explanation should be found regarding whether the creative sector contributes to employment growth and, in particular, to the employment growth of the creative sector. To the best of my knowledge, there are many empirical studies investigating this effect of human capital pooling, but there is no study focusing on creative capital pooling. Therefore, the first main hypothesis 1 is that the creative sector is positively linked to employment growth in Germany. Hypothesis 2 is that the creative sector significantly contributes to the employment growth in the creative sector. The two hypotheses are strongly interrelated. If regions with low shares of creative professionals grow faster in the employment of creative professionals than employment generally, those regions catch up with regions with higher shares of creative professionals. However, if regions with large shares of creative professionals lead to an increase in the total employment, and simultaneously reduce the growth of the same employment group, it can be concluded that there is no self-reinforcing process. If there is evidence for divergence, I may conclude that spillovers and local amenities have an influence on employment growth.

The last minor hypothesis 3 is that cultural amenities—here measured by bohemians and diversity—are linked to the growth in employment. The assumption is that cultural amenities affect the location of creative professionals.

A panel model based on data from 1977 to 2004 for all West German (planning) regions is applied to research these questions empirically. In the following, the data for the empirical work are briefly presented.

Data and Variables

In order to measure the number of creative professionals, the "IAB Regionalfile 1975–2004" data are used.[1] This is a representative sample of 2% of all German employees, who are subject to compulsory insurance deductions, and includes approximately 21 million employment career histories. A disadvantage is that civil servants, freelancers and the self-employed are not recorded in this employment sample.

An advantage is that bohemians reported to the German Social Insurance for Artists ("Künstlersozialkasse")—which is the most important insurance agency for employed and self-employed artists—are included in the data. Therefore, the results may be considered reliable for statements on the role of bohemians in employment growth.

In the IAB-Regionalfile, it is possible to identify 130 professional groups (by means of a three-digit code) and details on individuals' nationality or working place. The sample's time period is extraordinarily long and the data census coherent in time. In the following, the data cleaning and preparation and the variables used for the econometric model are briefly described.

Data Cleaning and Preparation

In the first step, only the years from 1977 up to 2004 and the Western German regions are included. Since the individuals working in the creative sector are assumed to work often with part-time labour contracts, both part-time and full-time employed individuals are observed. All agents in apprenticeship are excluded. Moreover, all observations with no valid information on the occupation and all observations with missing information on the region are dropped. After the first data cleaning, around 10% of the observations have no information on education. Since the education variable suffers from a relatively large number of missing values, in the second step values are imputed for the missing education data by following the imputation procedure IP1 (Fitzenberger *et al.*, 2005; Drews, 2006). In the last step of data preparation, the observations (10,932,559) are aggregated to the level of Germany's 74 planning regions.

Variables for Creative Professionals and High-Skilled Agents

For the purposes of measuring the creative sector, engineering, technical, scientific and IT professionals are aggregated into a share of the creative sector (CS) (Definition 1). This group is characterized by improving "technology in the line of business they pursue, and as a result, productivity and growth" (Murphy *et al.*, 1991, p. 505). This group is considered as highly creative and innovative, i.e. with the ability of technological creativity. Furthermore, the second agent group of the creative sector, the bohemians (BOH), is included in the analysis as an independent variable. It is assumed that bohemians—who are agents working as artists, publishers or audio engineers—are a locational amenity factor. Bohemians themselves are also, according to the hypothesis, an economic factor. They are regarded as agents with the ability of cultural creativity. The third group of

Florida's definition of the creative class, the agents with so-called economic creativity, is excluded from this definition. Since a clear-cut definition of what agents with the ability of "economic creativity" are and the concept of creativity are still fuzzy and nebulous (cf. for instance Glaeser, 2005 or Peck, 2005), this definition of the creative sector is introduced.

Alternatively, the second definition of the creative agents is the "usual" share of Florida's creative class (CC) (Definition 2). The variable CC captures the technological and economic creative ability of agents. Definition 2 is used in a further separate regression to test whether the creative class concept outperforms the creative sector definition.

The third alternative measure is the share of highly skilled employment (EDU) (Definition 3). Table 1 summarizes the three variables.

Table 2 presents the correlation matrix between the different variables. It is obvious that the relative share of the creative class CC is relatively highly correlated with the share of the creative sector CS (94.9%). The two definitions are interrelated, since the creative sector is defined as agents with the ability of technological creativity and the creative class is defined as agents with technological and economic creative abilities. The match between the creative sector and bohemians is considerably smaller (52.1%) than the ratio between CC and BOH (0.636). The correlation between the share of the highly skilled agents and CC is also relatively high (91.5%).

All the variables, the share of the creative professionals (CS, CC), the share of the highly skilled agents and the share of bohemians, are calculated on the basis of the employment data IABS Regionalfile 1975–2004 from the FDZ (2008). Tables A1–A3 in the appendix give a detailed overview of the three employment groups.

Dependent Variables

The dependent variable is the total employment growth (ΔEMP). Growth is calculated by using absolute employment data for the three intervals 1980–1986, 1989–1995 and 1998–2004, whereas the growth rate is approximated by: $growth_t = \ln(variable_t) - \ln(variable_{t-1})$. This calculation is chosen to reduce the possible effects of (real) business cycle fluctuations of four to five years. Second, the intervals are not too long to loosen further the number of observations. Last, with this computation of intervals, it is possible to have equal balanced growth periods (six years plus a three-year

Table 1. Variables definition

Human capital	Sector/group	Agents with	Variable
Creative (human) capital (acronym: creative professionals)	Creative sector	...the ability of technological creativity	CS
		...the ability of cultural creativity	BOH
	(Florida's) Creative class	...the ability of technological and economic creativity	CC
		...the ability of cultural creativity	BOH
Educational (human) capital	High-skilled agents	...an university degree	EDU

Note: Tables A1–A3 in the appendix give a detailed overview of the employment groups.

Table 2. Correlation matrix for the initial years 1977, 1986 and 1995 (average)

Variable	CS	BOH	CC	EDU
Creative Sector (CS)	1.000			
Bohemians (BOH)	0.521	1.000		
Florida's creative class (CC)	0.949	0.636	1.000	
High-skilled agents (EDU)	0.873	0.650	0.915	1.000

Note: Number of observations = 222.
Sources: IABS Regionalfile 1975–2004, FDZ (2008), own calculations.

lagged variable). Overall, with this computation, three observations for each region are obtained. The number of observations is 222. The variable for the growth rate of the creative sector is ΔCS. Alternatively, the variable for Florida's definition of the creative class is ΔCC and for the employed high-skilled agents ΔEDU. The growth variables are all calculated with absolute employment numbers. I analyse growth separately for the creative sector, creative class and highly skilled jobs to discriminate between the different groups.

Further Control Variables

Jacobs (1969) proposes that professional diversity contributes to regional development. The main argument is that diverse professionals bring diverse knowledge stocks into production processes. To operationalize diversity, the relative concentration of CS is measured by using an inverse Herfindahl–Hirschman Index, $DIV_{it} = 1 - \sum_{k=t}^{k} s_{kit}^2$, where s_{kit}^2 is the number of employees with (creative) profession k in region i in year t. This index thus takes into account the diversity among the creative sector (DIV_CS). An alternative measure is the diversity for the creative class (DIV_CC). Since the education variable has six different characteristics, a variable for the diversity by skill group (DIV_EDU) is constructed.

As an additional measure of diversity, the share of employees with no German nationality (DIV) is applied as a measure for cultural–ethnic diversity. Because of data restrictions, the variable is constructed by using the information on whether employees have a foreign or German nationality. Cultural–ethnic diversity is assumed to be important in the knowledge creation process, since the variety of knowledge stocks increases the possible combination of knowledge and knowledge networks (Florida, 2002; Lee et al., 2004; Audretsch et al., 2009). It is further an argument for externalities in processes and production. The share of employees with a foreign nationality is calculated with the IABS Regionalfile 1975–2004 (FDZ, 2008) data.

A control variable for the employment size of regions is also added (EMP). The variable is calculated by using the natural log of employment in the initial years.

Units of Observation

The units of observation are Germany's 74 planning regions ("Raumordnungsregionen"). Eastern Germany is excluded (former German Democratic Republic, GDR, and the city of Berlin), since the economic, political and social structures are still different from that of Western Germany. More importantly, no data before 1992 are available for Eastern Germany.

Table 3. Summary statistics

Variable	Mean	Std dev.	Min.	Max.
ΔEMP (Total employment growth)	0.054	0.076	−0.107	0.244
ΔCS (Creative sector growth)	0.124	0.115	−0.150	0.833
ΔCC (Florida's creative class growth)	0.043	0.086	−0.182	0.484
ΔEDU (High-skilled growth)	0.199	0.113	−0.082	0.667
CS (Share of creative sector)	0.067	0.022	0.022	0.142
CC (Share of Florida's creative class)	0.129	0.029	0.066	0.242
EDU (Share of high-skilled agents)	0.059	0.026	0.014	0.169
BOH (Share of bohemians)	0.006	0.003	0.001	0.020
DIV_CS (Diversity index of CS)	0.899	0.013	0.813	0.919
DIV_CC (Diversity index of CC)	0.917	0.015	0.852	0.939
DIV_EDU (Diversity index of EDU)	0.463	0.043	0.361	0.596
DIV (Share of employees with no German nationality)	0.070	0.036	0.011	0.192
EMP (log of total employment)	8.247	0.675	6.960	9.920
AGG_CS (Interaction var of CS and agglomerations)	0.025	0.041	0.000	0.142
AGG_CC (Interaction var of CC and agglomerations)	0.045	0.072	0.000	0.242
AGG_EDU (Interaction var of EDU and agglomerations)	0.023	0.038	0.000	0.169
AGG_BOH (Interaction var of BOH and agglomerations)	0.002	0.004	0.000	0.020
AGG_DIV (Interaction var of DIV and agglomerations)	0.027	0.045	0.000	0.192

Number of observation: 222; number of groups 74
Panel variable planning region: strongly balanced
Time variable: year 1977–2004

Notes: Growth (Δ) for 1980–1986, 1989–1995 and 1998–2004; control variables for 1977, 1986 and 1995; AGG_ are categorical variables (agg = 1, otherwise = 0).
Sources: IABS Regionalfile 1975–2004, FDZ (2008), own calculations.

I employ further various interaction variables measuring concentration effects in agglomerations. Hence, the creative sector is assumed to be highly concentrated in agglomerated regions; an interaction variable evaluating CS in agglomerated regions (AGG_CS) is included. With this categorical variable, it is possible to control for regional differences. Moreover, non-metric interaction variables for CC (AGG_CC), EDU (AGG_EDU), BOH (AGG_BOH) and DIV (AGG_DIV) are applied.

Table 3 shows the summary statistics of the variables with their mean, standard deviation (std dev.), minimum (min.) and maximum (max.). The mean over the three intervals of total employment growth ΔEMP is 5.4%, for the growth of the creative sector ΔTE it is 12.4%, for Florida's creative class ΔCC, 4.3% and for the highly skilled agents ΔEDU, 19.9% (Table 3).

Econometric Model and Specification

In a cross-section time-series analysis, it is investigated whether the creative sector has a positive impact on the total employment for the time period from 1977 to 2004. The basic regression equation for the growth of the total employment is:

$$\Delta \text{EMP}_{it} = \beta_0 + \beta_1 \text{CS}_{it-3} + \beta_2 \text{BOH}_{it-3} + \beta_3 \text{DIV\_CS}_{it-3} + \beta_4 \text{DIV}_{it-3} + \beta_5 \text{EMP}_{it-3} \\ + \beta_6 \text{AGG\_CS}_{it-3} + \beta_7 \text{AGG\_BOH}_{it-3} + \beta_8 \text{AGG\_DIV}_{it-3} + \epsilon_{it-3}, \quad (1)$$

where $\Delta\mathrm{EMP}_{it}$ is the growth of the total employment in three intervals from 1980–1986, 1989–1995 and 1998–2004 in region i.

CS_{it-3} and BOH_{it-3} are the shares of the creative sector and bohemians in the initial years 1977, 1986 and 1995. $\mathrm{DIV\_CS}_{it-3}$ is the diversity measure for the professional diversity, which is measured by the variety of the creative sector in region i in year $t-3$. DIV_{it-3} is the diversity of employees with foreign nationality. The size of employment within the regions and cities is controlled by EMP_{it-3}. The last three variables $\mathrm{AGG\_CS}_{it-3}$, $\mathrm{AGG\_BOH}_{it-3}$ and $\mathrm{AGG\_DIV}_{it-3}$ are interaction terms. To establish trust in the empirical results, Equation (1), but also the two following Equations (2) and (3), are estimated with interaction terms and without interaction terms. In general, in order to model the relationship between the independent input and the output variables, the input variables enter into the estimation with a time lag of three years. Using input variables with sufficient time lags improves the concerns about reverse causality. The error term is ϵ_{it-3}. The second equation is:

$$\Delta\mathrm{EMP}_{it} = \beta_0 + \beta_1 \mathrm{CC}_{it-3} + \beta_2 \mathrm{BOH}_{it-3} + \beta_3 \mathrm{DIV\_CC}_{it-3} + \beta_4 \mathrm{DIV}_{it-3} + \beta_5 \mathrm{EMP}_{it-3}$$
$$+ \beta_6 \mathrm{AGG\_CC}_{it-3} + \beta_7 \mathrm{AGG\_BOH}_{it-3} + \beta_8 \mathrm{AGG\_DIV}_{it-3} + \epsilon_{it-3}, \qquad (2)$$

where CC_{it-3} is the initial size of the creative class (Definition 2). $\mathrm{DIV\_CC}_{it-3}$ is the diversity of the creative class. $\mathrm{AGG\_CC}_{it-3}$ is an interaction term of CC_{it-3} and regions with a high employment agglomeration. The variables $\mathrm{AGG\_BOH}_{it-3}$ and $\mathrm{AGG\_CC}_{it-3}$ are again interaction terms. The other specifications and variables are given by estimation Equation (1). The third equation is:

$$\Delta\mathrm{EMP}_{it} = \beta_0 + \beta_1 \mathrm{EDU}_{it-3} + \beta_2 \mathrm{BOH}_{it-3} + \beta_3 \mathrm{DIV\_EDU}_{it-3} + \beta_4 \mathrm{DIV}_{it-3} + \beta_5 \mathrm{EMP}_{it-3}$$
$$+ \beta_6 \mathrm{AGG\_EDU}_{it-3} + \beta_7 \mathrm{AGG\_BOH}_{it-3} + \beta_8 \mathrm{AGG\_DIV}_{it-3} + \epsilon_{it-3} \qquad (3)$$

where EDU_{it-3} is the share of high-skilled agents (Definition 3) in region i and time $t-3$. The other variables are specified as in the above Equation (1); the exceptions are the variables $\mathrm{DIV\_EDU}_{it-3}$ and $\mathrm{AGG\_EDU}_{it-3}$. The variable $\mathrm{DIV\_EDU}_{it-3}$ measures the diversity of six different education degrees.

Alternatively, all the Equations (1)–(3) are estimated with the three dependent variables $\Delta\mathrm{CS}_{it}$, $\Delta\mathrm{CC}_{it}$ and $\Delta\mathrm{EDU}_{it}$. These three dependent variables are analysed separately to research the potential concentration of creative professional employment growth.

The initial idea according to the model specification is that creative sector growth should be stronger where the creative sector is initially relatively scarce. At the same time, a further assumption is that regions with a high endowment of creative sector agents will grow faster if there is a localized human capital externality that positively affects the productivity of the creative professionals. The assumption is that diversity and employment diversity raise the probability of externalities. Cities especially are characterized by the absence of physical space between agents and firms; this can further have a fundamental influence on sharing knowledge and flowing externalities. The creative sector agents are furthermore assumed to be attracted through the presence of unique local conditions, such as cultural amenities.

In the panel estimation, I include local area fixed and time period fixed effects.

Growth of the Creative Sector: Regression Results

This section presents the regression results, which illustrate whether the share of the creative sector, the share of Florida's creative class and the share of high-skilled employed agents contribute to employment growth in Germany's planning regions. This section is divided into two subsections to present separately the estimation results on total employment and group-specific employment growth.

Total Employment Effects

The regression equations are estimated with fixed-effects (FE) estimators. With this technique, it is possible to consider unobserved effects. Since each planning region has its own time-independent characteristics that may or may not influence the predictor variables, the FE model controls for this. Having tested with a Hausman test, Breusch–Pagan–Lagrange multiplier and the joint tests, it is concluded that the FE estimator is adequate for all the equations for total employment growth. For the estimation Equations (1)–(3), the test results for the cross-sectional dependence (CD) of Pesaran indicate substantial CD in the errors. This may arise because of the presence of neighbourhood effects. Calculating Pesaran's average absolute values, there is enough evidence suggesting the presence of CD in the estimations. De Hoyos and Sarafidis (2006), as well as Hoechle (2007), suggest calculating alternatively the standard errors (SE) with the Driscoll–Kraay SE, correcting for CD. Moreover, the Driscoll–Kraay SE produces heteroscedasticity- and autocorrelation-consistent SE. Table 4 presents the estimation results.

First of all, the overall fit of the first estimation is 62% (column 1). The estimated results indicate that CS_{it-3} and the initial share of bohemians matter for the total employment growth. The coefficient of the initial share of the creative sector is highly significant (3.587). The initial shares of CS increase the growth rate in the total employment. Holding the other variables constant, a one-unit increase in CS will lead to a 3.6% change in the future total employment. The explanation could be that the creative sector is related to other industries, such as business-related services, and is integrated into production chains and processes. It can further be assumed that the creative sector employment fosters creative processes, contributing to innovation, which leads to further (employment) growth processes.

The initial share of bohemians is also significant at any level. Both signs are positive, as expected. Bohemians are supposed to create new products, to have an effect on taste and to give impulses to product variety. More important, the interpretation is that employment is attracted by local cultural amenities, and bohemians themselves contribute to these amenities. The coefficients DIV_CS_{it-3} and DIV_{it-3} are significant at the 1% level (1.190 and 1.551). The diverse occupational composition of the creative sector is positively linked to total employment. The results' interpretation is that the diverse composition of the creative sector employment and the high numbers of creative professionals (critical mass) matter for employment growth. Hypothesis 1, that the creative sector contributes to employment growth, could be confirmed.

The overall fit of the FE regression for the creative class is 61% (column 3). In general, the results indicate the same direction as for the first equation.

The estimation results for the employed highly skilled agents are also highlighted in Table 4. The R^2 of the FE estimation is around 80%. At a glance, the results are not so

Table 4. Total employment growth (1980–1986, 1989–1995 and 1998–2004)

	\multicolumn{4}{c}{Dependent variable ΔEMP}		
Variable	Definition 1		Definition 2		Definition 3
CS	3.587** (0.091)		2.240** (0.093)		
CC		3.348** (0.103)		2.409** (0.058)	
EDU					4.494** (0.151) 4.259** (0.078)
BOH	12.082** (1.440)	10.682** (0.877)	10.968** (1.259)	12.748** (1.757)	2.671** (0.829) 1.116 (1.426)
DIV_CS	1.190** (0.187)	1.290** (0.201)			
DIV_CC			0.944** (0.334)	0.795* (0.325)	
DIV_EDU					−1.374** (0.127) −1.524** (0.120)
DIV	1.551** (0.218)	1.684** (0.238)	1.855** (0.287)	1.723** (0.310)	2.079** (0.101) 2.180** (0.061)
EMP	0.034 (0.044)	0.041 (0.044)	0.099† (0.055)	0.098† (0.056)	−0.051 (0.031) −0.033 (0.028)
AGG_CS	−0.335 (0.224)				
AGG_CC				0.056 (0.151)	
AGG_EDU					−0.585** (0.211)
AGG_BOH	−4.492 (3.377)			−9.260** (2.446)	−2.557 (3.156)
AGG_DIV	0.453** (0.133)			0.567** (0.244)	0.395** (0.127)
Constant	−1.715** (0.223)	−1.853** (0.248)	−2.120** (0.224)	−1.996** (0.179)	0.692** (0.238) 0.621** (0.204)
Local area fixed effect: Yes; time period fixed effect: Yes; N = 222					
R^2	62.2%	61.9%	60.5%	60.9%	80.4% 79.7%

Notes: Driscoll–Kraay SE in parentheses; control variables for 1977, 1986 and 1995.
Sources: IABS Regionalfile 1975–2004, FDZ (2008), own calculations.
† Significant at 10% level.
* Significant at 5% level.
** Significant at 1% level.

different from those of the first two definitions. The coefficient of the share of the high-skilled agents EDU_{it-3} is positive and highly significant at the 1% level (4.494). However, the coefficient for the interaction variable share of highly skilled agents and agglomerated regions is negatively significant at the 1% level, and the coefficient is -0.585. The coefficient of the variable DIV_EDU_{it-3} is also negative at the significance level of 1% (-1.374). The reason could be simply that the relative concentration of one specific knowledge group (high-skilled) is one of the most significant driving forces for economic development, resulting in employment growth. This result is also confirmed by many other authors (Glaeser, 2008).

In general, the results are in line with the empirical findings by, for instance, Suedekum (2006, 2008), Möller and Tubadji (2009) and Wedemeier (2010). They find significant effects on employment growth coming from the creative professionals and/or high-skilled agents. The coefficients for the cultural amenity variable BOH are positive and significant in all three estimations. In general, the results suggest that BOH matters in the context of economic growth. This is also discussed in the literature on the creative sector and on the attraction of human capital, and confirms Florida's assumption (2002) regarding the positive effect of the cultural input on economic development. The results from Boschma and Fritsch (2009), Wojan *et al.* (2007) and Falck *et al.* (2009), for instance, support this view. However, if the results are compared, for instance, with those of Möller and Tubadji (2009), these results are not empirically supported. This can possibly be explained by the differences in the measurement of the bohemians or the regional level of research.

Group-Specific Employment Effects

Once again, the above three equations are estimated in a panel model. However, the dependent variable is replaced with the growth of the creative sector ΔCS_{it}, the growth of Florida's creative class ΔCC_{it} and the growth of the employed high-skilled agents ΔEDU_{it}. In the first tests, all the results indicate that the FE model is appropriate. Furthermore, the CD test of Pesaran indicates CD between the planning regions. Therefore, the SE are calibrated with Driscoll–Kraay SE, which are robust to CD. The results are presented in Table 5.

The hypothesis of the self-reinforcing process (hypothesis 2) is that the initial size of the creative sector contributes to the growth rate of the creative sector employment. The overall fit of the FE estimator is relatively low (30%). CS_{it-3} is negatively correlated with the growth of the creative sector; furthermore, the coefficient is significant at the 1% level (-3.898). The impact of the creative sector CS on the growth rate of the same group of creative professionals is negative and significant at the 1% level. It significantly reduces the growth of the same employment group. The coefficient for the interaction variable of CS_{it-3} and agglomerated regions is positive and significant at the 1% level (0.707). It could be concluded that there is a self-reinforcing process within agglomerated regions. In contrast, regions with lower shares of the creative sector catch up in creative sector employment with the German mean. The effect in relation to hypothesis 1 is that large shares of the creative sector lead to an increase in the total employment, but reduce the growth of the same employment group. The growth in the total employment overwhelms the decline in the creative sector.

Table 5. Group-specific employment growth (1980–1986, 1989–1995 and 1998–2004)

Dependent variable	ΔCS Definition 1	ΔCC Definition 2	ΔEDU Definition 3
Variable			
CS	−3.898** (0.323)	−3.436** (0.058)	
CC	−2.948** (0.366)	−2.838** (0.104)	−2.632** (0.149)
EDU			−2.997** (0.177)
BOH	−4.798** (0.486)	−12.351** (0.997)	−7.165** (1.286)	5.268** (0.334)
DIV_CS	2.519† (1.319)		1.176 (0.929)
DIV_CC	3.059** (0.448)	0.226 (0.266)	
DIV_EDU	2.563** (0.546)		−0.316 (0.244)	0.108 (0.185)
DIV	−0.466** (0.139)	−1.247** (0.239)	−0.210 (0.224)	−0.026 (0.115)
EMP	−0.221** (0.076)	−0.285** (0.068)	−1.580** (0.219)	0.468** (0.148)	−0.272** (0.005)
AGG_CS	−0.242** (0.067)		−0.283** (0.062)	−0.245** (0.022)
AGG_CC	0.707** (0.054)	0.218** (0.078)		
AGG_EDU			0.740* (0.279)	
AGG_BOH	27.782** (3.198)	23.926** (0.798)	14.079** (3.295)	
AGG_DIV	−1.097** (0.257)	−1.433** (0.128)	−1.740** (0.076)	
Constant	−0.538 (0.808)	0.047 (0.853)	3.193** (0.277)	2.446** (0.078)	2.515** (0.091)
Local area fixed effect: Yes; time period fixed effect: Yes; N = 222			
R^2	31.8%	27.0%	72.3%	69.0%	34.8%	33.1%

Notes: Driscoll–Kraay SE in parentheses; control variables for 1977, 1986, 1995.
Sources: IABS Regionalfile 1975–2004, FDZ (2008), own calculations.
† Significant at 10% level.
* Significant at 5% level.
** Significant at 1% level.

Therefore, the results suggest that the polarization effect of creative professionals depends on the spatial level of the research. The external effect of human capital—possibly affected by diversity—might be greater in agglomerated regions than in peripheral regions. Furthermore, the value of local amenities—here measured by bohemians—is also higher in agglomerated regions. Both affect the location of creative professionals (hypothesis 3). An explanation could be that productivity gains through knowledge spillovers leverage wages and then leverage the number of creative professionals in agglomerated regions.

When focusing on the creative class CC (Definition 2), the results are consistent with the results of the first definition and they are also significant at the 1% level, both for CC and for AGG_CC. However, the overall fit is much higher (72%). The share of Florida's creative class is negatively correlated with the growth rate of the creative class. The coefficient is significant at the 1% level (-3.436). The variable AGG_CC$_{it-3}$ is positively correlated with the growth of Florida's creative class and the coefficients are significant at the 1% level (0.218). The negative value of the coefficient for CC could be explained by spatial differences. This result is consistent with Florida's (2002) assumption of the self-reinforcing process, which is that the creative class is heavily concentrated in urban places. Again, the coefficient of bohemians concentrated in highly agglomerated regions AGG_BOH$_{it-3}$ is positively significant at the 1% level (23.926). BOH$_{it-3}$ is negatively significant, which could be explained through self-selection effects in that the creative class prefers to live in urban places. Comparing the estimated results with the estimation without the interaction variables AGG_*$_{it-3}$, the coefficients and their signs and significance levels indicate the same direction as for the first equation.

Table 5 also presents the estimation results for the effect of the initial share of employed highly skilled agents on ΔEDU_{it}; the Driscoll–Kraay SE are reported in parentheses. The overall fit is 35%. Once again, the coefficient for the initial share of employed agents with higher education EDU$_{it-3}$ is negative and significant at the 1% level (-2.997). The interaction term share of employed high-skilled agents and agglomerated regions is significant and positive, here at the 5% level (0.740). It indicates a further divergence process between the regions, so that an increasing number of highly skilled agents are concentrated in urban places. The share of bohemians BOH$_{it-3}$ is positively correlated and AGG_BOH$_{it-3}$ is positively highly significant for the growth rate of ΔEDU_{it}. The result of the employed agents with foreign nationality DIV$_{it-3}$ on the growth of the employed high-skilled agents is different in some aspects, since the coefficient is now positively highly significant at the 1% level.

The results are consistent with the overall estimations presented by Suedekum (2006, 2008). He suggests that regions with already high shares of highly skilled agents will grow more moderate, i.e. regions with low shares of high-skilled agents will catch up with those regions with higher shares of skilled agents.

To sum up, large shares of creative professionals lead to an increase in the total employment, but also reduce the growth of the same employment group (Table 6 sum ups the main findings). According to theory, the growth in the total employment overwhelms the decline in creative professionals. On the contrary, the econometric results suggest that an initially large share of regional creative professionals further pushes the regional concentration of those professions into agglomerated regions. The driving forces for the concentration are cultural amenities (BOH, DIV), unobserved city-specific characteristics (controlled with the FE model) and assumed knowledge spillovers (forced by diversity

Table 6. Summary of findings: The impact of the creative professionals on employment growth

Variable	ΔEMP	ΔCS	ΔCC	ΔEDU
CS	3.348** (0.103)	−3.898** (0.323)	.	.
Agglomeration effect (AGG_CS)	−0.335 (0.224)	0.707** (0.054)	.	.
CC	2.409** (0.058)	.	−3.436** (0.058)	.
Agglomeration effect (AGG_CC)	0.056 (0.151)	.	0.218** (0.078)	.
EDU	4.494** (0.151)	.	.	−2.997** (0.177)
Agglomeration effect (AGG_EDU)	−0.585** (0.211)	.	.	0.740* (0.279)
Hypothesis accepted	Yes	Yes	.	.

Local area fixed effect: Yes; time period fixed effect: Yes; $N = 222$

Notes: Driscoll–Kraay SE in parentheses; control variables for 1977, 1986 and 1995.
Sources: IABS Regionalfile 1975–2004, FDZ (2008), own calculations.
†Significant at 10% level.
*Significant at 5% level.
**Significant at 1% level.

effects). Extending the assumption a bit further, the explanation could also be that the creative sector is related to other growth sectors, such as business-related services and industries. However, the results show that regions with lower shares of the creative sector catch up in creative sector employment with the German mean.

Regarding the employment diversity variable, the empirical findings are at odds. The hypothesis is that the creative sector's diversity fosters employment growth. For DIV_CS, but also for the alternative estimation for DIV_CC, the coefficient is positive and significant at the 1% and 5% levels. The interpretation is that diversity matters for the development of the total employment growth, i.e. the diverse composition of the creative sector and Florida's creative class, and not the clustering of one specific creative profession. Nonetheless, the results indicate that the regional concentration of creative professionals matters for employment growth, but the creative professionals should be diverse in their composition. This might have important consequences for economic and urban policies, since cluster strategies or complex networks and regional innovation systems are very often of relevance to policy-makers.

Conclusion

Using a FE panel model with sufficient time lags, evidence is found that high initial shares of the creative sector foster the growth rate of the total employment. In contrast, high initial shares of the creative sector remain negative regarding the growth rate of creative sector employment. In consequence, on the basis of the theory the interpretation is that a convergence in creative professionals' employment between regions is observable. Large shares of creative sector employment lead to an increase in the total employment, but also reduce the growth rate of the same employment group. The first effect overwhelms the decline. The results further suggest that local amenities—measured by bohemians and diversity—and assumed knowledge externalities—possibly affected by diversity—are great enough within agglomerated regions to accumulate and polarize creative professionals further. The assumption is that creative agents prefer to live in agglomerations with high levels of amenities, and that the productivity is higher through (assumed) externalities in agglomerated regions. One theoretical explanation could be that the clumping in agglomerated regions contribute to the exchange of (new and) diverse knowledge. Whether it is differentiated in the model by agglomerated and all other regions, there is strong (and probably long-lasting) divergent regional development. The distribution of successful regions is unequal in space.

Those arguments support Florida's assumption that the economic success of cities and regions is influenced by creative regional processes. However, this is not the full story on regional development and growth. Explanations for the dynamics of regions are manifold. However, one point is that most successful regions seem to be particularly concentrated in idea-producing sectors: And, the creative sector is part of those.

Acknowledgements

I would like to thank the participants of the 3rd Research Seminar on "Creative Regions in Europe", especially Roberta Comunian (School of Geography, University of Southampton), Caroline Chapain (Centre for Urban and Regional Studies, University of Birmingham), Nick Clifton (Centre for Advanced Studies, Cardiff University) and the local organizers for helpful comments and support. This research is based on some results of the author's thesis project "Germany's creative sector and its impact on employment growth". I thank Wolfram Elsner of the University of Bremen and an unknown referee for their input and worthwhile comments on this paper.

Disclosure statement

No potential conflict of interest was reported by the author.

Note

1. The analysis is based on data from the IABS 1975–2004. Access to the data is possible through a Scientific-Use-File, which can be provided by the Nuremberg Research Data Center FDZ (2008) ("Die Datengrundlage dieses Beitrags bildet die faktisch anonymisierte IAB Beschäftigtenstichprobe (IABS 1975 to 2004). Der Datenzugang erfolgte über einen Scientific Use File, der vom Forschungsdatenzentrum der Bundesagentur für Arbeit im Institut für Arbeitsmarkt- und Berufsforschung (IAB) zu beziehen ist").

References

Acemoglu, D. (1996) A microfoundation for social increasing returns in human capital accumulation, *Quarterly Journal of Economics*, 111(3), pp. 779–804.
Acemoglu, D. & Angrist, J. (2000) How large are human capital externalities? Evidence from compulsory schooling laws, in: B. Bernanke & K. Rogoff (Eds) *NBER Macroeconomics Annual*, Vol. 15, pp. 9–59. (Cambridge, MA: MIT Press).
Andersen, K. V., & Lorenzen, M. (2005) *The Geography of the Danish Creative Class: A Mapping and Analysis* (Frederiksberg: Imagine – Creative Industries Research, Copenhagen Business School (CBS)).
Appelbaum, E. & Schettkat, R. (1995) Employment and productivity in industrialized economies, *International Labour Review*, 134(4–5), pp. 605–623.

Audretsch, D., Dohse, D. & Niebuhr, A. (2009) Cultural diversity and entrepreneurship: A regional analysis for Germany, *The Annals of Regional Science*. doi:10.1007/s00168–009–0291-x.

Autor, D., Lawrence, F. K. & Kearney, M. S. (2008) Trends in U.S. wage inequality: Revising the revisionists, *The Review of Economics and Statistics*, 90(2), pp. 300–323.

Borcherding, A., Hansen, T., Reich, N., Stiller, S. & Zierahn, U. (2012) *Hamburg 2020 – Chancen nutzen, Zukunft gestalten*, Hamburg: Herausgegeben von PwC in Kooperation mit dem HWWI.

Boschma, R. & Fritsch, M. (2009) Creative class and regional growth: Empirical evidence from seven European countries, *Economic Geography*, 85(4), pp. 391–423.

Clifton, N. (2008) The "creative class" in the UK: An initial analysis, *Geografiska Annaler: Series B, Human Geography*, 90(1), pp. 63–82.

Clifton, N. & Cooke, P. (2009) Knowledge workers and creativity in Europe and North America: A comparative review, *Creative Industries Journal*, 2(1), pp. 73–89. Special issue on The Drivers and Processes of Creative Industries in Regions and Cities.

De Hoyos, R. & Sarafidis, V. (2006) Testing for cross-sectional dependence in panel-data models, *The Stata Journal*, 6(4), pp. 482–496.

Drews, N. (2006) *Qualitätsverbesserung der Bildungsvariable in der IAB Beschäftigtenstichprobe 1975–2001* IAB Paper number 5/2006, Nuremberg: Nuremberg Research Data Centre (FDZ) of the Federal Employment Agency at the Institute for Employment Research.

Falck, O., Fritsch, M. & Heblich, S. (2009) *Bohemians, human capital, and regional economic growth*. CESifo Working Paper 2715, Center for Economic Studies (CES), Institute for Economic Research (ifo) and the Munich Society for the Promotion of Economic Research (CESifo GmbH), Munich.

FDZ (2008) *IAB Regionalfile 1975–2004 (IABS-R04)*. Nuremberg Research Data Centre (FDZ) of the Federal Employment Agency at the Institute for Employment Research, Nuremberg. [Official statistical data].

Fitzenberger, B., Osikominu, A. & Voelter, R. (2005) *Imputation rules to improve the education variable in the IAB employment subsample* IAB Paper number 3/2005, Nuremberg: Nuremberg Research Data Centre (FDZ) of the Federal Employment Agency at the Institute for Employment Research.

Florida, R. (2002) *The Rise of the Creative Class and How it's Transforming Work, Leisure, Community, and Everyday Life* (New York: Basic Books).

Fritsch, M. & Stützer, M. (2008) The geography of creative people in Germany, *International Journal of Foresight and Innovation Policy*, 5(1–3), pp. 7–23.

Glaeser, E. L. (2005) Review of Richard Florida's the rise of the creative class, *Regional Science and Urban Economics*, 35(5), pp. 593–596.

Glaeser, E. L. (2008) *Cities, Agglomeration and Spatial Equilibrium*, (Oxford: Oxford University Press).

Glaeser, E. L., Kallal, H. D., Scheinkman, J. A. & Shleifer, A. (1992) Growth in cities, *The Journal of Political Economy*, 100(6), pp. 1126–1152.

Hansen, H. K. (2007) *Technology, Talent, and Tolerance—The Geography of the Creative Class in Sweden* Rapporter och Notitser 169, Lund: Department of Social and Economic Geography, Lund University.

Hoechle, D. (2007) Robust standard errors for panel regressions with cross-sectional dependence, *The Stata Journal*, 7(3), pp. 281–312.

Jacobs, J. (1969) *The Economy of Cities*, 1st ed. (New York: Random House).

Krugman, P. (1991) *Geography and Trade* (Cambridge, MA: MIT Press).

Lee, S. Y., Florida, R. & Acs, Z. J. (2004) Creativity and entrepreneurship: A regional analysis of new firm formation, *Regional Studies*, 38(8), pp. 879–891.

Lucas, R. E. (1988) On the mechanics of economic development, *Journal of Monetary Economics*, 22(1), pp. 3–42.

Marshall, A. (1890) *Principles of Economics* (Macmillian: London).

Möller, J. (2001) Income and price elasticities in different sectors of the economy: An analysis of structural change for Germany, the UK and the USA, in: T. ten Raa & R. Schettkat (Eds) *The Growth of Service Industries: The Paradox of Exploding Costs and Persistent Demand*, pp. 167–208 (Cheltenham: Edward Elgar).

Möller, J. & Tubadji, A. (2009) *The creative class, bohemians and local labor market performance: A micro data panel study for Germany 1975–2004*. ZEW Discussion Paper 08–135, Centre for European Economic Research (ZEW), Mannheim.

Moretti, E. (2004) Estimating the social returns to higher education: Evidence from longitudinal and repeated cross-section data, *Journal of Econometrics*, 121(1/2), pp. 175–212.

Murphy, K. M., Shleifer, A. & Vishny, R. W. (1991) The allocation of talent: Implications for growth, *Quarterly Journal of Economics*, 106(2), pp. 503–530.

Peck, J. (2005) Struggling with the creative class, *International Journal of Urban and Regional Research*, 29(4), pp. 740–770.
Rauch, J. E. (1993) Productivity gains from geographic concentration of human capital: Evidence from the cities, *Journal of Urban Economics*, 34(3), pp. 380–400.
Roback, J. (1982) Wages, rents, and the quality of life, *Journal of Political Economy*, 90(6), pp. 1257–1278.
Rosen, S. (1979) Wage-based indexes of urban quality of life, in: P. Miezkowsi & M. Strazheim (Eds) *Current Issues in Urban Economics*, pp. 74–104 (Baltimore: John Hopkins University Press).
Schlitte, F. (2012) Local human capital, segregation by skill, and skill-specific employment growth, *Papers in Regional Science*, 91(1), pp. 85–106.
Shapiro, J. M. (2006) Smart cities: Quality of life, productivity, and the growth effects of human capital, *The Review of Economics and Statistics*, 88(2), pp. 324–335.
Suedekum, J. (2006) *Human capital externalities and growth of high- and low-skilled jobs*. IZA Discussion Paper 1969, Institute for the Study of Labor (IZA), Bonn.
Suedekum, J. (2008) Convergence of the skill composition across German regions, *Regional Science and Urban Economics*, 38(2), pp. 148–159.
Wedemeier, J. (2010) The impact of the creative sector on growth in German regions, *European Planning Studies*, 18(4), pp. 505–520.
Wojan, T. R., Lambert, D. M. & McGranahan, D. A. (2007) Emoting with their feet: Bohemian attraction to creative milieu, *Journal of Economic Geography*, 7(6), pp. 711–736.

Appendix

Table A1. Definition of the creative sector ("Definition 1")

Occupational title	IAB-Label
Creative sector (excl. bohemians)	
Mechanical and vehicle engineers	63
Electrical engineers	64
Architects and construction engineers	65
Surveyors, mining, metallurgists and related engineer	66
Miscellaneous engineers	67
Chemists, physicists, chemical/physical engineers, mathematicians and civil engineering technicians	68
Mechanical engineering technicians	69
Electrical engineers technicians	70
Surveyors, chemical, physical, mining, metallurgists and miscellaneous engineering technicians	71
Miscellaneous technicians	72
Biological/mathematical/physical-technical assistant, chemical and related laboratory technician workers	74
Draft persons	75
Computer-related professions	99
Statisticians, humanists, natural scientists and pastors	120
Bohemians	
Journalists, publishers, librarians, archivists and museum specialists	107
Musicians, performing artists, performers, graphic artists, designers, decorators, sign painters, stage, image and audio engineers, photographers, artists and professional athletes	108

Table A2. Definition of the creative class ("Definition 2")

Occupational title	IAB-Label
Creative class (excl. bohemians)	
Mechanical and vehicle engineers	63
Electrical engineers	64
Architects and construction engineers	65
Surveyors, mining, metallurgists and related engineer	66
Miscellaneous engineers	67
Chemists, physicists, chemical/physical engineers, mathematicians and civil engineering technicians	68
Mechanical engineering technicians	69
Electrical engineers technicians	70
Surveyors, chemical, physical, mining, metallurgists and miscellaneous engineering technicians	71
Miscellaneous technicians	72
Foreman, work master	73
Biological/mathematical/physical-technical assistant, chemical and related laboratory technician workers	74
Draft persons	75
Computer-related professions	99
Statisticians, humanists, natural scientists and pastors	120
Analysts, entrepreneurs, leading administration and opinion makers	93–95
University professors and education	118
Financial services	80
Legal services, lawyers, officers and justice	104
Bohemians	
Journalists, publishers, librarians, archivists and museum specialists	107
Musicians, performing artists, performers, graphic artists, designers, decorators, sign painters, stage, image and audio engineers, photographers, artists and professional athletes	108

Table A3. Definition of the skill groups ("Definition 3")

Educational title		IAB-Label
Low-skilled		
	Basic education, no vocational education	1
	Gymnasium, no vocational education	3
Medium-skilled		
	Basic education with vocational education	2
	Gymnasium with vocational education	4
High-skilled		
	University of applied science.	5
	University	6

Index

Note: **Boldface** page numbers refer to figures and tables, Page numbers followed by "n" denote notes.

A8 migrants 17
"absolute agglomeration of artists, the" 121
Alliance Wales 67
amenities 117; local *see* local amenities; natural 122; and tolerance factors 122–3
amenity-related factors 117; of Florida 116–18, 122–3
Artistic Bohemian 76
Autonomous Communities (A.C.) 87–9

Barcelona: clustering policies in 91; contribution to national industrial GDP **85**; economic profile 84; for Olympic Games of 1992 92
Basque country: employment in creative sectors 90; as modernization 91
Belfast 48, 52–6
Bilbao 88; contribution to national industrial GDP **85**; economic profile 84
Birmingham 6; city of migrants 16–18; as Cultural Melting Pot 21–3; skilled migrants move to 19–21
bohemians (BOH) 144, 145, 149; coefficient of 153; creative *see* creative bohemians; lifestyle in relation to craft businesses in 76–7; shares of 148
bonding social capital 117
bridging social capital 117

"Caixaforum Madrid" 92
Catalan–Valencian culture 86
Civil War 86, 87
Cohesion, Sharing and Integration Strategy (CSI) 58
community impoverishment 38–9
community-orientated cultural activity 35
control variables 146
Convention for the Protection and Promotion of the Diversity of Cultural Expressions 104
Council of Europe 99

craft enterprises: in bohemian lifestyle in relation to 76–7; owner/manager characteristics of 70, **71**; research approach 72–3; results and discussion 73–5
creative bohemians 14, 18, 76; migration trajectories of 26
creative class (CC) 145; migration tendency 26
creative class (CC), spatial agglomeration of: distribution over time, change of 128–30; empirical approach and data 120–4; Florida, Richard 114–15; model 124; regional growth rates of freelance artists, variation in 130–4; spatial distribution of freelance artists in Germany **125**, 125–8; theoretical considerations 116–20
creative class (CC) workers 12–13; amenities, diversity and tolerance 13–15; Birmingham 16–18; hyper-mobility of 23; location choice 21; research methods 18–19
creative economy, polymorphic notion from cultural development to 102–4
creative professionals 140–1; on employment growth, impact of 153, **154**; group 119; polarization effect of 153; regional concentration of 154; shares of 143; variables for 144–5
creative sector 145, 147; employment growth in 142–4; growth of 149–54; shares of 148
creative-sector employment, diversity 22
creativity in fostering economic development, role of 46–7
CREAURBS Survey, Spanish cities 82
CRIME factor 123
cross-cutting approach to cultural policies 107–9
cross-section time-series analysis 147
cross-sectional dependence (CD) 149
CSI *see* Cohesion, Sharing and Integration Strategy
CUL_AMENITY factor 123
cultural amenities 143
cultural amenity variable, coefficients for 151
cultural development 102; strategies 107
cultural diversity 23, 103; challenge of 109–10

159

INDEX

cultural identity of territories 106
cultural individuality 38
cultural industry policies 33
cultural policy 100
cultural quarter (CQs) development policy in UK 32; from dualistic to differentiated 37–42; economic determinism of 33–7; role of culture 33
cultural–ethnic diversity 146

data cleaning and preparation 144
Department of Employment and Learning Northern Ireland 56
dependent variables 120–1, 145–6
"Deutscher Lernatlas 2011" 123
diversity 27; creative-sector employment 22; in Northern Ireland 56–7
Driscoll–Kraay SE 149

Eastern European migrants 59
economic creativity 145
economic factors 117–18
Economic Strategy for Northern Ireland 59–60
education in Belfast 55
educational opportunities 19–20
electoral wards in Belfast 54, **54**
employment diversity variable 154
employment in Mid and West Wales 69
entrepreneur 70
Equality Commission for Northern Ireland 49
"Espace culturel Grande Région" 105
ethnic diversity 116–17
EU regional policy *see* European Union regional policy
European California 107
European Capital of Culture 2010 106
European Construction, from Euroregions to 109–10
European Creative Industries Alliance 67
European cross-border scale: Council of Europe 99; culture, creativity and construction of territoriality in Euroregions 107–10; culture, creativity and cross-border development 102–4; Euroregional cultural development 105–6; Euroregional cultural policy 100; Euroregions 99; Greater Region 100–1, **102**; Pyrenees-Mediterranean Euroregion 100, **101**
European polycentrism 107
European territorial authorities 99
European territory, structures of 107, **108**
European Union (EU) regional policy 99
European Year of Creativity and Innovation 103
Euroregional cultural capital, strengthening of 106
Euroregional cultural corpus 105
Euroregional cultural development 105–6

Euroregional cultural policy 100, 110
Euroregional cultural project 109
Euroregional Franco-Belgian space 106
Euroregional policies 100
Euroregional projects 109
Euroregions 99; culture, creativity and construction of territoriality in 107–10; to European Construction, from 109–10; as territories of development 104
External Action Plan 109

fast-urban policy 43
fixed-effects (FE) estimators 149
Florida, Richard 114; creative class (CC), spatial agglomeration of *see* creative class (CC), spatial agglomeration of; creative class workers in 14–15; hypotheses 115; super-creative core 18
Franco-Flemish linguistic policy 106
freelance artists 121; correlation of growth rates and number of 129, **130**; in Germany, spatial distribution of **125**, 125–8; growth rates of **129**; total population growth, determinants of 130–4; variation in regional growth rates of 130–4
freelance visual artist 22
functional identity: notion of 106; territories 106

German Social Insurance for Artists 144
German Weather Service 122
Germany: development of freelance artists in 129, **131**; Florida, Richard *see* Florida, Richard; spatial distribution of freelance artists in **125**, 125–8
"global talent magnets" 14
Goldblatt, David 108
Good Friday Agreement 49, 56
Greater Region 100–1, **102**, 105; cultural cooperation in 109; as European Capital of Culture 104; reverse situation in 106
group-specific employment effects 151–4

high-skilled agents, variables for 144–5
highly skilled migration in Europe 15–16
human capital: external effects of 141, 153; externalities 142
Huntington, Samuel 110
hyper-mobile "creative class" 26

"IAB Regionalfile 1975–2004" data 144
ICT *see* information and communication technology
idealist 70
independent variables 121–4
information and communication technology (ICT) 67
INI *see* National Industrial Institute

INDEX

INKAR data set 122, 123
Innovation Strategy for Wales 76–7
Intellectual Property Fund 68
interaction variable, coefficient for 151
intercultural dialogue 110
international bohemians 16
inverse Herfindahl–Hirschman Index 146

knowledge-intensive sectors 142

large-scale cultural institution 36
late developer 70
lifestyler 70
local amenities: characteristic of 143; value of 153
Local Government Districts in Northern Ireland 52, **53**

Madrid: contribution to national industrial GDP 85; cultural industries development in 86; economic profile 84; government role as *de facto* metropolitan authority 88; top-down approach 89–90, 94; urban expansion 85
Madrid Network 89–90
MediaCityUK 39
Medialab 92
Merkel, Angela 110
micro-business strategy 69
Mid and West Wales: attributes of 68–70; bohemian lifestyle in relation to craft businesses in 76–7; craft enterprises in 70–2; employment in 69
"migrantdense" professional sectors 17
migrants: motivations, experiences and trajectories 19–26; workers in Northern Ireland 56
migration in Belfast 55
migration trajectories, mapping of 23–6

National Centre for Popular Music (NCPM) 41, 42
National Industrial Institute (INI) 85
natural amenities 122
NCPM *see* National Centre for Popular Music
neo-liberal economic development policies 7
neo-liberal policy-making 3; development agenda 50
Newcastle-Gateshead Initiative 40
"nomadic workers" 15
non-metric interaction variables for CC 147
Northern Ireland 46–7, 50, 52; diversity, tolerance and social cohesion 56–7; economy 48–50; executive policies 57–60; geography of creativity in 52–6; Local Government Districts in 52, **52**; parliamentary constituencies in 52, **53**; policy-making context 49–52
NVIVO software 18

OECD *see* Organization for Economic Cooperation and Development
"one size fits all" approach 67, 70
OPENCities Project 54
Organization for Economic Cooperation and Development (OECD) 103
Ouseburn Trust 40
Oxford Economics 44

parliamentary constituencies in Northern Ireland 52, **53**
peripherism 109
permanent migration 16
personal developmental opportunities 19
'post-conflict' society 7, 47
post-crisis recession 7
Programme for Government 50, 57–9; document 47
Pyrenees-Mediterranean EGTC 107
Pyrenees-Mediterranean Euroregion 100, **101**, 105, 106, 109; development of 107
Pyrenees-Mediterranean space, development of 104

Quality of Living in Belfast 55
quantile regressions 124, 130, **132**

Race Relations (Northern Ireland) Order 56
regional growth rates of freelance artists, variation in 130–3
regional policy-making in Wales 67–8
"relational complexity" 43
"relative number of artists per inhabitant" 121
"return to territory" movement 110
RIPPLE Producer Survey 70
Rosen–Roback framework 140

second-tier European cities 13
self-reinforcing process 153; hypothesis of 151
short-termism 41–2
skilled migrants, role of 17–18
skilled migration, literature on 13
snowball techniques 18
social capital 123; bonding and bridging 117
social cohesion in Northern Ireland 56–7
social diversity 14
social engagement cultural activity 35
social networks 24, 27
Spain: creative and knowledge sectors from urban diversity in 89–93; economic success elements identification, in urban regions transformation 93–6
Spanish cities: creative and knowledge sectors 82–3; CREAURBS Survey 82; cultural and institutional pathways in 83–8; cultural traditions emergence 86–7; economic activity transformation 80–1; economic capacity

INDEX

to accommodate creative and knowledge sectors 89–91; economic divergence in 83–8; economic profile configuration, early industrialization 84–6; economy of 81; elements of 81; path dependency 82–3; path dependency variables synthesis 94, **95**; shaping diverse governance frameworks 87–8; socio-economic characteristics of **81**, 81–2; urban competitiveness 82–3; urban economic development 82; use of culture to reinvent city 91–3

"Technological and Cultural Laboratory" 105
temporary migration 16
territorial cultural policies 102
'Together: Building a United Community' policy 58
tolerance14; Birmingham 21–3; factors of Florida 116–17; in Northern Ireland 56–7
"top-down" urban policy strategies 89
tourism 118; culture in Euroregion 107
traditional cultural institutions 34
trans-national migration in Europe 15
triumvirate model 37
'Troubles, The' 49

UK regional competitiveness index **51**
United Cities and Local Governments (UCLG) 111n4
units of observation 146–7
URBAN factor 123, 132

Valencia: autonomous communities of 90; contribution to national industrial GDP **85**; economic profile 84; modernization of 91; urban and economic development 85
variables: control 146; for creative professionals and high-skilled agents 144–5; definition 145, **145**; dependent 120–1, 145–6; employment diversity 154; independent 121–4; units of observation 146–7
visual artists 133

Wales: attributes of 68–70; bohemian lifestyle in relation to craft businesses in 76–7; craft enterprises in 70–2; economic progression barrier 69; regional policy-making in 67–8
"Wales: A Vibrant Economy" report 69
Welsh Assembly Government Creative Industry Strategy (2004) 68

zero-sum urban strategies 41